ADVENTURES IN
THE GOLDEN AGE

ADVENTURES IN THE GOLDEN AGE

Scotland in the World Cup Finals 1974-1998

ARCHIE MACPHERSON

BLACK & WHITE PUBLISHING

First published 2018
by Black & White Publishing Ltd
Nautical House, 104 Commercial Street
Edinburgh EH6 6NF

1 3 5 7 9 10 8 6 4 2   18 19 20 21

ISBN: 978 1 78530 191 9

Typeset by Iolaire, Newtonmore
Printed and bound by MBM Print, East Kilbride

CONTENTS

In memory of my father, who watched every minute.

ACKNOWLEDGEMENTS

I could not have written this kind of book without coopera-
tion from many of the leading figures of those World Cup
years. I am deeply indebted to the following players who
patiently responded to my questioning by directly and
eloquently recounting their versions of events.

Denis Law, Joe Jordan, Lou Macari, Tom Forsyth, David
Hay, Gordon McQueen, Danny McGrain, Alan Rough,
Graeme Souness, Willie Miller, Alex McLeish, Davie Provan,
Richard Gough, Maurice Malpas, Roy Aitken, Charlie
Nicholas, Frank McAvennie, Mo Johnston, Ally McCoist,
Murdo MacLeod, Gordon Durie, John Collins, Stuart McCall,
Tom Boyd, Colin Hendry, Tosh McKinlay, Kevin Gallagher,
Darren Jackson. And the man who never played in a World
Cup but was nevertheless there in spirit on the field, former
Scotland captain, Gary McAllister.

I am also grateful for the added information provided by
journalists Alan Herron (*Sunday Mail*), Alex Montgomery
(*The Sun*), and Hugh Keevins (*Daily Record*) whose World
Cup wanderings coincided with mine.

Iain Scott, formerly of the *Herald* and the *Daily Record*,
helped enormously in advising me on text and making

precious contacts, as did his former colleague Gary Ralston (*Daily Record*).

PR consultant Alan 'Fingers' Ferguson provided extremely useful background material from his time in a commercial advisory role with the SFA in certain years. And, for the eighth time, that wondrous football historian and author Pat Woods assisted me in providing essential perspectives from his research for this book. I would also like to thank the other talented football historian and author David Mason for checking out some essential statistics for me.

I am still in awe of those colleagues at the BBC for putting me on the air with a professionalism that lent confidence to any broadcast I was involved in. I'd particularly like to thank producer Bill Malcolm who tolerated my swings of mood with calm forbearance through many of these years. And I tug my forelock to computer expert Kenny Forsyth who helped me with innumerable problems.

INTRODUCTION

The title admittedly might seem contentious to some. The records will show that between the period of 1974 and 1998 Scotland won nothing on the global stage and indeed failed to qualify for the later stages of the six World Cups they were involved in. It is a period that is associated as much with anguish as pleasure, as much with hubris as triumph, and public wrath then was heaped upon national managers and players, as is the continuing nature of football to this very day. So why would I characterise it with such a glittering phrase?

It depends, of course, on how you wish to interpret 'Golden Age' itself.

There are many periods in history that have given rise to that phrase because we value their virtues above their vices and cling on to them as something worth preserving. We received a model of democracy from the Golden Age of Greece, when there were also many wars and famine. We understand why the Golden Age is often attached to the reign of Good Queen Bess, who presided over the age of Shakespeare and great triumphs at sea, but also treacheries and incurable plagues. But they both measure up to the gold standard because of the exceptional qualities we still cherish.

So, this period of international football that I lived and worked through did have its light and dark, its highs and lows, its controversies, its disputes, its frustrations, its embarrassments, but also those moments of rejuvenating, incandescent joy. But it stands out in sharp contrast to what went on before, and what certainly has happened since. Graeme Souness tells me distinctly, 'I used to get stick for saying that Scotland qualifying for the World Cup finals was, in itself, a great achievement, would you believe?'

Of course, I believe it. For despite many of the negative occasions and the uncertainties, this period was underpinned by regular, solid achievement, elevating us to a level in international football that was unprecedented and is a legacy we revere, but equally find difficult to live up to. We could in fact claim a legacy going back to the birth of the World Cup in 1930 in Uruguay. Five men born in Scotland, and who had learned the game here: Andy Auld, Jim Brown, Jimmy Gallagher, Bart McGhee and Alex Wood, playing in the USA at the time, represented their adopted country, and reached the semi-final. The trainer of their team was also Scottish, Jack Coll, who had been coach of Parkhead Juniors and whose entry into American football was through the help of the then Celtic manager, Willie Maley. So, we had exported success right at the birth of this global affair. By 1974 we were making realistic attempts to follow those pathfinders.

Before then Scotland's efforts to prepare for and play in World Cups might have given birth to the word 'shambolic'. And certainly, from that starting date of 1974 we can claim to have been part of an elite, compared to our international status of the twenty-first century, in which we have almost been rubbed off the map. Simply, it was the best of all times to pursue a national side. Countless thousands were lifted from their parishes and perhaps humdrum existences, and found themselves alighting in foreign lands for the first time, and with a combination of sign language and foreign phrase books could practically put to the test our old Scots belief that we are all Jock Tamson's bairns.

This was the world's best we were taking on, and the supporters followed in droves, advertising our identity eagerly to many uncomprehending onlookers, but doing so with a swagger that enlivened the Scotland dressing room itself. They could party with the best as a result. They could taste something in Dortmund called bratwurst, in Seville they could learn what genuine paella was like, in Mexico City they could devour *empanadas* and compare them to Forfar Bridies, in Cordoba they could sample succulent Argentinian baby-beef and then they could wash down all these new dishes, copiously, with whatever national drink was to hand, including supping from the now popular Malbec grape in the shadows of the Andes in Mendoza, before and after watching the most famous goal in Scotland's international history.

This wasn't just about players and officials, it was about all of us, or at least those who packed their suitcases and perhaps concluded, given some of the anti-climaxes experienced, that they knew what Robert Louis Stevenson meant when he wrote, 'To travel hopefully is a better thing than to arrive.'

Doing so gave us all personal adventures in an era which blew a gale through our dusty, cultural parochialism. We had become world travellers all because of events which pitched eleven foreigners against us with differing consequences. It was exotic and enlightening. And what I have found in later years is a heavily laden nostalgia for those times and a persistent evocation of the names which are still preserved in many minds, and preserved like highly revered cigarette cards of childhood. These names are still part legacy of those times.

Dalglish, Law, Souness, Bremner, Jordan, McGrain, Jardine, McStay, Cooper, MacLeod, Rough ...

Enough to be going on with at the moment.

We didn't have a Shakespeare to immortalise the vagaries of their history, but we had many redoubtable journalists who could attack like Rottweilers when necessary or make us clutch our throats with emotion.

Try this from the *Glasgow Herald* of Thursday, 27 September 1973. These are the words of journalist Ian Archer on what he witnessed at Hampden Park, the night before.

'Strong men wept as at a homecoming after a long journey. Others just stared in disbelief. No one remained unmoved or unemotional. It was a great and glorious night, a watershed.'

That evening, by defeating Czechoslovakia, Scotland had just qualified for the World Cup finals in Germany the following year. It was in fact the beginning of that era I identify as the halcyon days. Six World Cup finals ensued. In light of our present status in world football, it now seems an incredible feat for a nation of only five million to have maintained that level for so long. But at the time it did not seem so. It just felt natural for us to be elbowing for power amongst the best. We have never been short of a 'guid conceit' of ourselves and during that period we feasted on our belief that nothing could alter that status. But 1998, our last World Cup entry, seems like an eternity ago and leaves us wondering what has gone wrong since. Certainly, we have been left wondering if ever again a Scottish journalist will be able to write in such emotional terms about our national team as Archer did in the *Glasgow Herald* all these long years ago.

I feel privileged to have been a close witness to every second of these World Cups, from the night Joe Jordan headed the winner against Czechoslovakia in 1973 to qualify us, to the sad, sultry night in June 1998 in the World Cup in France, when fluent Moroccans put us to the sword in St-Étienne.

So, this record of events is admittedly highly subjective. It is a personal narrative. But it is about what happened in the background as much as what we saw on the field of play. It is about issues and policies and the unexpected. It is about the television lens as well, for in that period the game changed from one of partnership with the cameras to that of its virtual subjugation. It is about the nature of the support the public gave to the Scottish side and of how it started to develop a potential political shape as the country contemplated firstly devolution, which they did some months later, and then independence. Many politicians have always been avid football supporters, but through these particular years of the World Cups, as we shall see, they eyed victory or defeat of the national side as some kind of influence on how the public might vote.

People, however, voted with their feet during that period to follow Scotland, often inventively, like the man who devised the idea of trying to hire a U-boat to take supporters over the Atlantic to Argentina in 1978. The four corners of the earth are no longer ours to explore as our international football has sunk to a new low. Will we ever see their likes again? If not, and we must always hope that we will, then any record of this Golden Age must be preserved with the same diligence as that applied to the Dead Sea Scrolls.

THE 1974 FIFA WORLD CUP

GERMANY

1

SPIRITED LIFT-OFF

The British Airways flight, which rose into the air on the morning of 28 May 1974 from Glasgow Airport, bound for Brussels, was well loaded with fuel, talent, egos and seemingly enough liquid refreshment for a round-the-world trip. If anybody had stumbled onto this flight by accident they might have thought they had joined a stag party warming up for a stripper rather than a group of men embarking on the first stage of a journey which would take Scottish players to their first World Cup finals in sixteen years. Of course, the occasion was worthy of celebration and it would have been discourteous for anyone travelling to have turned down the offer of a bottle of champagne each, from BA, to ease the tedium of a one-and-a-half-hour journey to Brussels. From there we would travel on to that exquisite city of Bruges for the first of two friendly games, before reaching Germany, the host nation. Few of the bottles were left unopened. Mine was almost drained before the soggy chicken dish arrived. A fair proportion of the players had become very merry even before the aircraft reached the first layer of cirrocumulus cloud but were being outpaced by the media present who were no slouches when it came to accepting hospitality.

There might have been stray thoughts in some minds that all this euphoria might be slightly premature, but how were we supposed to behave at that juncture? We were all World Cup adolescents after all. Everything was new to us, packed in there. It was like we were being initiated into the new world of hedonism, all because Joe Jordan had ended years of misery by putting his cranium in the way of a Willie Morgan cross at Hampden that previous autumn, which effectively was like having a passport stamped at customs to send us into an entirely new world. It did not follow that we were now all a band of brothers hugely united in this new national venture, to right the wrongs of the past. For there was segregation on the plane. At the back were the press, who were regarded by the players as a pack of mangy curs whose bites could spread rabies. Indeed, Davie Hay, the Celtic midfielder who was to have an outstanding World Cup, tells me now that the identification of journalistic habits simply emboldened the players' attitude.

'Yes, there was drinking on the plane. It was just part of our culture at the time. And we were enjoying ourselves because in the past we had seen many journalists pissed and legless, and they were the ones who were telling us not to drink. Look, I admit it. At times we were daft boys about drink, but it just seemed like part of what football was like for us. We didn't think it got in the way of how we could play.'

Nobody could take issue with that view from a man who gave outstanding performances for his club and country. And he believed, like the rest of the squad, that in the previous month the treatment the media had meted out to Celtic's colourful and controversial player Jimmy Johnstone in the days leading up to their last game before setting off for Germany, had been grossly exaggerated. Johnstone had commandeered a rowing boat in the wee small hours, after, it is said, being at the bar for some hours, lost the oars and could have drifted from the shores of Scotland's west coast and ended up in Newfoundland had not the alarm been raised and he been rescued. This was generally written up by the press almost as a sign that the whole squad was undisciplined and treating their supporters with contempt, given the wide expectations amongst the public for success in Germany. Their reply was to beat England 2–0 at Hampden on 18 May and, for some of the players, to give two fingers to the men sitting in the press box high above Hampden. Now these very men were sitting at the back of the aircraft, hungry for stories and not in the mood now to let anybody off the hook. Although on this occasion clearly a truce was in play since none of the media pack there, of which I was part, was actually practising abstinence. At least there was unity in that regard.

There was another element on the flight: England had failed to qualify for Germany, so some of Fleet Street's big hitters were on board covering the only home nation to have reached the finals. Although they were to temporarily hold fire about what they were witnessing, there is little doubt that they were being alerted to the potential for some meaty headlines in future. They were not to be disappointed. This was no idle, meaningless passage in the great World Cup trek, because the images of revelry were to haunt this squad, and others following them, sometimes grossly unfairly so, over the next couple of decades.

Then there was a bitter division down at the front, where the officials of the Scottish Football Association sat near players with whom they were barely on talking terms. The SFA was in a dispute with the players about contracts, especially about the association's desire to take ten per cent of the proceeds that the squad might earn in total from its participation in the finals. Taking anything from the Scottish captain Billy Bremner would have been like trying to take a plateful of Chum from a Rottweiler. He had led the way in encouraging the players to open up their own squad bank account in defiance of the SFA whose secretary, Willie Allan, told the *Glasgow Herald* on the day of departure, 'I will not discuss the matter at all. We should all be concerned with the football and nothing else. If there is a dispute surely the correct time to do a deal is after the World Cup.'

A simple and sensible statement on the surface, but, in effect, words of evasion, and, in any case, Allan was incapable of making even simple pronouncements without lending the impression that the end of the world was nigh. Looking down the length of the aircraft at the players copiously imbibing and thoroughly lapping up their new celebrity, as carriers of the cause, it did not seem they would ever pay much attention to a man whose bearing was that of the pacemaker for a cortege.

So indeed, there was an ill-disguised nervousness to this flight, despite the buoyancy of the occasion. The pilot might have known what he was doing, but the Scots on board were flying blind. We simply did not know, either as journalists, broadcasters, officials or players, what really was in store for us. Joe Jordan, now virtually immortalised because of *the* goal, was nevertheless one of the innocents. 'Remember, I was only twenty-one at the time. Yes, I had played at Leeds with one of the greatest managers of the time, Don Revie. But this was a different world we were going into. We just didn't have a clue what was coming next.'

Given the dire, tawdry nature of Scotland's previous history in the World Cup, there was no consolation in thinking this squad could hardly do worse. This was a salvage operation, apart from anything else. For only the masochists amongst us spent much time talking over what had happened in Switzerland in 1954 and Sweden in 1958. And to resurrect the details of what happened at Hampden in 1950 was like entering a fantasy world.

For that is when the travesties really began. The Scottish Football Association had the tempting prospect of planning a trip to the World Cup finals in Brazil. You would have thought that would have been a succulent prospect to them, since many of the members were ravenous freeloaders. This is what Cyril Horne of the *Glasgow Herald* wrote about them, after England had beaten Scotland 1–0 on 15 April of that year.

'First of all, the foolhardy official expression of policy that the Scots would travel to Rio de Janeiro only if they retained the British championship – a draw on Saturday would have enabled them to fulfil that condition – imposed on the players, who represented their country, a tremendous psychological handicap. Having committed the error of insisting on conditional participation at Rio the public are entitled to know who forced that decision ... The truth of the matter is that certain legislators thought the defeat of England was only a matter of course.'

The *Daily Record* called the decision 'wicked narrow-mindedness'. And went on with a caveat, 'The ramifications of football today are such that Scotland is expected to do much more than it is capable of accomplishing.'

A refrain that has been echoed through the years. In fact, I watched Roy Bentley's goal for England in their 1–0 victory at Hampden in the sixty-fourth minute of that game, from the

13

schoolboys' enclosure, with a degree of pain accentuated by the fact that I had also witnessed the sturdy Willie Bauld of Hearts, the youngest player on the field, hit the underside of the crossbar from six yards near the end of the match; a dramatic miss which was like a stake being driven through the heart of a boy who from that very moment began to doubt the existence of God. There was certainly no Rio out there for us.

We did reach the Switzerland World Cup finals four years later, which produced a clash between modernity and stagnant orthodoxy that almost inevitably produced ignominy for the Scots. The man the SFA had appointed as manager, on a part-time basis, Andy Beattie, then with Huddersfield Town, did not come from the shock-and-awe school of management which sometimes lent the impression that these early Scottish international sides were responding to the sight of the Fiery Cross on the hill above the glens. He was more cerebral. He used blackboard and chalk. He would put diagrammatic plans on a board. He would move pieces around like a chess grandmaster trying to educate players to his ways of thinking. Meanwhile, in the background was the international selection committee comprised of men whose power to select managers and players was in inverse proportion to their lack of ability to do so properly. They looked upon his pointed arrows on the blackboard like kids trying to understand Egyptian hieroglyphics.

These men were sceptical onlookers of Scotland's first match against Austria on 16 June of that year. Before that game, a telegram was sent to the Scotland physio, Alex Dowdells from the 51st Highland Division, reading, 'Hope you play the same way that we played at Alamein with the Highland Division. We are a greater team, comrades, for we are brother Scots. Don't let auld Scotia down.'

14

Sadly, it did not work out that way as Scotland went down 1–0 to a goal scored by twenty-nine-year-old Viennese bank clerk Erich Probst. However, Scotland actually won universal praise for the way they had played, and were considered to have been unlucky, or, as the *Glasgow Herald*'s correspondent Cyril Horne put it, 'Every Scot who saw the match is proud tonight of his fellow countrymen who nearly succeeded in defying the efforts of eleven Austrians, a Belgian referee and a Swiss linesman, to beat them.'

The inference being that many dubious decisions went against the Scots, although Horne concluded his report in a tone which suggested harmony existed at the top, 'Whatever happens against Uruguay next Saturday, Scotland's name, thanks to the efforts of the team manager, trainer and players and those in authority who have been fit to encourage them, stands higher than it has for years.'

That sentiment lasted exactly twenty-four hours, for when the bunglers in the background intervened and tried to tell Beattie whom to select for the next game, in a manner that was effectively debunking all his methods, he quit on the spot. He didn't hang around for the next game in Basel. Not even endorsements by the sympathetic press could persuade him to stay and, despite risking the ire of those who might have thought he was being unpatriotic, he was not going to be forced to depart from his own way. What happened next was surely predictable.

They were now about to play Uruguay, the world champions, without a manager and with players both shocked and demoralised. It should be pointed out that the meticulous preparation of the SFA consisted of providing the players with thick woollen jerseys on the assumption that this was a country of snow and ice. Only if you are at the top of the

15

Matterhorn in summer, that is. In fact, it was searingly hot and humid, and Tommy Docherty admitted that, during the interminable Uruguayan national anthem, some of the Scottish players almost fainted. So, they were easy meat to the slick South Americans whose population it should be noted was then only half of Scotland's five million. They scored seven goals without reply, inspiring a blunt admission in the *Daily Record* headline, 'We Couldn't Lace Their Boots!'

In searing heat, Scotland had crumbled and been watched, incidentally, by Jock Stein, an interested spectator. Many people watched a game for the first time on television as the *Sunday Mail* front page reported, 'I sat through a pantomime yesterday only it wasn't funny. As least not for me or the thousands of Scottish TV viewers who watched the flower of Scottish football wither. Forty-three thousand were in the crowd to jeer the Scots demonstration of how not to play football. The Swiss were delighted. They invited the pipers to dine in the stadium after the match. The cameras gave a panoramic view of the scene which was very inspiring – until the match began.'

The *Glasgow Herald*'s Cyril Horne, who had been so upbeat after the Austrian match, hardly glossed over his wholly inaccurate prediction when he wrote afterwards of the Scots, 'I have never seen in any class of football, let alone in the top class, such dreadful passing. The spectators gave vent to their contempt by whistling and jeering as we went from one piece of fatuousness to another.'

The theme of anti-climax seemed to become uniquely ours and was amplified in the Swedish World Cup in 1958. Incredibly, the Scots had no manager. Matt Busby had been appointed on a part-time basis, but the Munich plane crash of February 1958, where he narrowly escaped death, put paid to him being fit enough for Sweden, and the SFA held off, out of respect to the man, from appointing an alternative. But, since at first, he had wanted to give up management altogether after the disaster, the dual task was certainly going to be too much for him, so he resigned.

Busby did return a year later; he took charge against Wales and Northern Ireland and in the first match gave an eighteen-year-old Denis Law his international debut in the hope of keeping tabs on him for Old Trafford. But, in that summer of 1958, he was still in recuperation and the task of managing was left to Dawson Walker, the trainer of Clyde FC, who, in the Scottish camp in Eskilstuna, had to deal with acute disgruntlement amongst the squad, because the SFA was refusing to pay pocket money to the players, unlike the associations of the other home nations involved in the tournament, England and Wales. Whilst their players were being handed out £2 per day, the Scots were on a simple match fee of £50, or £30 if a reserve. This rankled, and rankling was not what was needed for a squad still being picked by the SFA selection committee. Thankfully, none of them took the team talks. That was left to the goalkeeper, Tommy Younger.

The 1–1 draw with Yugoslavia on 8 June 1958 was therefore reasonably creditable, given the circumstances, but to follow that with a 3–2 defeat at the hands of Paraguay, after the South Americans had previously conceded seven goals against France, meant the selectors were sinking in a swamp of their own making. They were now about to face the French, who could rightly boast of fielding Raymond Kopa and Just Fontaine, two of the best attackers in the world. During this tournament, Fontaine was to go on to create a World Cup record of thirteen goals in a single tournament. Typically, they both scored in France's 2–1 victory over Scotland in

17

Orebro. The retreat from Sweden was a slow-motion replay of the earlier years.

On the flight that morning, we were hopefully leaving that badly blemished past behind us. But to accentuate that feeling, we were also refugees fleeing the sour mood of the nation in 1974. We had come through a winter of the Three-Day Working Week, established by the Heath Conservative government to conserve electricity and to counter the effect of the impending miners' strike in their fight for increased wages and new pension rights. Scottish football had been directly affected. In the context of saving energy, there was an obvious ban on floodlit games, so early kick-offs had been implemented. At a bitterly cold and wet Hampden on 15 December 1973, for instance, I commentated on the Scottish League Cup final between Celtic and Dundee, which was forced to kick off at 1.30 p.m., so that it could be played wholly in daylight, and produced a 1–0 victory for Dundee that, for the record, burst many a coupon.

So, at least in dressing rooms around the country and on the terracings, if not in boardrooms, where clubs were run largely by businessmen with political leanings to the right, there was a great deal of sympathy for the miners. Their culture had long been part of the fabric of the Scottish game. Matt Busby had been a miner. Jock Stein had worked at the coalface. Bill Shankly had honed his witticisms and corn-poke philosophy in the mines in the village of Glenbuck, which with only a population of 1,000 had nevertheless produced fifty professional players throughout the years. I recall Stein telling me how much he admired Mick McGahey, the Scottish NUM strike leader, and especially his comment, when some politicians had urged the government to send in troops to replace the miners, 'You can't dig coal with bayonets.'

Politics hardly ever entered the chatter of the stadiums; at least not then. Times, they were a-changing, though. Football was like any other institution in those days, in assuming that the current political structure was set in stone. But many of us were not reading the runes. For on the same week of that day of embarrassment at Hampden in 1950, a letter had appeared in the *Glasgow Herald* from an irate reader writing, 'For what is the real issue? Is it not whether Scottish affairs shall be dealt with by Englishmen or by Scotsmen: whether Scotsmen shall have the ordering of our country's life and destiny, or no?'

If that was almost in a whispering tone from halfway down the letters page in the sedately laid-out typography of that newspaper, twenty-four years later, as we prepared for Germany, the *Daily Record* blasted a headline on to its front page that was meant to identify a new era for the country, 'Scotland Strikes It Big'. It had nothing to do with the euphoric mood of the Scottish public, who were finding it difficult to bring their excitement for the World Cup under control. It referred to the biggest discovery yet of North Sea oil. News that was seized upon by Scottish Nationalists to support their slogan, 'It's Scotland's Oil'.

Would all this lead to a national football team taking on a new guise, a new kind of identity in the midst of seismic political change? Could its success or failure influence the emotions of those approaching the ballot box? Few on that plane would have given that notion much credence, even though, earlier that very week, the SNP at Westminster had threatened to withdraw its support for the minority Labour government on issues of devolution, thus initiating political turmoil that, much further down the road, would lead to an independence referendum in which football crowds

19

blatantly took sides on the issue. So, unknown to us then, we were being shadowed by political events that would last right through this period of six World Cup appearances, and make us ponder whether the emotional ties to our side might lead to political advantage of one kind or another. Certainly, prominent politicians did think so, as we shall see.

However, there was one man on the flight who was totally insulated from any other thoughts than simply how to get through this journey and get his feet safely on terra firma again. He was at the front, and at least I could understand why we saw little of him during this short flight. I had to assume that, no matter the great challenges facing him in Germany, the Scotland manager Willie Ormond was securely buckled in and almost certainly with a drink in his hand for most of the flight, because of his intense fear of flying. Gordon McQueen, who was awarded his first cap by Ormond, says almost affectionately of him, 'He liked a wee drink', as if indicating the man's geniality rather than a crucial weakness.

When he was manager of St Johnstone, and beginning to earn kudos for the way he was shaping this provincial club, I met with him at the end of season 1969 to talk about how he had inspired this club to finish that season in third place – ahead of Rangers, though – and qualify them for a European place for the first time in their history. He was a small, neat, dapper man with hair looking as if it were permanently slicked back with brilliantine. His rounded face almost gave him a cherubic appearance at times. That day we met, he was at pains to tell me of how the sight of an aircraft made him feel ill. It originated in a horrendous attempt at a take-off in Yugoslavia in winter, returning with St Johnstone from a UEFA cup-tie in December 1971.

'I could see we weren't going to make it. The branches of the trees were brushing against the wings and the whole plane was shuddering. I thought this was going to be it. I don't think I even prayed. I was too terrified to think of anything. Then, somehow or other, the pilot swung the plane round and I kept my eyes shut. But we landed. We got off the plane and I remember they told us they were going to have another go at taking off in about an hour. Not on your bloody life! I thought. But I knew I had to get back somehow, so I went back into the lounge and drank it dry. I was paralytic when I went back on and I remember bugger all about anything else until we landed back in Edinburgh.'

Reputations are easily made in football, however ill-informed they can be, and it is certainly true that the wee man who had been a magnificent left-winger in Hibernian's Famous Five in the 1940s and had played for Scotland in the 1954 World Cup in Switzerland, including the Uruguayan cataclysm, had his drinking habits emphasised most cruelly, by tagging him practically as a lush. This exaggeration was exacerbated by the fact that Ormond was never the kind of aggressive personality to put the fear of death into rumour-mongers.

A provincial manager with a club that had won nothing but had certainly punched above its weight was clearly not enough to satisfy the doubters in the media, including myself. After all, in his first game as manager against England at Hampden on 14 February 1973, on a bitterly cold night, with the ground as hard as granite, Scotland lost 5–0 to England, and, as commentator, I had to try to make sense of that to the Scottish public. It almost immediately dampened my enthusiasm for his appointment, and I found it difficult to recover from that, even though, on the countless times I talked to

21

him, I was impressed by his knowledge of the game, and by the courtesy he always extended.

And you could not dismiss lightly the fact that, under his management, Scotland had won only four out of their previous fourteen games. So, although I was exhilarated by the qualification for Germany, like everyone else, I also harboured doubts about his ability to manage at this exalted level. I was not alone of course. Most of us were comparing him unfavourably to the company he would keep in Germany; the likes of Rinus Michels of Holland, Miljan Miljanić of Yugoslavia, Helmut Schoen of West Germany and Mário Zagallo of Brazil. They were the managerial giants of the time, with lustrous pedigrees. In contrast, we were being led by a homely, pleasant little man whose credibility rested principally on that one evening at Hampden the previous September. Our World Cup group placed us awesomely with the World Cup champions, Brazil, the strongly fancied Yugoslavia, and the first African nation to reach this stage, Zaire.

However, it was the voice of the captain of the flight who reminded us of that challenge, when he wished us good luck, through the intercom, just before we drained the last of the champagne and bumped down onto continental soil. As we descended the aircraft steps shakily, everyone was offered another bottle of champagne, as if to celebrate touchdown. So, apart from the abstemious secretary, Willie Allan, there were few who did not see dull Belgium as Dorothy suddenly saw Technicolor Oz, after the monochrome of Kansas. We were, in fact, heading for the World Cup like tipsy bus-trippers bound for Blackpool at the traditional September weekend.

2

DOUBLE TROUBLE

The sentence that still clings to me from that brief stay in Belgium came from the lips of the manager of the Belgians, Raymond Goethals. It was at the post-match press conference in the Klokke Stadion in Bruges. Perhaps because his country had not qualified for the finals, he was more acerbic than he needed to be, or else he was just a miserable sod most of the time. He declared, 'Scotland played like blind men.' He was referring to Scotland's manifest discomfort throughout the entire ninety minutes of the friendly game which saw them beaten 2–1 in the match. Nothing was lost in translation because he repeated it clearly and distinctly in English after he had told his own countrymen in Flemish what he had thought of the visitors.

My own stated view on radio later was that our lads made you think of a pub team playing on Glasgow Green in borrowed boots. From the moment they had walked on to the pitch before the match, they looked hungover. The word had got around the press quickly that the drinking on the plane had spilled over into the hotel amongst some of the more prominent players. At least for some of them, that had seemed the case, for I recall in particular the palsied face of the Scottish captain Billy Bremner on the morning of the game, which had the dehydrated, creased look of an insomniac. What was unquestionable is that the hotel itself was a major factor – the SFA had chosen one that specialised obviously in sleep deprivation. It was surely at one of the busiest motorway junctions on the entire continent, with juggernaut lorries thundering past right through the night and seeming to hit a particular bump in the road, which sounded eventually like the banging of cannons in the '1812 Overture', and actually shook some of the rooms. On the back of a boozy outward journey, this proved fatal.

The game was played in this tiny stadium that reminded me of some of the junior grounds I used to visit in Ayrshire when I was following Shettleston Juniors in the Scottish Junior Cup as a teenager. It was Muirkirk or Cumnock without the atmosphere. As this imitation of a competitive fixture trudged its way to an end on a bumpy, hard, dry pitch, where unexpected googlies and leg breaks would occur, when the ball dropped from on high, it left the obviously disoriented Scottish players utterly confounded. They could hardly string passes together. It was sore on the eyes, and certainly on those of the viewing public back home. They were one down to a goal by the Belgian striker Roger Henrotay in twenty-three minutes, pulled back level through Jimmy Johnstone, four minutes before half-time, and then, looking as if they would rather have been on a beach somewhere in this month of June, conceded the winner to Raoul Lambert from the penalty spot, after Kenny Dalglish had been judged to push Van Moer in the box.

When you have played badly, you are as well fulminating against the referee, which Willie Ormond duly did, calling the official a 'homer' in the time-honoured tradition of someone who had nothing positive to say. It was left to Raymond Goethals to let rip with a candour that we hadn't heard from anyone before. We recorded him saying, 'Out there they looked like strangers together. I'm sorry about this, but I think Brazil and Yugoslavia will qualify in your World Cup section.' Although he was not coming across as a charmer, if truth be told there were not a few of us who welcomed this Flemish hero throwing a bucket of icy water over all of us. Not exactly the cold turkey treatment, but we had been stopped in our tracks by one of those typical, orthodox, robotic Belgian sides. To rub it in, we had been scolded by a manager who seemed to want to double as a soothsayer and whose prediction began to unsettle even those of us who were sceptical of our chances under Ormond. For, despite all, we did want to succeed, although not with the kind of dumb loyalty inferred by the English journalist Brian Glanville's description of the Scottish media at the time as 'Punters with typewriters'. Wisely, he had not travelled with the official party.

At this juncture it is well worth reminding ourselves of the entire squad of players whom Goethals was dismissing as not fit for purpose.

David Harvey (Leeds United) Age 26/Caps 7, Sandy Jardine (Rangers) 27/16, Danny McGrain (Celtic) 24/12, Billy Bremner (Leeds Utd, captain) 31/48, Jim Holton (Manchester Utd) 23/11, John Blackley (Hibernian) 26/3, Jimmy Johnstone (Celtic) 29/21, Kenny Dalglish (Celtic) 23/19, Joe Jordan (Leeds Utd) 22/11, Davie Hay (Celtic) 26/24, Peter Lorimer (Leeds Utd) 27/14, Thomson Allan (Dundee) 27/2, Jim Stewart (Kilmarnock) 20/0, Martin Buchan (Manchester Utd) 25/13, Peter Cormack (Liverpool) 27/9, Willie Donachie (Manchester

25

City) 22/11, Donald Ford (Hearts) 29/3, Tommy Hutchison (Coventry City) 26/8, Denis Law (Manchester City) 34/54, Willie Morgan (Manchester Utd) 29/19, Gordon McQueen (Leeds Utd) 21/1, Erich Schaedler (Hibernian) 24/1.

Looking at the names, and linking man with club, you can see how richly embroidered the Scottish tapestry was at that time, with top quality and credible experience. Joe Jordan put it simply to me, 'It is the best national squad I played in. And yes, better than 1978.' But, of course, this was a new experience they were heading for, as Danny McGrain is quick to point out. 'Not one of us had played in a World Cup before, of course. So there was nobody in the squad we could talk to about what it would be like. I know we all had experience, but not at this level. Even the most experienced among us, like Billy Bremner and Denis Law, had never been there before and although you might think professional players can take these things in their stride, it's not like that. We just didn't know how we would react. And I'll be honest. I admit I was scared, or to put it another way, nervous like I had never felt before, even in the big games for Celtic. I mean scared of making just a simple mistake. I know I had been in a lot of televised games before, but this was different. You felt the eyes of the world were on you, staring at you. Yes, it was frightening up to a point and yes, I did make a crucial mistake which I think might have cost us in the game against Yugoslavia. I still wonder why I made it. Maybe I'm putting too much blame on myself for it, but it still annoys me that something I should have known about an opponent I let slip.' We will come to that game eventually.

Joe Jordan still looks back on that period with a certain degree of awe though. 'What a breadth of talent. But you know what strikes me? The talent that came before it. Think of Baxter, Greig, Crerand, McNeill, for example – great players who never got near the World Cup itself. Why couldn't they qualify? That question preyed on me and, as a comparative youngster in the team, I realised I was faced with the biggest test of my life, especially as I had read somewhere in one of the papers, before the squad was picked, that Willie Ormond thought I wasn't quite ready yet. It was some challenge!' Even though he had played in European football under the great Don Revie at Leeds, like all the others, this was like venturing into the unknown.

Denis Law's presence gave the squad a lustre that you always associated with Scotland's greatest ever goal scorer. When I put Jordan's puzzlement about lack of previous success at this level to him, Denis offered me a partial explanation. 'Too many games. Too many injuries. In those days we had to fit in a heavy schedule of club football along with the international games. No "international week" like they have now. I lost count of the number of times we had to go into games minus key players. This lack of continuity cost us heavily.' But his own special effervescence, which had lit up all our lives so often, was no longer showing. It was just our misfortune that, in our hour of need, we were bothered by the nagging thought that this great player was probably past his sell-by date at the age of thirty-four, but still carrying the distinction of being Scotland's top scorer at the time, with thirty goals.

But Belgium had given us all a headache. For the first time since that great night at Hampden, a kind of squeamish uncertainty about the immediate future had already set in. The conversations I was having with others in the media, in the hours immediately after the Bruges game, had taken an interesting turn in contemplating what had never really occurred to us previously. Were we, in reality, out of our depth? Or was this just some skittish knee-jerk reaction on our part brought about by one friendly game and too easily panicked by the Grim Reaper, Raymond Goethals?

We were grateful to pack our bags and get out of Bruges, although it did feel like we had just been thrown out of town by the local sheriff. In contrast to the birthday-like party we had experienced crossing the North Sea, the flight over the fiords to Oslo was rather more like a convocation of Trappist monks heading for a spiritual retreat. There was a pall of sobriety hanging over the party. By that I mean it seemed unnatural, pessimistic, not at all like a group of players desperate to get into the fray. The next game against Norway was taking on a new and unexpectedly crucial dimension, although the first sight of Oslo hardly made the flesh creep, as sometimes it did when you flew into great footballing cities like Milan, Barcelona, Madrid, or Amsterdam, knowing that any team would have to pull out something special to come out unscathed. You could not avoid seeing the expanse of sea, and the wedges of fiords below as you descended into this city and when you left the airport you could not miss the looming presence of the huge ski-jump site as you travelled into town.

So, this was the country of people who skied and fished, was it? That was about all our preconceptions carried, not to mention a few other titbits, like knowing they had blown up their own heavy water plant in the mountains during the last war, which severely handicapped the Germans working to attain an atom bomb, and that Kirk Douglas looked great as a Norwegian hero in the film of the action *The Heroes of Telemark*. But football? Not to be taken seriously, that was the category we put them in. That is until you looked at the fine print of their record. They had only been beaten by a late and stupid goal in East Germany just a couple of weeks before, and, during their World Cup qualifying section, lost only to an even later goal against Holland, who had a considerable reputation and were strongly fancied by some to win the title in Germany. But it wasn't football itself that greatly exercised our minds over the next few momentous days. Instead, we were to study the frailties of men under stress.

Firstly, the setting. It was generally agreed that the claustrophobic hotel chosen for Bruges could have been used as the setting for a remake of *Psycho*. Now we had swung to the opposite extreme. We were all now in what was effectively a student hostel in the middle of a university campus. The rooms were no more than tiny cells into which you could manage a suitcase and yourself, plus, perhaps the odd termite. For everything, bar the soap, seemed to be made of wood. It was not my first impression that mattered. It is what I tried to imagine was going through the minds of the players as they reached their rooms, infinitely more accustomed to a standard of hotel where you could take the luxurious free toiletries, wrap them up and offer them as Christmas gifts eventually. Although Davie Hay offers this caveat, 'You know why we didn't complain as much as we should have? Because we were such crap against Belgium that we felt it would be better to shut our mouths before anything was cast up to us.' But they also knew it was manna from heaven for the media who, completely out of kilter with the SFA, did interpret this as lowering the tone of preparation for the greatest challenge of their lives.

Many of us had been used to travelling around Europe with various clubs, especially on big occasions. We were with Stein in Lisbon in 1967, when he put his players in a marble palace of a hotel in Estoril prior to the European Cup, which he knew would help dispel any feelings of inferiority amongst his men prior to taking on Inter. If they were going to be taking on the best, then they had to be treated like lords all the way. That strategy spilled over onto the field of play itself on that famous day in 1967. We were with Willie Waddell of Rangers when he housed his charges in one of the most luxurious hotels in Castelldefels, just outside Barcelona, before their triumph against Moscow Dynamo in Barcelona in 1972 in the European Cup Winners' Cup. It fitted the sense of being part of the aristocracy of European football.

And now this: the tradesman's entrance to the Cup. We had a full five days of preparation before the game against the Norwegians and in that time I failed to find one soul who applauded the SFA for innovatory thinking in bringing to an end the pampering of players and instead treating them like delinquents in boot camp. The events of the very first night and the subsequent consequences of the next few days proved the folly of that thinking.

The area was just outside the city in an almost sylvan setting with long lawns sweeping between the various buildings of the university and in the middle of which was a large student union which, as they always do, contained a long bar with easy access. We soon learned that the beer there was cheaper than in town and the décor was enhanced by languid, leggy blondes, all of whom seemed to be potential Miss Worlds. Unsurprisingly, this little oasis, in the middle of sober academia, had a magnetic pull on the players, who were immediately told by Ormond that it wasn't out of bounds, that there would be a curfew at night, and that, overall, he would trust them to be prudent in handling the odd bevvy. The ordinance seemed mature and manly in a trusting kind of way. It simply blew up in his face.

The night I walked into Ormond's nightmare was one I shared with a man who was at the embryonic stage of his career with the BBC: John Motson. He had joined me from London that day to film some previews for *Grandstand* and *Sportsnight* with a camera crew and a pugnacious little Cockney producer called Bob Abrahams. England had not qualified for the finals, so they were charged with the duty of putting their own slant on things for a network audience. I never thought at any stage that they were relishing that role. There was a patronising quality to their fraternising. Then came the moment when their new-found enthusiasm for Scotland was put to the test. Motson and I were sitting in the student bar having a pleasant chat and sipping our beer when we heard the sound of raucous singing that caught the ears. They were Scottish voices, drunken voices.

Down the short flight of stairs leading into the well of the bar came the Scottish captain Billy Bremner, his arms round the shoulders of his great mate Jimmy Johnstone. They were, as the Bard would have it, 'unco fu'. They saw us and made a beeline towards our table.

Motty froze. Whatever liberal arts education he had enjoyed in the south, it certainly hadn't prepared him for being confronted by two drunken Scotsmen in a Norwegian student bar, about to intrude on his privacy. 'Will we move?' he muttered out of the side of his mouth, preparing to get up and flee. Bad idea. I didn't need to say anything. I gripped him by the arm under the table and shook my head. There could be nothing more provocative than snubbing two of the undoubted stars of the Scottish side. I could tell from the state they were in that hell would have no fury like these two scorned. We held still and they thumped down beside us, Bremner's arms round Johnstone's shoulders and singing straight into his face. Johnstone, the better singer, was trilling like a linntie, as they say, but in between they were encouraging the bewildered students to join in. Those of them studying anthropology might have found this very interesting. I looked at my watch. It was at least an hour past the curfew limit that Ormond had set for the players. It looked as if they were begging for trouble now. I don't know how long we were there, but after a time Ormond appeared at the top of the stairs staring at the pair of them, his sickly pallor leaving us wondering whether he would scream or vomit. They had obviously been reported missing. He stood there for a minute or so, then just disappeared. Very shortly after that, the SFA and Celtic doctor Dr Fitzsimons appeared, marched down the stairs, put his arm round Bremner, whispered something in his ear, pointed towards the exit, and both of them, surprisingly meekly, quietly rose and stumbled off like two contrite lads who just been caught stealing crab apples off a neighbour's tree.

That pair were a contrast in personalities. I never warmed personally to Bremner, although I had the utmost admiration for him as a player. You felt he was only approachable if you had previously negotiated terms with him. Johnstone, on the other hand, was a lovely personality who surrendered too easily to drink, but had not an ounce of malice in him. Danny McGrain agrees about who the real culprit was.

'Billy was a strong personality. And he was clever. He knew what he was doing, taking Jimmy out. He needed company to support him on a binge and then, of course, things just got out of hand. Jimmy was just a harmless boy at heart. Wouldn't hurt a fly. Remember, Jock Stein had his problems with Jimmy's drinking at times, but he always handled it brilliantly. However, the pair of them had let us all down. A lot of us were angry, although we didn't say too much for this was our captain and a special player whom we banked on.'

I detail this scene because here was an opportunity for Ormond to stamp authority on two of his senior players. To our eyes, he had dodged the issue. However, Joe Jordan took a more benevolent view when he told me, 'I think it was Sir Alex who said, "Don't go seeking confrontations." There is enough happening inside the dressing room for you to confront. Don't chase after trouble outside it. I think Willie handled it his way, and in fact I'm sure that his view of Jimmy Johnstone, in particular, for the rest of the time in the squad, was altered completely. I think he had reservations about him after two poor displays and that night confirmed what he had to do with the player. And that is, don't play him.'

We had all assumed that players would approach this special task like men studying for the priesthood, or of soldiers doing nothing but bayonet drill before going over the top. We had believed this was the time for asceticism and that seeing a player so much as lick a stamp would be the act of a footloose libertine. And now what had we got? A couple of men who had brought Hogmanay to the fiords.

So, what would that tell us about how Ormond could cope in any crisis he had to face? When they had sobered up they would realise they were dealing with a man far removed from the occasional tyrannies of their club managers Stein and Revie. Although Motson and I were the only media witnesses to the incident and had vowed to say nothing, since we were not in the business of news reporting, we also knew that by daybreak the word would have spread throughout the camp. What we certainly did not know at the time was what Davie Hay knew.

'I spoke to the pair of them when they came back from the bar and wee Jimmy kept saying, "I'm goin' hame. I've had enough of this." Billy was ready to pack his bags and get out of there as well. I tried to argue with them about that, because they weren't the only ones that had been drinking. It's just that they had carried it too far, and somehow or other Jimmy was the one who always got caught, like the time of the rowing boat incident, because he wasn't the only one who had been out at sea that day at Largs.' Although the betting amongst the media at that stage was that the players would be sent packing, at lunchtime the next day, Willie Allan announced the result of the international committee's deliberations on the incident, effectively fudging the matter by stating that apologies had been accepted from both men. They were staying. As the first impressions had been given to the media that the men would be sent packing, the press let loose at the SFA with both barrels.

Alan Herron of the *Sunday Mail*, and one of the most respected of journalists, was uncompromising. 'The pair of them should have been sent home. Immediately. Full stop.' Jim Blair, in the *Glasgow Evening Times* wrote back that same Monday, 'It would appear that manager Ormond, who later refused to comment further, may well have saved the players from being sent home. Rather luckily, they got off with a severe reprimand. The fans back home must be wondering what has gone wrong at international level – but discipline will have to be tightened and had the officials carried out their original intention, there would have been no cause for a complaint.' In the *Glasgow Herald*, Ian Archer was making his readers aware of the image problem emerging from this.

'The affairs of the downstairs bar continue to reverberate, not only around this student hostel, but is stretching across Europe with the Continent's entire media making telephone calls.' He then added, most pertinently, '" I wonder," one of my colleagues sighed wistfully today, "when are we going to get back to the business of actually writing about football."'

And so said all of us. Perhaps Archer had identified the most salient point of all. Whilst there had been that overall drinking session on the original flight over to the continent, most players had indulged only moderately and some, while hardly teetotal, were models of restraint, like Jordan, Dalglish, McGrain and Jardine, just to mention a few. This would be little different from many other squads heading for Germany, where few squads practised total abstinence. But with two players hitting the news as they did in such a flagrant manner, the harm had been done, the stigma had been attached. Effectively, Scotland were now seen to be carrying booze in the team hamper. It was going to take some living down.

That wasn't helped by other news getting out. One morning we heard around the place that the players had left their breakfast table armed with the knives they had been using to butter their toast. What next? Kidnapping their SFA nemesis Willie Allan? They had hired a so-called agent called Bob Bain, of the kind of physique that suggested he was a legend in his own lunchtime and who had boasted to all and sundry he had been PR for the Bunny Club in London at one time. Dealing with female pulchritude hardly qualified him to take on Billy Bremner, of the grasping commercial hand, and who had learned a thing or two about negotiations from one of the masters of making deals, his manager at Leeds, Don Revie. Bain was predictably failing. His initial promise of earning the squad something like £10,000 was not even approaching half of that. They were particularly riled by the sports company adidas, which had not stumped up enough to satisfy them. I sat and had a meal with the main rep for the company, Jim Terris, and as he waded into his steak on a sizzling platter, he told me what the knives had been used for.

'You wouldn't believe what they did,' he told me, almost weeping into his beer. 'They took their knives up to their rooms and they ripped the adidas stripes off their boots for the official photograph for the newspapers. What kind of lunacy has taken over? Greedy bastards, eh?'

I've never placed Danny McGrain in that category at any time. But he simply recalls the need for unity under Bremner.

'We did do that. We had been let down. We didn't want to be promoting them when they just weren't meeting what we thought were reasonable terms. The funny thing is that when the *Daily Record* came to take the official photograph, they crowded us all into such a small room and there was no way the photographer could have shown our feet at any time anyway and what we were wearing on them. So, you could say that what we did was just a waste of time. But at the time we just felt we had to make a stand.'

Immediately, on top of that, the players learned that the SFA had simply ignored an offer from Tennent Caledonian Breweries to provide incremental financial inducements to the squad, at various stages of the competition, which would eventually earn them close to £100,000 if they won it outright and, in return, the brewery would benefit from advertising. The SFA members there, led by Willie Allan, preferred to go to a dinner with the Norwegian FA, rather than face a specific deadline meeting with the executives of the brewery company.

So, the potential revenue all disappeared into a void, to the disgust of players and press. But snubs were almost becoming a new World Cup fad. With Bremner openly describing some of the press to me as 'vermin', it was hardly surprising that when we all turned up for an evening training session, a Norwegian official was sent to the door of the stadium to say in laboured English, 'Not allowed in training. Mr Ormunn has said.' I could see startling anti-Ormond headlines being written on the faces of the journalists present, who were actually grateful for being saved from the tedium of watching players running around traffic cones.

Relations had now broken down completely, as was emphasised the following day when the respected journalist, John McKenzie of the *Daily Express*, was pulled aside from the press corps and told he was to be banned from the official charter flight when we left for Germany because of what they thought was ill-informed reporting of events. His press colleagues were actually very envious of him, as no doubt their editors would be demanding, 'Why weren't you banned?', given that this was simply an act of self-immolation by the SFA, which created great front-page headlines and boosted circulation.

For a spell, we in television were feeling slightly superior to the press in not having broken any rules or caused offence; and also because we had come to terms with Ormond, in the fullest sense of the word. Weeks before, the BBC had sent a London sports executive up to Glasgow to meet the manager and to take him to a splendid restaurant in the centre of the city, where he had been regally wined and dined. And in an act that seemed right out of John le Carré, by prior instruction an envelope was passed from the editor, under the table, to me, to pass on to Ormond, who obviously knew what was

37

going on and took it with aplomb, before secreting the bulky envelope into a side pocket. As this surreptitious manoeuvre could hardly be achieved without a trace of fondling of thighs, that in itself was embarrassing. As this ludicrous scene was enacted, it did pass through my mind at the time that he could have been passing the Scotland manager on a couple of tickets to the Chelsea Flower Show, for all I knew!

For, ultimately, in Germany, we were being given free access to move amongst the squad, so hooray for the Chelsea Flower Show! This was much to the disgust of an envious press who perhaps did not know that the BBC had also paid handsomely into the players' pool for the privilege. Then, one night, a roomful of players besieged by events, and not wishing to arouse any more hostility by breaking curfew, asked Motty's producer Abrahams if he would go out somewhere and get them some beers. He obliged. But when he returned and took the lift upstairs with several packs of lager, he opened the door and walked straight into Willie Ormond in the corridor. Abrahams apparently said simply, 'Good evening' to the manager and delivered his package. In return, Ormond delivered us a knockout. Like the press, we were now banned from any communication, with him and his men, for flagrantly encouraging players to booze.

Our swagger among the press had been taken away from us. Which is why we greeted the morning of 6 June 1974 with a sense of relief as well as apprehension, for now we were getting ready to actually go to a football match. What would it tell us of the mood of men who were only days away from leaving for Germany?

Here were the men who would be the first to seek redemption:

DOUBLE TROUBLE

Tommy Allan,
Sandy Jardine, Danny McGrain, Martin Buchan, Jim Holton,
Jimmy Johnstone, Billy Bremner (*captain*), Davie Hay, Peter
Lorimer,
Tommy Hutchison, Joe Jordan.

In the first half, Scotland looked to be a chain gang hobbled by their own recent experiences and misdemeanours. They were a goal down to the talented Tom Lund, an elegant striker whom Ajax were trying to woo to Holland to replace Johan Cruyff, but who would never move out of Norway professionally, because of his fear of flying. He was that good, and made the lumbering Jim Holton at centre half, who had just passed a late fitness test, look ominously uncomfortable. There was no such fear of heights for Joe Jordan, who rose splendidly to equalise with a header with only sixteen minutes to go, and then Kenny Dalglish, who had come on for the wholly anonymous Jimmy Johnstone, tapped in from almost on the goal line to win the game with a couple of minutes left. A 2–1 win in the rain, against so many semi-professional players, did nothing to ease our football concerns as we packed our bags for Germany, with the classic headline in the *Daily Record*, the day before, succinctly capturing the mood of what had happened so far, 'The Tour De Farce'.

3

ENTER THE WITCH DOCTORS

It was the Black September terrorist movement that had effectively organised our reception into Frankfurt on 7 June 1974.
The airport was crawling with armed policemen. The over-
arching concern about terrorism, and the dreadful Munich
massacre in the Olympics of 1972, had stirred the German
authorities to protect all incoming teams like precious assets,
and to enhance their reputation for efficiency and organisation. We had hoped that all this meticulous scrutiny, with
guns at the ready, had been explained to the players as being
the result of a terrorist threat and not because of their new-
found, and hardly justified, reputation for dissolute living.
Before we left the airport, and without intending to mention
the fumble under the table and the envelope, I tried to make
contact with Ormond to point out that, although he had
obviously taken umbrage against the BBC because of the
drinks lark, and given his assurance he would be available
for information at any time, that he should keep his word.
But in the general melee in the airport, as the players and
officials made their way to their bus surrounded by padded
men with guns sloped against their chests, there was no
chance of a private word in his ear.

So, parting was certainly no sweet sorrow, as we saw the team bus leaving for what we assumed, given the SFA's track record so far, would be some godforsaken spot in the Taunus mountains to the north of the city. Our hotel, in contrast, was in an area devoted to the architecture of commerce. By 6 p.m., when businesses closed down and folk departed the scene, the tall soulless glass and steel buildings felt like you had come across a Druidic meeting place. And after a few days the hotel itself seemed as congenial as Colditz. It almost evoked nostalgia for Oslo and that damned student bar, which, for the moment, had become almost as famed as Rick's Bar in *Casablanca*. Then one night I suddenly felt a lurching sensation inside me, like I was about to levitate.

It was the sight of commentator David Coleman that shook me out of a kind of post-World Cup lethargy. The games still seemed so far off that it was almost as if we were on holiday. Then, on the second night there, I saw this figure marching through the lobby barking some orders to a flunkey or two around him, which Coleman was wont to do, with a voice you instantly identified with the highest level of sports broadcasting. He was top dog. Nay, a demi-god, if you listened to what was said about him in broadcasting circles. He was fully aware of that and acted accordingly, regarding all around him as Lilliputians set to bugger him up, and, as a consequence, treated them like serfs. But he was a marvellously articulate broadcaster.

There is no doubt he resented the fact that I would be working for BBC Scotland while he was on the national network, when, in fact, he would like to have monopolised the whole UK output. I was an intruder, someone from the backwoods. But the politics had been agreed in advance and Scotland, in this sense, would have its independence in this broadcasting matter – or at least we thought that position had been cleared.

We also had Jock Stein. He would be my co-commentator for some of the games, although it was clear that Coleman wanted to put a claim on him, like a prospector sensing gold in the offing, given Stein's enormous reputation. And, as if he wanted to make it perfectly clear of his omnipotence, when we were all in the dining room one night, sharing a table, in walked the editor of *Grandstand*, Jonathan Martin – who was supposedly in charge of everybody in the whole World Cup operation – who started to ask his commentator to turn up for a recording the following morning at a particular time. Coleman's barked reply was instantaneous, 'There are big pricks, there are small pricks, but you are the biggest small prick of them all.' Thus, in one sentence, he had revealed the true hierarchy within BBC Sport and that nobody, but nobody, could push him around. I knew though, that I was safe enough in having Stein beside me for the first game against Zaire, because Coleman was to commentate on the opening ceremony, immediately followed by Brazil against Yugoslavia in the opening match of the tournament the day before our match. That was enough on his plate even for a demi-god.

That same night turned out to be educational, though. Stein opened up about Scotland for Coleman's benefit, for although the Englishman was meticulous in his preparation and would have done much homework, listening to a giant of the game discuss particular players was penetrative insight of the highest order. I noticed there and then, and throughout the entire tournament, that Stein liked to lavish praise on Kenny Dalglish. Not without some justification, of course, but it went on so much, even in his interviews for

42

the English in particular, that at one stage I asked his close friend, the Glasgow bookmaker Tony Queen, who had accompanied Stein to Germany, 'Is he actually trying to sell Kenny?' I deferred from asking the man himself.

I recall fragments of the conversation with Coleman. He talked about the defence. 'Two great full backs. They move Danny McGrain over to the left to accommodate Sandy Jardine, but that makes no difference. Danny can play anywhere. Jardine has pace. You need that. And we've got fighters in midfield. Nobody will take the mickey out of Davie Hay and Billy Bremner. But Denis? I wonder about him.'

He didn't pursue that much further about Law, and he almost dried up when Coleman asked him about Jimmy Johnstone. All he did, at first, was cover his eyes with a large hand in a kind of mock despair.

'Jinky? In the mood, he's the best. In the mood.' This was in distinct contrast to what he had told Hugh McIlvanney of the *Observer* just before the team had left Scotland, when he said, 'Even the Brazilians have never seen anything like him. If Willie Ormond can keep a grip on him, Jinky may show some of the old stuff.' The reports from Oslo, it seems, had put doubts about Johnstone in his head. He clearly didn't want to say much more and abruptly changed the subject by stating, 'You know something, I think Yugoslavia could actually win this group. Maybe even get to the final.' He went on to give his reasons, including the fact that they were individually talented, had a great coach, and would have a huge support, almost as if they were playing at home. My overall feeling was that he wanted to be very measured about Scotland's chances, and didn't want to be seen by the English as some kind of flag-waving zealot, of which there were more than enough in the vicinity.

Now, though, it was down to business. And business meant beating ITV to the ratings. This was not simply a domestic duel between my good friend Arthur Montford for Scottish Television and myself. The metropolitan clash between ITV and BBC network dominated the whole tournament. London was calling the shots for both of us. The BBC was getting slightly concerned about the burgeoning popularity of the relatively new sports output on the other channel, which was initially led by its first outside broadcast editor Frank Keating, who relished taking on what he called, 'the scornful strut of the BBC, who had all the experience as well as the watertight contracts.' The channel he led was now much stronger and more aggressive, to the extent that the editor of *Grandstand*, Sam Leitch, had warned all BBC men not to frat-ernise with the opposition in the bar of the hotel, which both sides were sharing, for fear of letting slip one of our ploys. 'Careless talk in the bar could cost professional lives,' he told me, mimicking the wartime poster slogan. Seriously. In that context of being highly competitive, I wanted to impress upon Leitch, my fellow Scot, that I could get things done for him. So, getting Ormond to speak openly and frankly for us before the opener had become an obsession with me, even though I knew that anything he had to say would not be laced with Socratic wisdom.

The morning after that dinner together, Coleman, Stein, Queen, myself and an entire camera crew took off for a little village called Erbismühle in the Harz mountains an hour and a half away. This is where the SFA party had based itself. It was pretty as a picture. They were housed in an old German hunting lodge, which was also used as a ski centre in winter. Whoever had selected this deserved the SFA's Distinguished Service Medal, given what they had chosen in Oslo. The main temptations of life, though, were miles away. Isolate footballers and their thoughts don't automatically think of whiling the time away over a chessboard. Frustration is the enemy of good preparation, but at least their accommodation and training facilities were of the highest order. The factor that helped keep any wayward thoughts out of their minds was that they knew they were now being mocked by many European journalists, most of whom had distorted the news of drinking on the way to Germany, into evidence of a weakness of Scottish character that would crucially undermine any chance of success.

This was absurdly out of all proportion since other continental journalists I knew talked about drinking and dissent, of one kind or another, amongst other squads in Germany. The Dutch, who always gave us the impression that infighting was a national pastime, had threatened to strike, however remote that may have seemed at the time, if financial demands were not met. The German squad had made a last-minute demand to be paid £10,000 a man if they were to go on and win the tournament, and some even threatened to refuse to play. But players trying to screw another quid out of the system was something of a bore to the press, who knew they would come to nothing, and would rather make hay about a couple of men drinking a bar dry.

In this much more pleasant setting, the players were working actively to salvage their reputation by being much more amenable to the press, except for a few particular journalists whom they still considered almost leprous. They had become cheery diplomats, particularly with German kids, who flocked up there for autographs. There was one day, though, when word came that a threat had apparently been made by the IRA to assassinate a couple of Protestant players

45

in the squad and suddenly the cheeriness had a certain hollowness to it, and the guards looked sterner, and got to frisking anybody who moved an inch towards the hotel. After some official spokesman for that organisation utterly denied that such a threat existed, the atmosphere became more relaxed and some of the security people began wearing tammies and looked more as if they were Redcoats at Butlins.

Dortmund beckoned now. This first game was against an unknown quantity.

'I knew absolutely nothing about Zaire,' Joe Jordan tells me. 'We didn't really get much information from the manager. We weren't going to take them lightly but, honestly, we thought we couldn't lose. That's how it balances itself out in your mind, how could the first African team to play in the World Cup beat us?'

We had travelled the night before the game to the city and in the morning walked to the SFA hotel to pick up any news of team selection. The long hours before any big game can sometimes be agonising, as you try to while away the time in your own meditations. You kick every ball in advance. You are the kid at heart trying to put your team ahead, seeing moves, goals, near misses. It always works out better before-hand in the sense that I have never visualised a Scotland defeat pre-match. I saw us as three up by half-time against Zaire, with goals by Dalglish, Law and Bremner.

With this fantasy still in mind, Stein and I walked into the Scotland team hotel on 14 June, the morning before the game, on the prowl for any team information. We hadn't been sitting in reception all that long before we saw Billy Bremner heading towards us. It was time to stop dreaming. He sat beside us, making it clear from his body language that he was pleased in particular to see Stein, and, almost without taking breath, launched into an attack on the press and made it clear he was not happy with some managerial decisions either, since they had left Glasgow. It was an eruption that seemed to be based on the assumption that the Celtic manager would be sympathetic to him. He wasn't. Stein's anger was well enough telegraphed in advance to people through the years. When he was about to explode you could see a tightening of the lips, the eyebrows seeming to clash together and the broad shoulders pulling back to expand the chest. Bremner was suddenly seeing the Incredible Hulk emerge in front of him. A big fist was suddenly thrust towards the Scottish captain until it was just under his nose.

The tirade came in spurts. 'Don't bloody well lie down to all of this … stick it right up the press … get out there tonight and show us you're in a different league from these pygmies you're playing … think of the faces of everybody who's upset you and think of stuffing it up everybody tonight … get out there and show us all.'

Bremner barely said anything in reply. He did put out his hand eventually and shook Stein's with a mumbled few words of thanks. But when he left the table he was a chastened man. Two issues emerged in that one scene. It was clear the Celtic manager would be a father confessor figure to certain prominent players who would seek him out with their worries. So, even though he was there on behalf of the BBC, it was emerging that he would play a part in maintaining morale within the group. The second point was the increasing influence of Bremner in team talks. Clearly, he had not been impressed so far with Ormond. Alan Herron of the *Sunday Mail*, one of the most influential and respected journalists in Scotland, knew Bremner well through previous encounters and, despite Bremner's antipathy towards some of the press, knew he would get access to him. He told me, 'Maybe it was because I was a Sunday journalist and didn't need to hassle the manager and the players daily that helped me. I could lie back a bit and choose the right time to make an approach. Anyway, Billy and I went way back. I remember travelling in a train with him to Glasgow's Queen Street after a long journey from the north. When he got on the platform he was so drunk and staggering all over the place that Eddie Gray, his teammate, was so embarrassed that he refused to walk into Glasgow with him and slipped away and left him on his own.'

So far this would seem like a wholly negative picture that is being drawn of Bremner, but what has to be stressed is that, whatever his personal social frailties, on the field nobody was more influential. Clearly, he liked a beverage, but equally, he never lost sight of why he was a player in the first place. Throughout his career, whatever the fluctuations of his form, and despite his fondness for a refreshment, his powers of recuperation were obviously miraculous, and rarely was he anything other than a dynamic personality on and off the field. This is something Alan Herron of the *Sunday Mail* recognised.

'I did get a long interview with him at Erbismühle. We sat down and discussed all kind of things about Scotland. And do you know, as I sat there listening to him, I was actually saying to myself, "This wee man is actually running the team."'

But Bremner, like the others, was now about to go into the unknown. Zaire had an immensely charming man as their coach, Zoran Vidinic, who was part of the great Yugoslavian diaspora of coaches who could be found in many parts of the world. He had guided them to a 3–0 victory over Morocco in the final African round to be the only side from that continent to reach the finals and the first ever from sub-Sahara. Willie Ormond had taken the trouble to travel to Egypt to see them play in a friendly a couple of months previously, but apart from giving the *Daily Record* a picture of himself dressed like a sheikh and seated on a camel, which, as you can imagine, was a gift from God for cartoonists, his summary of the visit was really summed up in one sentence, 'If we can't beat Zaire then we should pack our bags and go home.'

These were the words of an ingénue. You wouldn't have heard such statements uttered by experienced men accustomed to the vagaries of the game, especially at World Cup level. It was, in fact, a self-limiting prophecy which, unnecessarily, put the emphasis on a win-or-else challenge to his players, and it left some of us with the lurking thought that there might be, looming in the distance, the prospect of an outcome to which, at this level, Scotland had historically become accustomed: embarrassment. Ormond had not taken into account that the African players had been given huge incentives by the Zaire dictator Mobutu who, it was reported, had awarded each of them a new house and a Volkswagen car and, above all, had ensured that witch doctors would accompany the team to Germany to provide occult protection to the squad. The Scotland manager probably thought the witch doctors would offer less trouble to him than the Scottish press anyway.

The Westfalenstadion in Dortmund was in its embryonic state then. Now it is the biggest stadium in Germany, holding over 80,000 people. Then it was a box-shaped arena, with a capacity of 54,000, which proved to be the prototype that attracted Willie Waddell of Rangers, who was then planning a new Ibrox and who eventually decided to copy what he had seen there. It had also been inspected by the Scottish Sports Council, on my own recommendation as a current member of the council, who were seeking a design for a new Hampden Park. But something obviously got lost in translation on that particular venture for Mount Florida in the following years. For the new Hampden which emerged from that visit lost a great deal of its raw grandeur. By comparison, this modern stadium was only a basis for increased capacity in the future, whilst Hampden, significantly, was not. However, up in the television platform, Jock Stein and I were sweating. The humidity was intense. It was almost beyond belief that the Zaire players would wear vests under their shirts, even though Dortmund was trying its damnedest to be like Kinshasa. We hadn't thought of climate. Now we were. It wouldn't be a factor, would it? Were we actually in defensive mode already, testing out a ready excuse just in case? Certainly. Old habits die hard. It was like holding confidence close to your heart, but with a get-out clause in your back pocket.

Then we were handed the official Scotland team sheet.

David Harvey,
Sandy Jardine, Danny McGrain, Jim Holton, John Blackley,
Peter Lorimer, Billy Bremner (*captain*), Davie Hay,
Kenny Dalglish,
Denis Law, Joe Jordan.

No Jimmy Johnstone. Or more broadly speaking, no wingers. The Zaire side were no giants, as we had noted in their training session. Jordan would be an obvious threat in their midst. Was this situation not made for wingers to ply him with the stuff he loved? A blunder? Then the Zaire team sheet came to us and, at first look, was a shock to the system.

Kazadi Mwamba,
Mwepu Ilunga, Mwanza Mukombo, Bwanga Tshimen, Lobilo Boba,
Kilasu Massamba, Mayanga Maku, Mana Mamuwene, Ndaye Mulamba,
Kidumu Mantantu (captain), Kakoko Etepe.

It was time to offer a pertinent prayer that the numbers on their shirts would be easier on the eye than their names were likely to be on the tongue. They were. The worry of identification having been eased, I did actually throb with anticipation as Joe Jordan kicked Scotland off into a new era, to a massive roar from their supporters, in the echo chamber that was a superb characteristic of this new stadium. What followed in the opening quarter of an hour was an anti-climax. My nervousness about commentating on a World Cup match for the first time made me almost leave my seat in excitement, like the fans in the stands below us, when a Lorimer cross in only two minutes was headed by Jordan just inches past the post. I had to remember I wasn't on the terracings. I had a mike in my hand. Stein beside me, was amused, like he had come to the game with a kid. But we both felt this was just a taste of a lot more Scottish pressure to come. It didn't quite work out like that. Certainly, Scotland were looking much more professional and determined, and there were moments in the earlier stages when you thought the Africans might suddenly wilt. But they didn't. What was evident was that the Zairians were in no sense overawed by the occasion. For it was as if Scotland had stirred up a hornets' nest. The Zaire players were harassing, covering, snapping at heels, running like the wind, filling spaces, cramping Scotland and launching tackles with gay abandon. Yes, in the earlier stages, there was a Holton header and a Law shot which brought out the best in the elastic-looking arms of their goalkeeper, Mwamba Kazadi, but there was no tidal wave towards their goal.

Indeed, some of our players looked as if they had got stage fright. Everything seemed predictable and laboured. We hadn't written this into the script. Stein and I were subdued, trying hard not to reveal the sense of disappointment that was now creeping up on us. Something wasn't quite right. For one man the explanation was ridiculously simple. Billy Bremner confessed to Alan Heron of the *Sunday Mail* a day later. 'I couldn't believe it. My legs weren't working right. They felt like rubber. I never thought I would feel as nervous as I did. I just couldn't get going. I kept thinking "This is the World Cup. I'm at the World Cup." I couldn't get that out of my head.'

So, the thirty-three-year-old captain, who had once played nervelessly in front of 136,505 at Hampden in a European tie for Leeds against Celtic four years before and scored a stunning goal from thirty yards, had been virtually neutered inside a much smaller stadium, which held only 25,800 that day. This special platform they were on seemed to have affected the players negatively. The fact is, they didn't know how to handle these newcomers. They were making it up as they went along. And on top of that, they had got an early warning as Danny McGrain clearly recalls.

'They surprised us. They were eager and up for it. And don't forget in the early part of the game one of their players had a great chance to score and it took a marvellous save from Davie Harvey to prevent them. I tell you, it might have been a different game if they had scored then.'

As soon as Ndaye had brought out that special save by Harvey, the local German crowd had taken them to their hearts, as if Scotland were bullies taking on weakened underdogs, and proceeded to cheer every tackle they made, or even a simple pass completed, and you could tell the Africans were responding, not with any particular guile, but just with the enthusiasm of kids bursting to play at the interval with a ball in the playground. The Scottish supporters in the stands were relatively subdued and being outshouted by the so-called neutral Germans, even though some 7,000 Scots were there. But that did not herald an imminent onslaught. Scotland still looked cagey, wary.

After about twenty minutes of trying to make sense of this uneasy performance, Stein threw me a rueful grimace of a man who had expected Scotland to be at least two or three up by now. Then events changed after twenty-four minutes of sparring. Firstly, Peter Lorimer drove in a shot that seemed to be handled in the box. With nothing rewarded and the play raging on, Davie Hay fired in a typically fierce twenty-five-yard shot which hit a post and rebounded down the pitch. Two minutes later, the previously cautious Danny McGrain advanced down the left and swept over a cross which reached the head of Joe Jordan, who turned it towards the feet of Peter Lorimer, who could not have hit it harder into the net, as if all the frustration of the previous week was in its very venom. One up. We couldn't say, 'Thank God!' on the air but my overreaction, like we had just won the World Cup itself, shouted its own truth. Seven minutes later came the second goal. It was bizarre. Bremner had to take a free kick on the left. Perhaps the Zaire defence had interpreted the award as indirect. For, with the ball in the air, they stood stock still, like rigor mortis had set in, allowing Joe Jordan to rush forward unimpeded to head towards the line. The keeper, obviously dumbfounded by his static defence, allowed the ball to slip greasily from his hands over the line. 2–0. And counting? This was the bland assumption we made at half-time.

Scotland's performance in the goalless second half could best be summarised by pointing out that they were heartily booed off at the end of the game by the German spectators, who really enjoyed the spectacle of Zaire continuing to frisk around like colts let loose from the corral. They had made the Scottish defence look cumbersome and had it not been for two superb saves by Harvey in goal, then embarrassment would have been complete. Apart from that, the Africans had many other opportunities, but their shooting was woeful. So, obviously, were the floodlights. For a few minutes in the second half, they failed altogether – for several minutes, in fact. Then they came to life again to show us that there was no alteration to the dour pattern Scotland had apparently set themselves by being simply content to pass the ball amongst themselves with no thought of adding to the tally. This was noted by some supporters as a kind of dereliction of duty, in that the goal difference which could be important at the end of the day was seemingly not a singular motivation out there.

'Easy enough to criticise, especially if you were not down there on the pitch,' Davie Hay said. 'It was damned hot, like I thought I would sweat away to nothing. Remember, we had taken some stick for the way we had played in the two friendlies, and, of course, for some of the antics off the field as well. We were going to play the world champions in four days' time, and it was the first-ever victory by a Scottish side in the World Cup, and this was Zaire's first game when they would probably be at their best. That was going through all our minds. Just get the win.'

Scotland had looked exhausted. No amount of tactical nonce or long-distance objectives like goal-difference could be taken into account when the legs have gone.

Bremner told me to my face a couple of days later, 'Look, I was gasping for air at the end. So were the others. We couldn't lift up the pace. I tried to calm things down. That's why we tried to keep possession a lot. We weren't trying to take the mickey out of Zaire.'

Joe Jordan thought there was a mix of factors.

'I think it was a wee bit of naivety and a wee bit of profes-sionalism at the same time. We thought we had done enough. It was Scotland's first game in this tournament for sixteen years and all we wanted was a win and to see the game out, particularly with two big games to come. And remember, everything was new to us. We were just beginners in this.'

The victory was gratefully accepted by the media. They had moved on from gripe to grin.

4

BREMNER REDUX

Erbismühle in the mountains was a happier place after the players' return from Dortmund. The weather had changed. It was now dry and sunny as opposed to the drenching rain that had preceded that for the first few days. The change neatly reflected the inner mood of players and management, for apart from their own result, they had taken some comfort in having watched the opening goalless game between Brazil and Yugoslavia on television, like the rest of us, which meant Scotland had gone top of their group. That opening ceremonial game had introduced boredom to the competition in a manner that was almost difficult to comprehend. Brazil were astonishingly pedestrian and they simply did not relish the heavy pitch which had been saturated by torrential rain. This was like some team of understudies trying to ape the style and finesse of 1970, but ending up being booed of the stage as impostors, which in a sense they were, by the disapproving German crowd who felt they had been cheated. When they had become world champions, their play had been like poetry in motion, now it looked like pedantic prose.

I had first seen a Brazilian team in action in 1966 at Hampden when they played a friendly against Scotland and, although the great Pelé was on the field, the outstanding player of that 1–1 draw was Jim Baxter, in perhaps his greatest ever performance. However, there were still lyrical qualities to their play, which had augured well for their World Cup appearance in England weeks after that match at Hampden. But, it is what happened to them there in 1966 that influenced their views on how they would set themselves up on their return to Europe eight years later. Peter Pullen, an elegant Brazilian diplomat, with impeccable English, who at the time acted as PR for the Brazil team, reminded me of that when I met him at a Brazilian training session before the game, in discussing his team's apparent new attitude.

'In England in '66,' he said to me, 'we were chopped down. They really had it in for us. I've never seen so many wild tackles. Remember the Portugal game? They might speak the same lingo as us, but not on the football field. They're European. They almost killed Pelé. He had to be carried off and you should have seen his legs at the end; covered in hacks and bruises. We didn't get past the first stage in '66 and we vowed then that, if we came back to Europe, we'd be better prepared.'

Judging by their first game in the Waldstadion in Frankfurt, they had 'Europeanised' themselves, as they saw it. Gone were the eloquent expressions of play that seemed to stem from any area of the field when they had the likes of Pelé, Tostão, Gerson and Carlos Alberto. Now, although they retained Jairzinho and Rivellino, of the immense left foot, even that pair looked much more cautious when they played Yugoslavia. Perhaps the man who had made the most impact was the flamboyant blonde left-sided wing-back Marinho, who, either under instructions or through natural inclination, didn't take prisoners. In a sense, it was disappointing to see the transformation, because whatever national loyalties you lived with, you always wanted to see a Brazilian side being true to their apparent birthright. What we had seen in their opening game was a hybrid, something that confused their real identity. Still, on the credit side for Scotland, if they were prepared to shape up like that against us, then we knew we had battlers who would not be easily marginalised.

The man who could summon up magic in the past for us, Denis Law, had barely been seen in the Zaire match. This was central to the chat among the press. Stein's doubts about his relevance to the team in his advancing years seemed to be prescient. He did not look remotely like the Denis who had captured our imaginations with the thirty goals he had already scored for his country. You could hardly blame Ormond for having given it a fair shot, though. Denis himself showed no sign of being perturbed by the conjecture about him. In all the time I have known him, either as a player or as colleague with the BBC in his pundit days, he seemed to breeze through life. The mop of hair, the shoulders thrown back to emphasise his erectness, the snappy smile, the quick wit, the notion that he would never age in appearance; all these were apparent in the few days before the selection for the Brazil match, for he was mixing with the others in the full knowledge that, whatever befell him in future, the players around were still in awe of Law, like Donald Ford of Hearts.

Ford had little chance of being selected, but became almost a valet to his idol for the remainder of the tournament and, to the amusement of the rest of the squad, he staged a performance of being a kind of Jeeves to Denis, with the pair of them playing it up like old troupers. Ford even went public about his feelings and penned a special article for the

Glasgow Herald in which he wrote, on the morning of the Brazil game, 'To be with him is exciting, interesting, amazing and exhausting all at the one time. The simple fact is that he loves life and the way he is living it. Intentionally or not, he passes it on to all who pack his room to chat, to play cards, talk about football or be bombarded by tea bags.'

Davie Hay had been playing alongside a boyhood hero.

'It was just inspirational to be in the same team, just that. No, he was far from his best. But, importantly, not once throughout did he act like Denis Law the Superstar. He was one of the boys. That's how I'll remember him.'

Ford, converting a genuine admiration for his favourite player into helping make Denis's room a temporary shrine, was helping divert attention away from the public discussion about selection. For the man who preferred to go out on to the golf course on that Saturday in 1966 to avoid watching England win the World Cup, still desperately wanted to play, especially against Brazil.

Most in the press were hoping Ormond would also give Johnstone a fling, even though some of them had originally advocated sending him packing from Oslo. We all knew he had special qualities but my closeness to Stein in Germany made it clear that even his manager and, do not forget, his benefactor, given the way he astutely handled Johnstone's turbulent career, was unsure that he could rise to the special demands at this level any longer. We were kept guessing. But then I was given a clue. The day before the game we had travelled to Erbismühle to interview Ormond, now that the envelope had at last played its part. As a television spectacle it was hardly Frost v Nixon. But I recall it vividly, not for what he was saying and what, perforce, we were obliged to transmit, but for what I was seeing in the distance in the background. Walking around one of the lawns stretching out from the hotel was Stein accompanying the Manchester United winger Willie Morgan. It was a heated and clearly intimate conversation, which went on long after Ormond had left the interview area. At one point, Stein put his arms around Morgan's shoulders and gave him what looked like a quick fatherly hug. When they parted Stein made his way into the hotel for what he had told me in advance would be an arranged private chat with Ormond. He said nothing about the meeting on the way back to Frankfurt, but I did ask him how Morgan was feeling about being at a World Cup.

'He's a bit down in the dumps,' Stein admitted. 'I told him to be patient. His chance will come.'

A day later, Morgan's name was on the team sheet in the Waldstadion. Would I dare to think that Stein had recommended Morgan before his own player? As Davie Hay points out, Stein at no stage offered any support to his own Celtic players. 'We saw Jock from time to time during the tournament, but he never got us together as a group to advise us about anything. It might be because he didn't want to give the idea there was a Celtic clique in the squad that would get the benefit of his experience. We were just Scottish players under another manager. That was that.'

That, of course, does not mean he had no influence on Ormond at all. It wouldn't stay out of my mind. Or had Ormond already decided on playing Morgan anyway? There is little doubt that the Scotland manager wanted some input from Stein, or else their pointed meeting would not have been made so public. Everybody in the media had wanted their meeting of minds anyway. Scotland's most famous teetotaller wasn't going to sit down with Ormond simply to warn him off the demon drink. I am sure Stein endorsed

Morgan to the exclusion of Johnstone and, in a way, started the decline of one of the most emotional relationships between any manager and player, for, exactly a year later, the man he treated like a son, albeit at times a wayward one, was shown the door at Parkhead in an almost heartless way.

Then came a poignant conversation about Denis Law. Stein didn't think he would be picked, or else, as I suspect, he simply knew what the team would be anyway. But the gist of what he said to me, with an element of sadness, was that he felt he would not like to see this iconic figure muddy the reverence attached to him by the public by being made to look like a relic.

Not that I was approaching the Brazil game with equanimity. For a couple of days before, I received a message from Alec Weeks, the executive producer for the World Cup, that BBC Scotland would be excluded from coverage of the game because there were no commentary spaces left for them, given the great demand by broadcasters around the world to cover a Brazil match. It would be left to Coleman and London. I was assured that this decision had nothing to do with them, but was made by the German World Cup authorities. Likely story. I simply didn't believe it and knew that BBC London didn't want us within a mile of that game. So I contacted BBC Glasgow and made it clear to them that I would make sure this would reach the public ear, for there were many journalists around who would welcome an assault on the Corporation, and whilst Coleman and Co would make a hugely acceptable professional job of it, and largely be accepted by the Scottish public, nevertheless BBC Scotland's sudden exclusion would make them look like country cousins or, in the eyes of the increasingly voluble nationalists, dupes of a colonial power. I even phoned my friend Norman Buchan, the Labour MP for Rutherglen, and put that delicate situation to him. He was sympathetic and told me he would see what he could do by speaking to the Controller of BBC Scotland.

Whether or not it was through his influence, or someone else along the chain of command, the organisation grasped the implications of this and, on the morning of the game, I was given the clearance to commentate. I arrived at the Waldstadion with the usual gear, but feeling a little like an alien just awarded a work permit. The intriguing point was that there were plentiful empty commentary positions around me in the media area. It exposed the original banning of BBC Scotland from its rightful place as an internal political scam. And, in a sense, they were partly successful in their machinations because they had purloined Stein for the London output. This was now a solo act for me.

We looked at the team sheet. Willie Morgan had been preferred. And Martin Buchan was in for John Blackley in defence. No Peter Cormack of Hibernian, whom many of the press had been touting for a place, and whose exclusion provoked him in later years into an autobiographical denunciation of Ormond. And, of course, no Denis Law. We were not to know at the time that the game against Zaire had taken on an almost historic hue with the final departure from international football of one of the most inspiring Scottish players ever. In 2017, when I talked to Denis on the day he received the Freedom of the City of his hometown Aberdeen, he was still conscious of his feelings then.

'Even at that stage of my career I had hoped to play against Brazil, so, of course, I was always disappointed to be dropped from a team, although it didn't happen too often. But you just accept it. And remember, at that time there were so many good players about. That's what it was like in the past for Scotland. Take Dave Mackay for instance. He was one of the great midfield players of his time, but he didn't get many caps. Why? Because there were so many other alternatives around. That was a luxury compared to what it is today. And yes, I didn't think I would play for my country again. Yeah, it was inevitable. Sad though.' The last two words were accompanied by an almost defiant but typical smile on his face.

The full side was:

David Harvey,
Sandy Jardine, Danny McGrain, Martin Buchan, Jim Holton,
Peter Lorimer, Billy Bremner (*captain*), Davie Hay, Willie Morgan,
Kenny Dalglish, Joe Jordan.

The Brazilian side still sent a shiver of apprehension up the spine.

Leão,
Nelinho, Pereira, Peres, Marinho,
Piazza (*captain*), Rivellino, Paulo César, Jairzinho,
Mirandinha, Leivinha.

Only one change from the Yugoslav game: Peres in for Valdomiro.

So, they had brought in a more defensive player? Trying to interpret the significance of that was eventually lost on me when the body started to palpitate at the sight of the yellow jerseys striding out onto the pitch. Now the Waldstadion itself was not as daunting as Borussia Dortmund's, where the players must have felt the crowd was intimidatingly close. This one had the comfort zone of an athletic track necklacing it. But at that moment it was not minimising the world champions for me. They simply looked bigger, more loose-limbed, lethal, and you could not help but feel that their first game had been a cunning ruse to lull us into a false sense of security. I could not have foreseen that I was about to commentate on one of the greatest individual performances in a Scotland jersey.

But all was put on hold as we heard the national anthem; The Queen was again booed and whistled at by the sizeable Scottish support of around 10,000, which led to puzzled faces among the foreign commentators around me. An explanation to them at that time would have been importunate and lengthy. The Huddersfield Town supporter in the stands did not need an explanation. He was Mr Harold Wilson, the Prime Minister.

But now the nerves were semaphoring me the message, 'For God's sake, this is Brazil we're about to play!' That was finally getting through to me – right down to the sphincter muscle! So, what was it like down there on the pitch for those walking out beside them?

'Awesome,' admitted David Hay to me, simply echoing my own sentiments as a non-participant. 'The sight of these yellow jerseys got to me. They didn't have Pelé right enough, but they had Rivellino, Jairzinho, Paulo César, and they had that magic aura about them. And I suddenly thought, "It doesn't get better than this, does it?" For there is no animosity ever against Brazil. I suddenly felt I was privileged to be there. To be honest, the first ten minutes or so were a blur. I didn't know what was happening around us. They were pinging the ball around at some rate and I felt we were going in circles. The pace of the game was astonishing. I thought, "This mob are going to give us a doing." Then, just after that, Rivellino whacked me. He had great skills and a great left foot. Remember that famous drag-over he had? Well, he could whack as well. It was sore. It was what I needed. I felt I was coming into my own.'

There was much whacking in the game in fact; some of it brutal. They were finding out about *new* Brazil. Crunch for crunch was swapped as Hay and Bremner began to test the Brazilians' new emphasis on physicality, although, certainly on occasion, the South Americans would find some space and let loose their shots, all of which seemed to have swerve and dip in them. Their full back, Nelinho, tried one first, which slipped past the post, making Harvey in goal look static. Rivellino bent one in, which Harvey again diverted brilliantly past the post. Leivinha then hammered a volley against the bar, which buckled in respect. In between, it was a battle of attrition in midfield with the Brazilians becoming fully aware that Scotland were increasingly more confident and that any awesome regard for these yellow jerseys was dissipating. That is why the second half turned into one of the best forty-five minutes in Scotland's World Cup history. One sight certainly spurred them on as Danny McGrain explains, 'We came on at half-time and looked at the scoreboard, which said Yugoslavia 6–0 against Zaire at half-time. It hit us then that this could all come down to goal difference. I think that put some fire into us.'

Their performance then was based on the refusal of the players not to be dazzled by the reputation of the Brazilians. That original deference to them had been neutralised by being able to defend well against their quick thrusts and long-distance shooting, and the gradual realisation that they had more running power in them in midfield than the South Americans. That is where the difference lay. It was also down

to player power, as Hay explains, 'We made our own decisions on the park. This had nothing to do with the manager.
I remember us telling Kenny Dalglish to come back deeper to
help us out in the middle of the park and let Peter Lorimer go
forward more beside big Joe up front. And Billy and I didn't
need to do much talking together because, at that stage, we
had developed a kind of telepathic understanding between
us. I could feel we were getting the upper hand because of
these changes.'

Hay was tireless, but it was Bremner who really stoked the
fires of this performance. He did not have Hay's shooting
power, which the Celtic man demonstrated time after time
– particularly with a superb twenty-five-yard drive which
Leão did well to tip over the bar, and another angled shot
which the keeper fumbled, with nobody there to pick up the
rebound. The way Hay was continually hammered by Rivellino and other accomplices, but refused to flinch, certainly
had me thinking that, even with a Brazilian team on the
park, pure football was being sabotaged. But it was Bremner
every Scot there was proud of. This was his finest forty-five
minutes in a Scotland jersey; this is what we had come all
this way for. True grit. A wee Scot fighting his quarter in
what we had assumed might be an unequal battle. I had a
pal at school who was prepared to fight some battles for me.
That was my relationship with Bremner down on the pitch
during that second half – me aloof on the viewing platform.
So, there he was in almost every nook and cranny of the play,
fearless in confrontations, urging his men on by example
and encouraging his full backs, McGrain and Jardine, to raid
forward with little fear of the reprisal counter-attack. And he
had struck a chord with the crowd. The Germans were now
roaring on Scotland. There was obviously delight in seeing

the yellow shirts panicking in defence. Then came THE MISS. Or was it?

It occurred about twenty minutes from the end, when Scotland was virtually parked around the penalty box and Leão in goal looked increasingly nervous. Lorimer, who himself had tested the keeper four times with thundering shots from a distance, looped over a corner which was headed down towards the goal by Jordan. The keeper could only scoop it up in front of him and the ball rebounded toward the figure of Bremner only a couple of feet away. It was at his toes. Suddenly, the ball wasn't there any longer; it was slipping past the post with the open goal gaping. How had that happened? Bremner had been presented a gift. Hadn't he? That was my first reaction, which I expressed in a muffled tone of horror – like condemning a culprit. It is still etched in some people's minds to this day, like that incident in the motorcade in Dealey Plaza. So many times I urge that ball to slip in on the right side of the post, just as I always want that bullet to miss in Dallas. Bremner's colleagues, though, are still staunch counsels for the defence. Davie Hay was almost at his elbow at the time, 'Look at the photographs and you'll see I'm beside him. It just happened in a flash and it was like a pinball just bouncing too quickly to get any real touch on it. People say it was a miss, naw, not for me.'

Danny McGrain was not far behind Bremner at that moment either.

'Billy got stick for that for a long time, but he had no chance. The ball rebounded from the keeper and it was all over in a flash. He didn't have a chance to control it or strike out at it. He was off balance and he couldn't even lift his foot back.'

Joe Jordan, as a striker, feels he could not have done any better himself.

'Put simply, the ball hit Billy rather than Billy hitting the ball. There was neither space nor time.'

It was cruel to witness though, and it remains the dominating image of the entire game and, in a sense, unfairly, has tended to divert posterity away from the truly magnificent performance of Bremner that inflamed the passions in that glorious second half. And yet it wasn't enough. At the end, with the cold statistic of a goalless draw failing to reflect an astounding Scottish performance, it was difficult to summarise the match live to the television audience without an emotional throb to the voice. Difficult for me. Difficult for them down on the pitch, trudging off. They had effectively diminished the world champions and, whereas before the game they would have settled for a draw, they now felt slightly cheated. Slowly that sense of disappointment ebbed away, and I relished the other foreign commentators coming around me in the media area, praising the Scots. If bursting with pride can sometimes make you feel kind of childish at times, then I surely had gone back in time to Primary One.

5

'GROWN MEN ARE ALLOWED TO CRY'

By the time they had arrived back in Erbismühle that night, they were in the mood for a party: an orderly one. Billy Connolly, then an emerging comic force, came from Frankfurt to rock them with laughter, easing the pain of virtually all of them bearing the scars of battle. Bremner's legs looked like he had been bombarded by bricks in a gang fight, covered as they were with scarring bruises. It was the stark evidence that the heritage of Pelé, Garrincha, Carlos Alberto and co had been publicly ditched. Although, as Davie Hay admits, 'We handed it out as well, don't forget.'

Life seemed sweeter to them now, which was a remarkable transformation for the men who had slunk out of Norway only eleven days previously. The headlines back home were screaming praise.

Ian Archer in the *Glasgow Herald* commented, 'Scotland should have beaten Brazil in the Waldstadion, and beaten them by the width of the Atlantic Ocean.' The Glasgow *Evening Times* succinctly declared, 'Super Scots Rock Brazil'.

But back at base some concerns were now being raised about the implications of goal difference, especially when the news of Yugoslavia beating Zaire 9–0 sank in. What we had not realised was the real reason for the collapse of the Zairians. There had been dissent in their camp over money, and some of their players refused to play. One of their players had claimed that the German organisers of the tournament had come up with some cash to enable this impoverished association to continue playing, rather than spoiling the image of the World Cup with a default. So, play they did, and to underscore their dissatisfaction with the lack of financial support from home, the coach himself Vidinic, at 3–0 down after only twenty minutes, seemed to have lost interest by deciding to substitute his main keeper with one who was only 5ft 4in. So, for the rest of the game, they had someone about the size of Jimmy Johnstone between the posts. It was an advert for annihilation. Another six goals were conceded, leaving Scotland needing to win their last game to make absolutely certain of qualification, while the Yugoslavs could settle for a draw.

I could not meet anybody outside the players themselves who felt comfortable with that scenario, given that goal difference might still matter hugely. When I interviewed Ormond the day before the game, he expressed great confidence in his players, but after their achievement against Brazil, he was a trifle prickly when I mentioned goal difference and their 2–0 Zaire victory, in light of their thrashing by Yugoslavia. But he then revealed he had a problem: Willie Morgan had an injury, which was so painful that he had to be taken to Frankfurt for a scan. 'Fractured toe,' Ormond told me, with a wistful smile on his face characteristic of a manager who knows that, even after an exalted performance, nothing ever runs smoothly. This gave rise to those highly enjoyable guessing games among the media as to who might be played in his place. Johnstone? Cormack? By common consent, both could have played against Brazil. Cormack, in particular, was

70

strongly fancied, given his recent club form, but somehow hadn't convinced the manager.

And then there was Kenny. He was never called Dalglish by anybody during that tournament. He had developed an identity with his outstanding form for Celtic that seemed to be like a favoured kid on the block you couldn't call by any other name. The problem was, we hadn't seen the Celtic Kenny. We had all waited patiently for it to emerge in the first two games, but it never had. By domestic standards, he had become anonymous, regardless of Stein, in many of his television interviews, praising his talents. It just wasn't happening. So, would they simply drop him? It was more than a passing thought among us. But on the day of the game we heard that Scotland would be unchanged from the Brazil match. Morgan had recovered after treatment at a special medical unit that had been set up in Frankfurt for such eventualities. Kenny was being given another chance. Scotland would be unchanged.

Harvey,
Jardine, McGrain, Buchan, Holton,
Lorimer, Bremner (*captain*), Hay, Morgan,
Dalglish, Jordan.

So back to the Waldstadion then on 22 June, again without Jock Stein, who was now under the command of London, who, after all, was paying his wages. Deprived of his services, I couldn't help the feeling that I was getting into this tournament by the back door. And, not to my liking, it was warm again. Not as oppressively humid as Dortmund, but you knew they would be sweating buckets out there. After the special pressure of taking on world champions, I hardly felt relaxed, but at least my stomach was not in knots, as it had

71

been during the previous game. The Yugoslavs had a huge and boisterous support, as we had expected, but although they had decimated Zaire, we knew they had problems inside the dressing room. It mostly centred round their captain and superb dribbler Dragan Džajić, who had been played sparingly over the past few months. He had broken his leg the year previously, been in a car smash and had a spell in the army for six months. His undoubted brilliance was only intermittent, and the Yugoslav journalists were telling us that it was time for him to go, but they placed their faith in him again, much to the discomfort of Danny McGrain eventually.

Their full team was:

Marić,
Buljan, Habžiabdić, Oblak, Katalinski,
Bogićević, Petković, Ačmović, Bajević,
Surjak, Džajić (*captain*).

I do not draw a veil over this game, but although it had huge significance for both sides, it exists in the memory only as preface to its last seven minutes. It is those last minutes, and the hour after the game, that ejects all the other images. Yes, there were chances in a match in which, for the most part, Scotland looked the better side, even though Yugoslavia started powerfully, and, ominously, Džajić looked as if he had preserved his best for us. But they were crude. For some reason, they had decided the boot was mightier than the mind. They went for Bremner, in particular, who took blows that might have emitted chopping noises. Of the chances, the best fell to Jordan in the first half when Jardine, who perhaps had his best game in a Scotland jersey, had a shot blocked by defender Katalinski, with the rebound falling to Jordan's feet only yards from goal. He seemed to stab at it, but the keeper, well out of his goal, parried it at his feet. It was a stalemate, which, of course, suited the Yugoslavs. Then came the sickener. It was in the eighty-third minute, much of the play had been concentrated around midfield and a certain amount of tiredness looked to be creeping in. Then Karasi, a foraging midfielder, found time and space to send a low pass to the right side of the Scottish penalty area. Danny McGrain now completes the story of deep regret he started earlier.

'I was playing against somebody I didn't think had a left foot. Well, I don't know why, but near the end of the game I was defending out wide on the left side and I forced him on to his left foot to turn him away from what I thought was his best, the right. And didn't he just swing round and send over a great cross with his left foot, which beat Sandy Jardine at the far post and the Yugoslav there headed it into the net. I should have known. I can only put it down to tiredness or weariness on my part, but I felt sore about it because it had put them in the lead.'

And with only three minutes left too. McGrain's *mea culpa* rings with a certain honesty after all these years and reflects well on both his integrity and the feeling of desperation that must have swept over the players as the clock ticked mercilessly towards a crushing and saddening finale. For the player he thought didn't have a left foot was in fact Džajić who, having been frustrated throughout by Jardine, had decided to move out to the right for a spell. Hence the accuracy of the cross met by the man who had provided the pass in the first place, Karasi.

All over? We thought so. The impact of that goal was like seeing one of your family fall under an express train. But I had to keep going, mouthing words that I think may have conveyed the hard-luck story all over again. Then, with one minute remaining, Tommy Hutchinson, who had come on for the under-performing Dalglish, sent a ball into the crowded Yugoslav penalty area which just eluded Lorimer, but broke to Jordan who scooped it up into the air in front of him and then poked the ball between the keeper and the post for the equaliser. Enter complexity, for about that time we heard that Brazil were only leading Zaire by 2–0, and, if it stayed like that, then Jordan's goal would qualify us for the next round. Complex in the sense that you could scarcely believe this circumstance, and what to say about it. Inside the dressing room, the reality eventually hit the players with three minutes of the other game remaining. Then they heard: Brazil had scored again.

You could not have made up a crueller exit from any competition, let alone the World Cup, particularly as the third Brazilian goal, scored by Valdomiro in the seventy-ninth minute, came through a blunder by the Zaire goal-keeper Kazadi, who had been brilliant throughout, but let an innocuous shot from the right slip under his body.

'I've never felt worse,' Joe Jordan says. 'Yes, I had played in Europe and had some defeats at different levels, but this sank me. I was young, remember, but even the experienced ones in the dressing room looked more badly hurt. They were crushed.'

'It bit into me,' Davie Hay told me, like it was yesterday. 'You couldn't believe things could end that way. Was it all down to what we did against Zaire? I've heard that so often. You can't just say that. People can be too clever about the way they analyse these things. There were a hundred things that could have been different.'

A Dutch commentator I knew well came across to me some minutes after I had stopped broadcasting and I will always remember his words to me, 'Grown men are allowed to cry, you know.' I don't know whether it was a reflection on his own condition or of the zombie-like creature he was seeing in the BBC Scotland commentary position, unable to move, and staring vacantly into space. You can imagine what any Scot felt. Afterwards, Hugh Taylor of the *Daily Record*, and a man surely hardened by the unpredictable nature of football through the years, admitted to me over a few drinks that he had had tears rolling down his cheeks. The mood among the supporters there was that odd mix of despondency and pride. But, overnight, as the outcome sank in, so also did the realisation that Scotland would return to their ain folk, undefeated, and having played, particularly in the last two games, with a vigour and style that justified their presence there.

This manifested itself at Glasgow Airport. To the astonishment of everybody on the aircraft, flying in the following day, the pilot congratulated the team and then announced that there was a welcoming party waiting for us at the airport. That was an understatement. In fact, there were thousands there. The players were landing as heroes. It struck me at the time that there might be something delusional about this reception, since nothing had been won and we had left earlier than we had aimed for. But, only weeks before, they had been the subject of universal derision. In that sense, it was magnificent redemption.

At first, in these early days in Belgium and Norway, with all the clashes with companies over sponsorship deals, the battle with the SFA over bonuses, two players offering the European press the opportunity to tarnish Scotland as a squad of drunkards, and with two weak games against Belgium and Norway, it looked like capitulation before we had even started. Instead, they were actually too talented to succumb that way. Some of the conduct early on blinded us too easily to that basic fact. It was only when they sensed that an awful fate was beckoning them that they used that talent, backed up by great leadership on the field, to make a transformation that was as if a new species had emerged.

For Bremner became a giant. Watching him in that bar in Oslo, you couldn't help but think this man is heading for the gutter. Twelve days later we had Pelé saying to the world's press, 'This man is one of the best players in the tournament.' His authority and personal commitment infected everyone around him, and Ormond benefitted hugely. Not that he was a rebel, as Davie Hay points out, 'Billy never questioned the manager. Never. He'd listen and then throw in his bit and there was never an argument. It's what he did on the park that mattered in the way he could talk to players and sometimes move them about. They listened to Billy all right.'

I would go so far as to say that, without him, our fate would have been worse. That is not to say that Ormond did not deserve credit. Joe Jordan had admiration for the way he handled himself.

'He was dealing with experienced players like Law, Bremner, Johnstone, who had played at higher levels than he had ever been associated with, but he listened to them and won respect for that.'

Danny McGrain realises why people like myself, accustomed to bruisers like Stein and Waddell, might have had serious reservations about him.

'He was not an abrasive man. There was no bawling and shouting. Everything was calm and clear. And he definitely knew the game. He was no amateur.'

But there was one gamble he did not take. He refused to field Jimmy Johnstone. Just after Yugoslavia scored in the last game, he had told the wee man to warm up. He never came on. It was said in explanation that there hadn't been a sufficient break in the action for him to do so. If that is the case, it should have been done earlier, as Davie Hay agrees.

'That was the big puzzle. The Yugoslavs might have been scared of him. Remember the night he destroyed Red Star Belgrade at Parkhead? So why not give the wee man a go? I know he hadn't been in his best form, but you know what he was like. He could turn the game in a few seconds with his trickery. Not playing him at all was a mistake. Although I have to say this, I roomed with Jinky for the whole five weeks, and not once did he sit down with me and say, "That bastard hasn't picked me again", as I know a lot of them would do. Not once did I hear a word of complaint from him.'

When the dust had settled, the records were to show that Scotland was the only unbeaten nation in the entire tournament. It was another indication of the success of Scottish football at that time, which irritated one gentleman in particular, who, by the sound of it, must have thought Hadrian's Wall was not doing its job properly. In a book just published then, *Football Handbook To End All Football Handbooks*, Chris Lightbown wrote 'Nearly all English football teams are managed by Scots and no team is complete without a few vicious Celts. This arises from one of the lesser known clauses of the Act of Union between England and Scotland that says there must be at least three Scots in every English football team and that teams should all have Scottish managers.'

The vicious Celts were about to gird their loins for another four-year battle.

THE 1978 FIFA WORLD CUP

ARGENTINA

6

A TOUCHY CONTROVERSY

A blunder started it all. A blunder by a referee, by television commentators, by journalists, and seen by millions. Or not seen, as the case may be. It should have been staring us in the face, but it wasn't as easy as that. On the evening of 12 October 1977 at Anfield stadium in Liverpool I told the biggest ever television audience for a Scotland international game that a Welsh player had handled in the penalty area, thus resulting in a goal from the spot by Don Masson, which effectively began Scotland's long trail to Argentina. The morning after, scrutinising the replay over and over with an intensity that could only have been equalled by those underwater cameras seeking out Nessie in the deeps, Jock Stein, my co-commentator and I, concluded that it looked like the hand touching the ball belonged to Joe Jordan. Of course, it was obvious, once you've had the chance to pore over these images, but, in the instant of having to make a live decision, we went with the opinion of the French referee, Robert Wurtz.

So, you could say our World Campaign to qualify for Argentina in 1978 was based originally on a deception. Not deliberately by us, but, nevertheless we were innocently complicit. We were not the only ones who went initially with the referee. The late Jim Reynolds of the *Glasgow Herald*, from a vantage point nearer than ours, wrote the following, 'Anfield erupted on seventy-nine minutes when Scotland took the lead. Johnston took a long throw on the left; the ball was going straight to Jordan and AND DAVID JONES PUNCHED IT AWAY. The referee seemed to take an age to point to the penalty spot, AND WITH JONES HOLDING HIS HEAD IN SHAME, Masson the coolest man in Anfield, stepped up and blasted the ball past Davies.'

I certainly hadn't recognised the body language of 'shame' by the Welshman. Disgust perhaps, if anything.

Mike Aitken of *The Scotsman* wrote, 'It took a needless and incomprehensible concession of a penalty twelve minutes from time to break the deadlock. Dave Jones handled in the box and the memory of that incident will haunt this particular Welshman for the rest of his footballing days.'

Ally MacLeod had been appointed as Scotland's manager in May 1977 with the typically infectious statement, 'My name is Ally MacLeod and I am a winner.' Since he was that night, he issued a statement to Alex Cameron of the *Daily Record* the following day, obviously indicating how highly he valued Scottish jurisprudence and its tradition of the 'not proven' verdicts.

'Jordan told me immediately after the match that if he touched the ball he couldn't remember it and certainly didn't intend to.' And this is what the latter still maintains to this day.

This is the team that surrounded Jordan that night:

Alan Rough,
Sandy Jardine, Willie Donachie, Tom Forsyth, Gordon McQueen,

Don Masson (*captain*), Asa Hartford, Lou Macari, Willie Johnston, Kenny Dalglish, Joe Jordan.
(Martin Buchan came on for the injured Jardine in the eighty-second minute.)

Frankly, this incident did not cause Stein and I to be guilt-ridden for the rest of our lives, for, overall, Scotland had deserved a victory by scoring a superb second goal, netted by Dalglish. On balance, the Welsh had done rather well and, early in the second half, John Toshack, the Welsh striker, brought out one of the best saves in Alan Rough's career when he had to arch back and tip a vicious, curving shot from him over the bar. The game was ultimately clinched with the second Scottish goal, a magnificent header by Kenny Dalglish from a Martin Buchan cross three minutes from the end, which produced a sound from me which viewers must have thought was the rebel yell. It was an eruption of relief in more ways than one because, at the start of the game when we looked at the massive 30,000 Scottish support that had squeezed itself into Anfield, it made Stein worry about a potential aftermath.

'I hope to God we win,' he muttered before the commentary, 'if we don't I think they'll take Liverpool apart.' Outside the ground we had witnessed drink-fuelled arrogance and belligerence that suggested defeat for Scotland was inconceivable. Lou Macari still remembers what it was like when he walked on to the pitch.

'I remember coming out of the tunnel and the noise was incredible. I couldn't believe the size of the Scottish support. The first thing that went through my mind, as soon as I heard the blast of sound from them, was that the Welsh FA had made the mistake of their lives. If they had taken this game to another of their own grounds, with smaller crowds but with Welshmen in the majority, they might have won this tie. But they were after the cash. Remember, it was a close game and, in these circumstances, crowd support matters. They handed the game to us by going to Anfield. So, although I still joke with my Welsh friends about the disputed penalty, I point out that the biggest mistake of that game was not committed by the referee, but by the Welsh FA.'

The degree of trouble was therefore minimal. There were some bottles thrown in anger at the police for not allowing the Scottish team to take a lap of honour, but that was quickly submerged below the fact, slowly sinking in, that we were World Cup finalists again. And we were off to the other side of the world. At that stage, like so many others, I knew little about Argentina. There was Eva Peron. They had lots of cattle. There was some place called the Pampas and a novelist named Borges whom I had always been recommended to read, but had never got round to. That was about it. Now if I see the name, or have it mentioned to me, a flood of images sluices through the mind.

That goal in Mendoza ... Ally MacLeod almost drowning at Le Blanc beach in Rio ... spits flying through the air in Cordoba stadium ... the bullets that were meant for Sheila Cassidy ... the damnable saves of the eccentric Peruvian goalkeeper ... the concentration camp with football posts ... a commentary that never happened ... Cubillas's act of deception ... listening to a Hollywood scriptwriter rewrite the Mendoza result ... the stunned face of Ernie Walker talking about drugs ... the insufferable smile on the face of Johnny Rep ... Ewan McGregor's sex scene ...

Usually they come randomly. Here I now put them in order.

It begins with the decision of the SFA to tour South America in 1977, even before they knew they would qualify for the finals. Such a decision took many of us by surprise, since we believed that the insularity of the SFA was well established and had been from that day in 1950 when they spurned the opportunity to go to Brazil for the World Cup finals, which was clearly on offer, without any qualification. I think their sober analysis of that prospect was that they didn't want to pick fights they couldn't win, and that it would be greatly expensive.

But after 4 June 1977, when we took to Wembley and beat England more handsomely than the 2–1 scoreline suggests, but with a support which disfigured the stadium in some creative ways, we began to feel we could square up to anybody again. So we welcomed this new initiative. However, the decision to play Chile, Argentina and Brazil might have appeared innovative and forward-looking, but not to the British government, nor to a sizeable element of the Scottish public. The news of their decision to play a game in Chile provoked outrage, particularly among trade unionists and people of the left, because, four years previously, the first-ever democratically elected Marxist president in the western world, Salvador Allende, had been killed in a coup engineered by the Chilean generals commanded by General Augusto Pinochet, later to become a buddy of Margaret Thatcher.

There was no hiding place for football in all this turmoil, for the Pinochet regime had used the Estadio Nacional, where the game was to be played, as a concentration camp from which many captives were then led out for torture or execution. To be playing on that grass would be like dancing on a grave, many thought, and, at that early stage, I felt very uneasy about that prospect. The Wilson Labour government of the time asked the SFA to cancel the trip. Ernie Walker refused, and, additionally, would not meet a deputation of survivors of the coup, who wished to argue for a cancellation. The SFA's obduracy inspired the splendid Scottish folk singer and poet Adam McNaughtan to write a song of protest, 'Blood upon the Grass', one verse of which addressed the players personally.

> Will you go there Alan Rough
> Will you play there Tom Forsyth
> Where so many folk met early
> The Grim Reaper with his scythe
> These people weren't terrorists
> They weren't party hacks
> But some were maybe goalkeepers
> And some were centre backs
> And there's blood upon the grass
> And there's blood upon the grass.

It made no difference to Walker or the others around him. The BBC too had made up their minds. They had decided to cover the trip in various ways and, as a member of their staff, I had little option but to travel with the party. That was the excuse I offered my left-wing friends, who thought I was being hypocritical. But, of course, I did want to go, despite my sympathies with those protesting. It wasn't just a contractual imperative; I wanted to see this tragedy with my own eyes. And they were truly opened only an hour or so after we had arrived in the smog-shrouded capital of Santiago, when a silver-haired Chilean gentleman suddenly walked into the pool area where players and press were lounging, after an almost insufferable twenty-six-hour flight on a British Caledonian aircraft, which really was only spacious enough inside for a trip around Arran. Savile Row-suited and in perfect English, which might have suggested he was an Oxbridge graduate, he started to pontificate about how great Chile was and not to believe those detractors and critics of Pinochet and that people were happy with their lot and to go back home and tell Britain the truth about the place. This caught the ear of Kenny Dalglish, whose retort could not have been bettered by a graduate of political philosophy. 'You're talking a load of crap. Piss off!' And, when the man tried to continue, was berated by Dalglish until he slunk away under verbal duress. Round one to the democrats, you could claim. It was creepy though and gave us an insight into the murky, sinister society we had come to.

But it was the following day that we really did feel we were dupes in this baleful attempt to lend credibility to this horrendous regime. A little man with a broad Scottish accent turned up to see the players. He was Father Jimmy Small, a Catholic priest who hailed originally from Shotts but who was in the country as part of the worker-priest movement, which was strong in South America at the time. He invited some of the media back to his mission for a very humble lunch, and as we were about to enter it, he pointed out the bullet holes pockmarking the walls. 'This is where the police tried to kill Sheila Cassidy when she was seeking asylum from us. She just made it, but her housekeeper was killed,' he told us. Cassidy, a Scottish doctor, had offended the regime by simply ministering to the poor, and when she was able to escape back to the UK, became famous for revealing the widescale torture in the country which she herself had endured at length. Some of us found ourselves simply touching the bullet holes automatically, as if in respect for her. We were genuinely moved by his story, which seemed to make our interest in football a wanton indulgence.

Which made it all the more difficult the following night to sit in the Estadio Nacional and try to make sense of a friendly game which attracted only a handful of people – although afterwards the authorities issued a figure of 60,000 to the press, which seemed in keeping with the customary distortion of facts in a dictatorship. Fake news, as it is now named. Our presence there at all had been justified in advance by Ernie Walker, who lectured us on the importance of giving the players the South American 'experience'. That evening, though, felt more like a raw night on Fenwick moor, for nature played its part in reminding us of the illicit nature of our presence there. Mist descended; Jack the Ripper kind of mist. The cold, damp kind that enveloped the ground and increased the feeling that you were in a mortuary, given what we knew of its recent history. Alan Rough felt rather blasé about this fixture until he reached the dressing room.

'I couldn't believe it. There were bullet holes round all the walls. I sat there thinking, "They must have killed people in here." I had started off thinking that if you're asked to play for your country then you do it and it's got nothing to do with politics. But I have to say, it felt creepy in there.'

The visibility became so bad that, when Alan Rough was substituted by Jim Stewart at half-time, I couldn't recognise the difference and still had the Partick Thistle goalkeeper playing until the end of the game. Scotland won comfortably 4–2, with goals by Dalglish, Hartford and a couple by Lou Macari. A win at the start of this expedition was comforting though, and maintained Ally MacLeod's unbeaten record since taking over the management. But that was all. All we now wanted to do was get out of this sad country, pronto, for next stop was Argentina itself. Or Buenos Aires, to be precise.

As had been the case in Germany, the security police were

in force at the airport. However, they made their German counterparts seem like bridesmaids. Unsmiling and bullish, but nervous and carrying heavy weapons, they told us of the danger of a terrorist group called the Montoneros. After a private discussion with Ernie Walker, the head of this operation informed us that, rather unusually, the press bus would go ahead of the team bus entering the city. When I asked why this stood protocol on its head, he informed us in sanguine tones that he had told the SFA that, if there was to be an attack by the Montoneros, it would be the first bus in the convoy that would get it: 'Mr Walker then instructed us that the press bus should go first.'

Our gratitude for that knew no bounds, of course. But, as we raced at breathtaking speed into the city and saw an officer lean out of a police car window in front of us and punch an old man who was daring to cross the road in front of us, leaving him in a crumpled heap, we concluded that, if somebody going shopping could be considered a threat, then we were not anticipating a dull time in town. And this was the real thing. Buenos Aires was a football city; a city that reminded you of Milan, or Barcelona or Madrid. And the host nation preparing for next year's finals was taking games deadly seriously. The clash would be in Boca Junior's stadium *La Bombonera* (The Chocolate Box), named so because of its shape of a flat stand and three steep – nay, vertiginous – stands round the rest of the stadium. An historic day approached. For it was there on 18 June 1977 that Scotland played its first game on Argentine soil. The only change in the Scottish side from the Chile match was Archie Gemmill replacing the injured captain Bruce Rioch, which meant that Martin Buchan was to captain Scotland for the first time. The full team was:

Alan Rough,

Danny McGrain, Willie Donachie, Martin Buchan (*captain*), Tom Forsyth,

Don Masson, Archie Gemmill, Asa Hartford, Willie Johnston, Lou Macari, Kenny Dalglish.

England, failing to qualify for the finals, of course, had played in that very stadium six days before and achieved a 1–1 draw, a very creditable achievement that had set another challenge. But we now had accepted that nothing ever ran smoothly in world football. About an hour before kick-off, the police found a large and suspicious-looking parcel sitting in the well of stairs leading to the commentary position, which I had actually seen myself on the way up. Pandemonium ensued. An announcement was made that the kick-off would be delayed. Floods of police came into the stand and we were told to move out smartly. When we returned, we learned that it had been a parcel of sandwiches, left there by a steward.

It is entirely possible that the whole militaristic ethos that existed in the country had fed into the mentality of the Argentinian players, for this was arguably the most brutal game I had witnessed up to that time. From the outset you could tell, in the ferocity of their tackles, that they wanted Scotland to cower. We timed the full back Pernía flooring Willie Johnston in precisely twenty seconds. Nobody buckled though. Scotland put the emphasis on keeping possession, their passing sharp and confident, and with an energy now that showed they had shaken off their travel weariness. Their amount of possession was clearly irritating the Argentinians. Solid-looking at the back and with Dalglish, in particular, looking as if the talk of him about to leave Celtic was actually stimulating him, they looked the more likely team to score. It was heartening to watch, since we had no way of telling in advance how they would react to this different aggressive football by the home side, backed up by screaming fanatics in the 60,000 crowd. 'You felt the crowd were falling on top of you in that place,' Lou Macari recalls. 'And the noise was deafening. It was one of the most intimidating stadiums I have ever played in.'

Pernía, who could have played Hannibal Lecter had he possessed an Equity card, had decided that he wanted to get rid of this pest Johnston. He achieved that in a bizarre way. Having tested Johnston to the point of cracking with severe tackles from the rear, he then spat clearly in Johnston's face. Even from the monstrously high television platform we could see what happened. Then came the kidney punch from Pernía on Johnston. A replay clearly revealed that. With the referee at the other end of the ground, the linesman flagged for an offence, reported it and Pernía was rightly sent off. Johnston, who was in agony, got to his feet and to his – and our – astonishment, was ordered off as well. He did so in tears. Not that he was unaccustomed to this experience, since this was the eleventh time he had been sent off in his career. The referee's error was compounded when, four minutes after Scotland had gone in the lead in the seventy-seventh minute from a Don Masson penalty, the home side were, entirely predictably, gifted one by a referee who had turned a blind eye to much of the thuggery and was now showing his imaginative powers. Tam Forsyth was appalled, 'I honestly did nothing untoward and, to be honest, I felt that after the Willie Johnston incident they would get a penalty for anything that happened in the box.'

The great defender Daniel Passarella, who was to captain his country in the World Cup finals the following year, made no mistake with it. So, an eventful day had ended with a 1–1 draw and the Scottish media so incensed by the on-field indiscipline, and by the refusal of Argentina's chain-smoking and lugubrious coach, Carlos Menotti, to answer questions about the violent conduct of his side, that, in protest, we rose from his press conference and walked out.

Scotland had played sound, well-organised football in an entirely hostile arena, and against a side that was so cynically crude in its approach that it clearly brought to mind Sir Alf Ramsey's 1966 inference that the Argentinians England had faced were 'animals'. Although, curiously, in that game at Wembley, records show that England committed thirty-three fouls to the South Americans' nineteen. In the Boca stadium that day, Scotland had fourteen fouls against their name, Argentina forty-one. However, lest we were utterly biased or had imagined much of what had gone on, one Argentinian newspaper bravely expressed concern.

'How are we Argentinians going to respond satisfactorily to the millions of British football fans who, after the matches against England and Scotland, are asking if it is really suitable to play the 1978 World Cup here, bearing in mind the brutality of the home team and the complicity of foreign referees?'

But it was a huge learning process. These ninety minutes alone seemed to make the trip to this continent worthwhile. But there was another consequence: there had been a huge television audience back home in Scotland that was rightly enthused by the performance. Add to that the press response to the result, which was ecstatic, then you can understand how the seeds of the wild expectations which followed the team to the World Cup the following year were sown that day in the Boca stadium.

'You might be right,' says Lou Macari to me. 'I've always tried to work out when this incredible hype about us winning the World Cup began. And yes, Ally began to talk about that even back then, after that game. It certainly caught on.'

It was one thing to have beaten England at Wembley two weeks before and break crossbars and dig up turf, but taking on the host nation on its own turf and drawing a game that Scotland should have won, started to give rise to another reaction: that we had players who could take us all the way the following year. This certainly was engaging the mind of Ally MacLeod. He was blooming in the days after that result. But we were all blooming, in fact, because we had now come to Rio de Janeiro.

7

ALLY'S WANDERS

Coming to that city seems to take years off you. The atmosphere in our hotel in Leblon beach was more a smooth *bossa nova* than a boisterous samba. Everything slowed down, except Ally. He held open court and spoke gushingly about the importance of the trip. We lapped him up. It was lulling us into a curious acceptance that, somehow, Ally was almost invulnerable. We were all on a high of positive thinking about this man, unblemished so far, and were feasting at his court. But then something occurred that gave us pause for thought. A couple of days before the game we were indulging in the sybaritic lifestyle of those who fortunately have been washed up on the shores of one of the most seductive coastlines in the world, and with sights on the beach that were decidedly pleasing on the eye. Ally, in a similar mood, decided to take to the water for a swim.

He was quite unconcerned about the fact that he was in no fit state to swim the length of himself, having had a heavy liquid lunch with Hugh Taylor of the *Daily Record*, who had a constitution for these endurance tests few could equal. We watched Ally splashing about like a kid on a school trip, watching indeed from a safe distance, because the further he went out, the higher were the breakers, causing him to bob up and down like a piece of driftwood. He was well out from us on the shore when we saw him disappear. At first we thought he was entertaining us, given he was in a merry mood. But it was when he didn't reappear that we thought this was no joke. We started towards him and then saw his head reappearing, but he looked as if he was unconscious. There was a rush then towards him. He was definitely stunned and had to be dragged back towards the shore. He could hardly speak. As I looked around at our colleagues, it was as if there was a general reluctance to be first to leap into mouth-to-mouth resuscitation for Scotland's manager. Then he started to bark up the water himself. He was trying to tell us his head had hit the bottom. There we were hauling him out of the water like an irresponsible kid. You could tell he was suffering as well from the indignity of being saved by some of the press, including Alan Herron of the *Sunday Mail*, who was beside me at the time. We were not slow to see the symbolism of this.

However successful Ally was at the time, like any other manager, he would have his bad times and, perhaps, there were people in the press who would be less likely to make up a rescue squad in the future. Indeed, in the bars that same evening, those who at the time were uncritical of Ally, but still bridled at some of his vocal ostentation, openly wondered if this incident would subdue him significantly.

They got their answer the following night when Ally went in front of the Brazilian cameras and was as subdued as the Edinburgh Castle's one o'clock gun in announcing what people would see if they turned up at the Maracanã. 'In fact, Thursday night's game could be a dress rehearsal for the final,' he told the locals. That PR gene in his make-up had responded. He was back in fine form and had said the right thing, drumming up public support on an evening of heavy rain, for 60,000 turned up to see a one-sided affair that sobered us up a great deal.

'I wasn't selected for that one,' Lou Macari says, 'Ally put in Archie Gemmill for me, the only change from Buenos Aires. But I knew what was getting to the lads: the travel had got to us. We were weary by that stage. Thousands of miles we'd come. Three games in two weeks. It was too much. But something else; we were all looking forward to playing in the Maracanã. Actually, the place looked like it was falling apart. The facilities in the dressing room area were awful. What a disappointment. The most famous stadium in the world? It was a dump.'

On 23 June, Scotland played like Macari himself felt that day, weary, jaded and needing to get back home. They lost 2–0 to a Brazilian side that, nevertheless, took all of seventy minutes to break Scotland down, which they did in the space of five minutes – firstly with a superb free kick by Zico, then, through stunning inter-passing, a second from Cerezo. Alan Rough recalls his own personal dilemma before he walked onto the pitch. 'Back then you were allowed to take a Mogadon to get some sleep. And I certainly used them. Now we always had a sleep in the afternoons before games. That was not when to take them, of course. I had a sore head that day and I decided to take Paracetamol before I had my sleep. And yes, I know what you're thinking, I took the wrong pill. I took the Moggie instead. The sleeping pill. I woke up, but I certainly was far from right. I tried my best. I poured coffee into myself, and there's plenty supply of that stuff in Brazil. By the time I arrived at the stadium, I was beginning to clear up, but I wasn't quite sure about myself.'

He needn't have been. He was the star of the night for Scotland, producing saves that could have been used as an advert for Mogadon, the obviously new alacrity drug. For Scotland were not even able to win a single corner in a one-sided game. It was that Rough performance which was to win him the Player of The Tour award from the accompanying media.

Ally's first defeat since taking over from Willie Ormond did not dampen his enthusiasm for the cause. Nor were there great lamentations over being beaten by favourites for the World Cup itself. What Ally kept repeating, over and over again, before we boarded the plane home, and during the flight, to those who talked to him, was what we had achieved in Buenos Aires. That's what he wanted people to pay attention to, and it is that theme which continued right up to that memorable night in Anfield four months later. Two men would be the principal leaders of this expedition; personalities of polar opposites.

Ally MacLeod could only fail to sparkle when he was asleep, although lending the impression he never actually did so. This made him immensely likeable, since much of what came out of him was an outpouring of optimism. You could not fail to be infected by it. Joe Jordan recognised his positive qualities, but with a qualification.

'He was so completely different from Willie Ormond. He was flamboyant, spoke a lot, great for the press, really built us up to think we could win our first group in Argentina. But although he was identified as a motivator, to be honest, anybody playing for Scotland doesn't need motivation. It should be there as soon as you're picked. So, although that was his reputation, it just wasn't needed.'

Lou Macari still puts it neatly, 'He was more like your pal than a manager.'

After Anfield, and prior to leaving for the World Cup, Ally and myself embarked on a tour of hotels, sponsored by a brewery firm, throughout the length and breadth of Scotland, in the spring of 1978 like a king accompanied by his consort, to offer himself to an adoring public. This is the period that the comedian Andy Cameron had astutely tapped into the frenzy and, with his song, 'We're On The March Wi' Ally's Army', gave it wide appeal by appearing on the BBC's *Top Of The Pops*. My English colleagues thought it faintly amusing, while to many in tartan it was a modern interpretation of 'Scots Wha Hae'.

I did the driving during that period. Ally sat beside me, talking and talking. His stories were highly entertaining, particularly about his time under fellow Scot manager Dally Duncan, when he was transferred to Blackburn Rovers in 1959. He enjoyed telling of his duties as the dressing room's teetotaller. And how, one night, Ally, acting as a gofer to the likes of teammate Derek Dougan who, it has to be emphasised, was not teetotal, had helped a group of nurses climb up a ladder to gain access to his mates waiting eagerly in their hotel rooms. I assume, from the story, they had plans in store for the maidens which went beyond a few hands of whist. Then didn't one nurse, perhaps in eager anticipation of what lay ahead, go and fall from the ladder, breaking her leg, resulting in the clamorous sound of an ambulance arriving on the scene.

The point of the story is that Duncan, and the rest of the management team, slept throughout the night, completely unaware of what had occurred, whereas the players had met them at breakfast, successfully hiding the fact from their coaches that none of them had slept a wink. They went out that same afternoon and won 6–2. I doubt if Ally was assuring me that you didn't need to sleep the night before a match, but more that he understood the subterranean world of the randy professional footballer; knew of all their wiles, their love of the flesh, and that nothing would get past him as a manager, not even at international level.

He certainly was in effective command as Ayr United manager, early in his career. He knew how to incentivise in his days there. It wasn't just with the tongue, but with money. He paid his players better than all clubs, bar the Old Firm, and had an intricate bonus system in operation at £5 a point until they got thirteen points and then £20 a point until 31 December when they reverted to £5 a point, until they accumulated another thirteen points. Since he reckoned that twenty-six points would make Ayr safe, you could tell that this man was not just all mouth, but had a definite grasp of what the pound sterling meant to even those of his charges who were not good at arithmetic. And, of course, as we would find out during the approaching World Cup, he could merrily plunder commercial opportunities that came his way, as many did.

However, the wildly enthusiastic crowds that turned up for these soirées were offering unswerving allegiance to him as he boldly assured them we would bring back the World Cup from South America. In retrospect, the way they hung on his every word seems almost like criminal gullibility. At one hotel I ventured an opinion. As chairman of the evening, I mildly suggested to him that Bruce Rioch of Everton and Don Masson of Queen's Park Rangers were no chickens and that we might not get the best out of them in the summer. He rebuked me for such a suggestion, which aroused the crowd. They turned on me. I was howled down, with Ally openly enjoying the spectacle. It was then I thought, 'What happens if it all fails?' He might end up making Icarus look like a swallow. I thought so, because even though there was wide public acclamation for his appointment, there were others who didn't see it quite the same way.

Jock Stein was quite stark and abrupt about it. 'It's a joke,' he said bluntly to me after Ally's appointment in 1977. He was infinitely more diplomatic in public, of course, and even though he held quite deep reservations about the appointment, always offered encouragement to Ally and his players. In this case, adopting harmony with a Scotland team manager, Stein was simply bowing to the inevitable. Although, with the benefit of hindsight, I now wonder if he was beginning to develop a taste for that post himself, even at that stage, when Ally had, nevertheless, seemed invulnerable.

Then there was the other man. Not exactly at Ally's elbow, but certainly always within earshot, would be Ernie Walker, who had replaced Willie Allan in 1977 as secretary of the SFA. He would call the operational shots. Thankfully, he seemed to embody the increasing perception of the SFA at last growing up. His predecessor had simply been an apparatchik. Walker was, by stark contrast, a genuine lover of the game. And of a good whisky, of a stout cigar, of patriotic Scots, of golf and of Robert Burns. He was a middle-class upright citizen, but certainly not a stuffed shirt, since I had sat beside him at a Burns Supper where he clearly enjoyed his drams and openly chortled at the savage satirical assault on pomposity and hypocrisy in 'Holy Willie's Prayer'.

He was to attract critics very quickly in his career, as is the inevitable fate of the holder of that office. But his elegant rebuttal of criticisms, from any quarter, was almost a visual delight. He would stand very erect, looking at his detractor with a cool, unemotional gaze, and sometimes, whisky-glass in one hand, cigar in the other, delicately dropping ash into any handy receptacle like it was a ritual to intimate rejection, would then calmly utter his quiet put-down that even as an onlooker could make you shiver. The future of the organisation looked to be in sound, intelligent hands. But even though he was, by a considerable distance, the most outstanding leader of the SFA of this or any other generation, he did make mistakes, as we shall see. Walker could also portray genuine anguish about our poor performances, like his very soul was in peril.

But not in the early months of 1978. Life was good for him. I interviewed him after he had returned from the draw for the finals. Both he and Ally were virtually purring with delight at the outcome. Peru, Iran and Holland, the opponents. There was also good public reaction, despite the obvious realisation that Holland, the previous World Cup finalists, would be difficult to handle. Of Peru and Iran, we knew hardly anything at that time, and it was good for the Scottish public to discover that they actually played football in Iran. Then I noticed a date in the calendar which I thought might be of some interest. Argentina were to travel to Peru and play them in a friendly on 23 March, only three months before Scotland's first game in Cordoba against, of course, Peru. I talked BBC London into an interest in this game as a preview for the finals. They were also interested in having Ally MacLeod accompany us, at our expense, to offer us his assessments on both sides. I contacted him with this offer, assuming that he would be going on a spying mission anyway, as was the custom of managers in these situations. I reminded him that Willie Ormond had gone to Egypt to see Zaire as a necessary precaution before the 1974 finals. He said he would get back to me, but he never did. I tried to contact him several times, but it was clear he simply didn't want to go, despite everything being at our expense. London could scarcely believe this. I could. The fact of the matter is that Ally was busy. He was mopping up all he could from the commercial deals coming his way like iron filings to a magnet. He was entitled to what he could get out of his current success, but I felt it was odd that he would pass up this opportunity to see the host nation again and, more importantly, to size up, in the flesh, Scotland's first opponents, Peru.

We left without him. Nor could the Peruvians believe Ally had missed this opportunity. For the moment my producer and I arrived in the capital, Lima, we were pursued by journalists and television cameras for interviews. Unknown to us, British Caledonian's press officer in Lima had told the media that I was here to spy for Ally MacLeod, which meant that my picture, taken at the airport on arrival, ended up on the front page of their national newspaper, under the caption 'El Espion' (The Spy). So, I played it up. In a television studio I said Ally had SFA duties to attend to but that I would be reporting back to the Scottish manager with every detail of the Peruvian side. In a sense, that was true, but all unofficially. We were given the regal treatment though, which might not have been just as grand had I admitted I was a mere television commentator. In any case, I was trying my best to cover for Ally, who back home was earning a fortune, I assumed. They might not have been as genial had I really explained that Ally couldn't be bothered to come to analyse their team. But, in my new honorary position, I learned very quickly that this was a country obsessed by the game.

The poor played football everywhere. Out of their shanty towns they would come to the long dusty pitches which ran for mile after mile, stretching out from the outskirts of the city as far as the eye could see. It was certainly much less romantic than Copacabana's beach games, but it had something of the natural quality of that, as the youngsters performed miracles of control on hard, powdery surfaces. The sun rose and set on these games, which suggested they were helping stave off the effects of a life of horrendous poverty. Our guide pointed out the one outstanding talent to emerge from this, 'This is where Cubillas started his football,' he told us. Teófilo Cubillas posters were on display everywhere. The country's greatest ever player had led his country to only their second ever Copa America title three years before and obviously the feting was still going on. They called him affectionately 'Nene' because of his boyish looks. This was the man I wanted to see above all others.

Peru's game against Argentina was played in their national stadium on 23 March on a bright sunny afternoon. A look at the visitor's team sheet revealed men the world, at that stage, knew little about, but within a few months would become names to conjure with.

Fillol, Luis Galván, Passarella (**captain**), Ardiles, Rubén Galván, Ortiz, Valencia, Luque, René Houseman, Gallego, Bottaniz, Pagnanini.

They were the superior side, strong, oozing with confidence, and their three goals that came in the first half were based on lightning counter-attacks. The first was scored by Luque, famous for his flowing hair, who Stein regarded later as the Argentinian he most enjoyed watching, and whose arms raised aloft were to become the poster symbol of Argentina '78. Peru were well beaten, although the man who scored their second-half goal, Oblitas, a left-sided player of pace, was their most effective player. As for Cubillas, he looked tricky but had been

largely marked out of the game. You could tell he had something in him, though in brief interludes amidst Argentinian
superiority. I left with the genuine feeling that Scotland could
handle them with not too much trouble. However, the problem
with 'El Espion' is that I didn't have any evidence to show.
We had hired a Peruvian film unit to cover this game to show
highlights, allied to some scenes of the country and the passion
for football, all in documentary fashion, and present all that
for Ally to study. And since we were the only UK television
people there, we knew the footage would be in great demand.
But when we returned with the film stock back to Glasgow and
processed it, we discovered that it was not transmittable.

All we could salvage were tiny fragments, which added up
to nothing. In film terms, I had produced a 'turkey'. I should
have known better, for the cameraman had used equipment
that looked as if it dated back to the days of the Keystone
Cops. Internally, within the BBC it was an embarrassment to
have gone all that way, spent all that money, and come back
with virtually nothing. We kept quiet about it, just as much
as we kept quiet about the absentee Ally having ducked an
offer to help him out. But, as we shall see, these things all
come out in the wash. He was at great pains to tell the press
eventually that, much later, he had seen video of that game,
without disclosing the fact that he had spurned an offer to
see the game for himself in the flesh, and for which there is
really no substitute. After all, Marcus Calderon, the Peruvian
manager, had taken the trouble to travel to see Scotland play
an international in Italy – or so he had thought. In fact, it was
a Scottish League Selection that was there on that occasion,
which led to him being pilloried by his own media for having
made that very expensive mistake. Events would eventually
show who had made the bigger mistake of the two.

8

PILLS AND PURGATORY

So, there was this man with a U-boat. His name was Jim Tait. A very personable small-time bookie from in and around Glasgow, an affable Nicely Nicely Johnson type, who struck an essentially whimsical tone that had suddenly arisen from contemplating the furthest journey any national side supporter would have to travel. The BBC were so taken by his story, that he was hiring a U-boat, supposedly with a captain wearing an Iron Cross, which would transport privileged punters across the ocean, that they sent me with a camera unit to interview him for a segment of national news. This would compete with other items like a Labour government defeat in the House, meaning a penny was coming off income tax, or the opening of the Frigg gas field, jointly by the UK and Norwegian governments, the biggest in the North Sea. Yes, there it was, with the po-faced Tait speaking like the trouper he was.

Now, of course, nobody at the BBC believed a word of this. None of us did, but it fitted the mood that was besetting the nation now preparing for another World Cup. On the one hand, it was like the gathering of a great social effort to talk up the forthcoming campaign as if it were the biggest initiative since the Darien Scheme in the eighteenth century.

On the other hand, at supporter level, it was like embarking on a jolly escapade following Ally's credo that nothing was impossible. So, Tait had put a smile on our faces, just as Ally was announcing his squad for South America, which he did with the usual gusto in front of a hypnotised media.

Alan Rough (Partick Thistle) Age 26/Caps 18, Sandy Jardine (Rangers) 29/33, Willie Donachie (Manchester City) 26/32, Martin Buchan (Manchester United) 29/28, Gordon McQueen (Manchester Utd) 25/20, Bruce Rioch (Derby County, **captain**) 30/22, Don Masson (Derby County) 28/16, Kenny Dalglish (Liverpool) 27/54, Joe Jordan (Manchester Utd) 26/30, Asa Hartford (Manchester City) 27/24, Willie Johnston (West Brom) 31/21, Jim Blyth (Coventry City) 23/2, Stuart Kennedy (Aberdeen) 25/3, Tom Forsyth (Rangers) 29/19, Archie Gemmill (Nottingham Forest) 31/26, Lou Macari (Manchester Utd) 28/22, Derek Johnstone (Rangers) 24/11, Graeme Souness (Liverpool) 25/6, John Robertson (Nottingham Forest) 25/2, Bobby Clark (Aberdeen) 32/17, Joe Harper (Aberdeen) 30/3, Kenny Burns (Nottingham Forest) 24/11.

You can tell from their ages that those in the squad who were regularly selected for the starting elevens were extremely experienced. On the other hand, the key players were hardly youthful. At this stage little thought was given to the relative consequences of maturity or immaturity and how it might affect the outcome in an alien environment. All these players had come through the mill in the normal pressures of a long season in both British and European football. But not much attention was paid to detailed analysis. It seemed more like the launch of a new product on to the market, which itself would determine its fate. Ally's audi-

106

ence was pleasantly complacent, but he was gaining attention from other quarters. He told me on our travels that he
was delighted that politicians were trying to climb on board
with him.

In the week of 22 May 1978, the Labour Prime Minister,
Jim Callaghan, sent a message to George Robertson, Labour's
candidate for the by-election in Hamilton, which he won with
51% of the vote but where the charismatic Margo MacDonald
for the SNP had been running strong. The message read,
'The best double I can suggest is Robertson for Hamilton,
Scotland for the World Cup.' Callaghan had obviously been
informed that, just before his message, the SNP had written
to FIFA demanding assurances that Scotland would still
compete in the World Cup as an independent nation. They
were flying the flag at every opportunity now. This was at
a time when Scotland were preparing for a referendum on
the issue of devolution with an opinion poll revealing, at the
time Ally was announcing his squad, that 64% of the population wanted a devolved assembly, against 31% in opposition.

With politicians clearly becoming sensitive to the possibility that populism might spread outwards from the
terracings, you had to hope that they would come up with
something less patronising and less naff than Callaghan's
few words. If judged by that week in May, it looked like the
results of Ally's team would be seen by certain politicians
as having currency at the ballot box. He himself was an out-
and-out patriot at a time when people, whatever their views,
were getting properly embarrassed by the barracking of the
National Anthem before games. So, it was surprising to learn
that, at the official draw for the cup in Buenos Aires, Ally,
who could whip up nationalist sentiment with ease, when
asked which flag should represent Scotland at the official

107

line-up, chose the Union Jack. He thought that it would be fair on the large presence of Anglos in the side and that everybody in the British Isles would be supporting Scotland anyway. Ernie was incensed, failing to see the sophisticated nuances of that argument and, according to what Ally told me on one of our trips, he was told by the SFA secretary where to stick the Union Jack. It was replaced by the Saltire. Common sense, if not political correctness, had prevailed.

Thankfully, though, I missed the departure for Argentina. I had travelled ahead of the official party to do some pre-match filming. I could scarcely believe that about 25,000 had turned up at Hampden just to wave goodbye. Much of this, I imagined, had been stoked not only by Ally's extravagant predictions, but by the fact that although Scotland, in their last game before departure, had been beaten 1–0 by England at Hampden on 20 May 1978, they had been the superior side, playing the kind of football that clamped the English into a more defensive mentality. It was a grotesque result and they received from the crowd the biggest ovation I have ever heard of a defeated Scottish side. That would have been a positive enough farewell, but no. That staged, calculated farewell tableau at Hampden, looked as if Walker, on this occasion, was dancing to Ally's tune.

But I was there all right with a camera crew to greet them in Alta Gracia, the little town about an hour outside Cordoba, where the first two games were to be played. They were delayed. The bus had broken down near the hotel. A bad omen for those of us sensitive to the possibility of the fates conspiring against Scotland? Not to Lou Macari.

'At the point where the bus broke down I saw Trevor McDonald of *News at Ten* there. Now, if one of the biggest faces in British television was there to greet us, then it suddenly hit me that we were in the big time. It really did sink in then that we were at the World Cup. And that was something few players of my generation could claim.'

The problems for Lou, and others, started as soon as the security guards let them through the gates and then closed them like they were in state detention. From the outside, the building on a hill looked like a badly run-down Gleneagles. Alan Rough's description of the place inside was nearer that of a doss house. 'It was terrible. It was a downer right from the start. There were two to a room. No windows. One cupboard. Small bathroom. That's what we had to live in for three weeks. There was a swimming pool, which for the whole duration had no water in it. There were no relaxation facilities as they have now. And the training facilities were poor. And I'm not making excuses, but these things affect players. Morale goes down, because after training sessions there was nothing to do except watch Argentinian television. Can you imagine? In fact, at one point we had been served this awful uneatable soup every night. Eventually, Gordon McQueen could take it no longer. He stood up and shouted. "See this bloody soup. Could you not take it and throw it in the bloody swimming pool. If you had done that sooner, we could all have had a bloody swim by now."'

In a sense, it is no wonder they made a break for freedom. The breaking of this story of their escape, from what now seemed a Gulag to them, was unusual. Alex Montgomery, a Glaswegian journalist but at the time chief football correspondent for *The Sun* and author of several football books, was in at its birth.

'Saturday was my day off and I would spend some time of it at the bar in the Jockey Club in Cordoba with Hugh Taylor. But that day there were several journalists about because Ernie Walker had joined us. Now, I always thought

Ernie was a great guy and liked a dram himself. Well, out of the blue, he casually tells us that the lads had climbed over the wall of the hotel one evening to get to a casino. And had been stopped by police. Just like that. That little anecdote suddenly became a major story.'

It is paradoxical that the kind of story that newshounds had been prowling around for, since the squad had arrived in the country, had been presented to them on a plate by the secretary of the SFA. His innocent recounting of something he thought inconsequential was plundered.

The relations between media and the SFA never really recovered from that slip.

'Suddenly,' as Lou Macari says, 'we were invaded. There had just been the usual faces in the press around us. Now we were mobbed. And we knew what they were saying about us. The rumours were flying. We were bloody angry, but what could you do about it? We were trapped in there and they were making stories up about us.'

This was the aggravating background to the preparation for the Peru game. What did not help the mood was that Joe Jordan had strained a thigh muscle and it was doubtful that he would be fit to play. His height and ability in the air would be invaluable against a moderately sized Peruvian defence. Derek Johnstone, who could have substituted in an emergency, had also gone over on an ankle. Ally did not seem overly worried, which suggested all the talk might just have been pre-match prattle. He did not seem to be twitching nervously. So, on 2 June 1978, the day we had heard from home that Alex Ferguson had just been appointed manager of Aberdeen, and three days after Billy McNeill had replaced Jock Stein at Celtic Park, Ally announced his team.

Alan Rough,
Stuart Kennedy, Martin Buchan, Tom Forsyth, Kenny Burns,
Don Masson, Bruce Rioch (*captain*), Asa Hartford, Willie Johnston,
Kenny Dalglish, Joe Jordan.

There was only one change from the side that had beaten
England – Buchan in for Donachie. I pencilled that in for my
commentary notes. Not that I needed them, for the commentary
never happened. You come all this way and you find out
just minutes before kick-off that the all-important line linking
you to Glasgow is non-existent and that somebody back at
base has forgotten to book the line, you then feel you need
an oxygen tent to recover. You are now simply a spectator
amidst the other 46,000 in the Cordoba stadium as you tell a
colleague to get to a phone, which is not all that easy at that
time, to tell your wife watching at home that the Montoneros haven't abducted you. I felt almost emasculated. My
commentary that day was muttered to the self with an angry
dispatch, as if I was being denied my witness statement in
the court of public opinion.

So, from the outset, it was a different and difficult game for
me. If you are in a jaundiced – nay, murderous mood – you
need uplift, you need therapy, which was potentially there
on the field. Well, in truth it looked heartening to start with.
We looked on top. The ball was moved about confidently
and Peru were on the back foot. When Joe Jordan knocked
in the first goal in fifteen minutes, when he pounced on a
rebound from the goalkeeper called Quiroga, I was beginning to relax. That, however, was the only mistake that man
made. In fact, this Argentinian-born keeper was the stake
upon which Scotland was eventually to impale itself.

At 1–0 up, some of that early energy and drive seemed to seep from Scotland as Peru began to move sweetly about the field and show their pace, particularly Oblitas on the left. Ally, you could say, had revealed his almost total ignorance about the Peruvian players by giving an interview to Tony Gubba of the BBC before the game in which he said, bewilderingly, that Martin Buchan would be the man to deal with Oblitas. In fact, Buchan was guarding the other side of the field in the left back position. So, this left-sided player was as prominent as Cubillas in the early stages, although I recall a brilliant dribble by the national hero, ending up with Rough having to make a brave save at his feet.

Brutally, their equaliser came with only two minutes of the half left, when Cueto's shot from six yards went under Rough's body. At half-time I knew the game was going to be more difficult than we had assumed; they simply looked increasingly stronger and fresher. Jordan should have scored early in the second half with a header that just touched the outside of the post. Shortly after that came the save of the match from Quiroga when Jordan blasted a shot from only six yards after being set up by Kenny Burns, but which the keeper brilliantly touched over the bar. Jordan actually patted the keeper on the back in appreciation of that save. Only five minutes later, Scotland were awarded a penalty when Bruce Rioch was chopped down in the box, by Cubillas of all people. Masson's spot kick was the kind that enrages – lacking in belief, soppy and eminently saveable. Quiroga palmed it away with ease. By that stage Joe Jordan was sick of the sight of him.

'He was immense. We had heard he was eccentric and all that, but I still can't believe how he kept some of my efforts out. That sort of thing can dishearten you. We should have been right on top. People forgot all that after the game.'

Cubillas, inspired by that Quiroga prompting, and throwing off the shackles of his age, played like a gazelle with boots and scored two goals in the space of six minutes.

With the Scottish defence laying off him, he had time to take a ball with his right foot and, from twenty yards, it seared into the net. Crushed. Sinking sensation. Slightly dizzy even. That about summed up the sensations of this spectator. Even then it looked to be all over. It was. Just six minutes later, Peru was awarded a free kick just outside the box. One of his colleagues made a dummy run over the ball and up stepped Cubillas behind him to take it. He did, with the outside of his right foot. He sent it into the net with an almost absurd ease. It looked like he had been making goals like that since he had played as a kid on those dusty pitches we had seen back in Lima.

Alan Rough still sees it vividly.

'Now, I'm not blaming anybody, but if you look at it again you'll see who was at the end of the wall: Stuart Kennedy and Lou Macari. They turn away from the ball as it flies towards them. But yes, it was a great kick. You don't see many taking a dead-ball like that and making that kind of contact. But in the World Cup we played with the Tango ball. It was different from the Mitre ball that we were used to. It swerved and did all kinds of movement. And I'm not talking about myself. Look at all the other goalkeepers that were letting in long shots, like the famous Dino Zoff of Italy.'

Lou Macari had only come on as a sub for the exhausted Bruce Rioch just six minutes before that incident.

'Marvellous technique,' he told me. 'Cubillas is the difference between good and great. But I knew when I came on that, physically, the lads were struggling. People have to understand that the Peruvians were accustomed to that humidity and heat. Even though we had come to South America the year before to get a taste of it all, when we got here it was like we were experiencing the conditions anew. It was murderous out there.'

However valid that may have been, at the final whistle, the mood I was feeling around me, even in the media area, on the back of that 3–1 defeat, was instant hostility. You could tell the players were about to have unleashed on them the full venom of a press, who would be crucially unmindful of the fact that they had been largely complicit in helping whip up the expectations, almost to the point of hysteria. I wandered lonely as a cloud through the streets of Cordoba that night trying to make sense of my non-commentary day and trying to avoid any Scottish supporter, because I felt I was as much to blame for encouraging so many to spend fortunes to get here. I was embarrassed. But that was nothing compared to what was to follow. For, back at Alta Gracia, a telegram had arrived informing the SFA that one of their players had failed a drug test.

As Ally was to tell me years later, nobody from the International Committee was in the hotel when the telegram arrived informing them of Johnston's failed test. He went straight to Dr Fitzsimmons' room to find out the medical background to the reported use of a banned substance. He walked straight in on the Celtic doctor, an extremely devout man, who was at prayer. All Ally could say was, 'You'd better say one for me, Doc. Look what I've got here!'

I took a phone call from the BBC office in Buenos Aires telling me they had heard that Willie Johnston had failed a drugs test. The order then promptly followed for me to take a camera crew and head for a reception, being given by Denis Howell, the Minister for Sport, to track Johnston down and confront him with this allegation. Anybody with a camera was heading precisely for that venue, including the aforementioned Trevor McDonald, who, as you might have expected, was trying to winkle the facts from Johnston when he was interrupted by an incensed Ally Macleod, who actually tried to push him out of the way. A sort of melee developed in which the SFA made the quick decision to smuggle Johnston out of the reception. There followed, soon after that, the decision to send him home immediately.

It transpired that Johnson had been taking a banned substance, Fencamfamin, for a hay fever complaint. Ernie Walker made his official announcement to the world's press looking so pale and shaken by events I thought he might actually collapse in front of us. Alan Rough explains that the SFA were supposedly vigilant about these matters.

'Doc Fitzsimmons would come into every room at the start of the day and would read out a sheet with the names of the banned drugs and ask us one by one if we had been taking any of these. Now, to be honest, there were a lot of medical names there that you wouldn't have recognised easily. Maybe that was it. But I can also say that what Bud had taken was used a lot in English football as a kind of pick-me-up. He took all the bad news like he couldn't understand what was going on. It was when the SFA decided to get rid of him right away, and we went for a drink in the town, that he broke down. He really lost it that day. What I certainly didn't like was how they slipped him out of the hotel in the middle of the night in the boot of a car like he was a criminal.'

But although Rough reports the incident in a kind of sympathetic vein, nevertheless, Johnston ought to have told the doctor that he was taking something – anything. He had deceived him, whether deliberately or not. What further emerged was the admission by Don Masson that he had taken this same drug because he felt it was commonplace and therefore OK. He then quickly denied it. We were now expecting the Mad Hatter to turn up for a Fencamfamin tea party. On the back of that, Ally decided to trawl through the hotel with the doctor and pocketed over a couple of dozen such tablets from different rooms. Years later I asked Ally if he could name the players who had them, which he naturally refused to do. One good reason, of course, is that they may have been in their possession, but had not used them. But, of the consequences, Joe Jordan is clear of mind.

'The scandal about Willie Johnston did not cause our failure in Argentina. That had nothing to do with it. It was the way we played poorly against Iran, in particular, that brought about our downfall. We got bad publicity over the drugs issue, but that was immaterial. We all let ourselves down on the field. Willie Johnson taking whatever it was, and all the noise about it, didn't put me off my game one bit. I still knew what I had to do.'

But others were now simply emboldened to write or say anything about the Scottish players. Much was made by the hawkish world media about the astonishing remarks of the Tunisian coach, Majid Chetali, whose team had shared the Scottish squad's hotel for part of the time. The world's press quoted him as saying, 'The Scots do no work. They lie on the veranda and drink and eat, drink and eat. They have whisky for breakfast, whisky for lunch, whisky for dinner. You would think they were tourists.'

It was preposterous. Even some of the press who wanted it to be true knew it was fantasy. But printing it simply made it seem true. A report, sadly, was also transmitted on BBC television which said that the players had drunk the hotel dry, and that they had sent out a 'drinks-trolley', whatever that may have meant, for more of the same. Ernie Walker was so incensed about that suggestion of bacchanalian orgies taking place that, on return to Scotland, he perused that film at the Corporation with his legal advisers with a view to possible legal action. In the end, he thought it wasn't worth the trouble and, in any case, at that stage he simply wanted to bury Argentina as quickly as possible and not stir the embers with litigation.

So, with the Fencamfamin now flushed down several toilets, I travelled with Martin Tyler, who was to become one of the most prominent national football commentators in the future, to see the Iranian team in training. Of our next opponents Tyler just murmured to me, 'They look as if they should be out herding cattle.' They were tall dark men who looked as if they had learned football by correspondence course. Nevertheless, we were all on edge moving to the Iran game, where previously it had simply looked like a banker.

Lou Macari was selected for this one.

'Everybody in Scotland was conditioned to think this would be a walkover, I know that. But in the World Cup there aren't all that many walkovers. Look at what Scotland were supposed to do to Zaire, but, as I understand it, the conditions weren't great for us there. And that's what was going through my mind. Iran are used to the heat and humidity. And remember, you and all the others from the media were expecting to return to Scotland with the World Cup, that's what had been pumped into everybody. This was a pressure game all right.'

Alan Rough agrees.

'I've played in many a big game but believe you me, I felt more pressure going into this game than any other. We'd had a bad result. Then came all the terrible headlines about drugs and drinking. So, we knew we had to win. And win against a team we knew nothing about. I really felt as nervous as I've ever been about a game.'

We had to settle down and return to football thinking again, which led us into conjecture about who would wear the jerseys for this one. Most of us were advocating two players in particular to be included: Graeme Souness, who was starring for Liverpool, and Derek Johnstone of Rangers, whose height and ability in the air would be a decided asset. Neither were picked. There was no Rioch, who was injured, and Masson had been dropped. Gemmill was to come in from the start. The final selection was:

Alan Rough,
Sandy Jardine, Willie Donachie, Martin Buchan, Kenny Burns,
Archie Gemmill (*captain*), Asa Hartford, Lou Macari,
John Robertson,
Kenny Dalglish, Joe Jordan.

We were back to the Estadio Olímpico Chateau Carreras in Cordoba on 7 June 1978, a stadium devoid of atmosphere with only 14,000 sprinkled around it and, of course, including a bold bunch of Scots. This time the commentary line had been booked for BBC Scotland, and there are times when I wish it hadn't been. Alan Herron of the *Sunday Mail* was by my side in the commentary position. Of course, I had watched the Iranians in training, and was hardly overawed by them. They were big strong players, but they gave the impression they had no wiles about them, that they were indeed football learners. But they were obviously very fit. That was what had been on show when Holland had beaten them 3–0 in their opening game, although it had taken the Dutch until almost half-time before they had scored their first goal. And surely we had enough guile and experience in our side to see them off?

What transpired in the next ninety minutes was as if all the Scots there, in whatever capacity, were members of a jury waiting to pass judgement on more than winning a game of football, given the scurrilous headlines of the previous few days. The reputation of our national identity seemed at stake. Somehow, we had to convince the world that football was our way of expressing the work ethic and creativity for which we were renowned throughout the world. Sadly, though, the performance we were eventually to see could hardly have been stamped with that great imprimatur, Clyde-built. It looked more like it had been drummed up in a sweatshop in the Far East.

From early on, you could tell that they had no idea how to take on a very fit side, full of running and certainly far from the amateurish outfit we thought they would be. They had, surprisingly, a couple of very tricky players and certainly pace, whereas you felt increasingly you were watching a Scottish side almost in sleepwalking mode. It was infuriating to observe, because nobody seemed to be playing as we knew they could. There was barely a moment in the game when I thought Scotland would actually score. There was one really decent save by Iran's goalkeeper, Hejazi, from a John Robertson free kick and again from a Dalglish header, but nothing really to make the pulse beat quicker. It did, two minutes before half-time, but accompanied by laughter all around me. Kenny Burns drove a ball into the penalty area but, in the confusion between Hejazi in goal and his defender Eskandarian, the ball fell from the grasp of the keeper and, astonishingly, the defender knocked the ball from about twelve yards into his own net. Remarkably all this did was produce a more plodding Scottish performance in the second half, which was notable for Donachie accidentally kicking Buchan in the head, who had to be replaced by Tom Forsyth.

Their equalising goal was a cause of lamentation for any full-blooded Scot in the stadium, because it seemed to underline the puerility of the entire campaign. But, as Danaifard on the left, with only thirty minutes remaining, slipped past Gemmill and then, from a narrow angle, beat Alan Rough at the near post, I had enough composure left to show appreciation for a player who actually looked more Scottish than those on the other side. Ally had sent on Joe Harper of Aberdeen to replace Kenny Dalglish with fifteen minutes to go. Harper had not played international football for three years and was about to play his last game for Scotland. Derek Johnstone, with recent scoring form, remained on the bench. It didn't make sense. Nothing was surprising any longer. It was the end. 1–1. It was another humbling. In many ways you could understand the wrath of the Scottish support there for barracking Ally as he walked round the ground at the end. But there was also something distasteful about it. I saw a couple looking as if they were spitting at him. All this was distinctly unhealthy and, at that moment in time, with Holland still to come, you had to feel that only an outbreak of food poisoning in the Dutch camp would save us from annihilation. To qualify for the final stages, we would need to beat Holland 3–0 because they had surprisingly drawn with Peru 0–0 in the other game. However, that simply sounded like a sick joke.

9

TRAINSPOTTING IN MENDOZA

Ally's press conference the following day was like a police announcement on an abduction. Like an identity had been stolen. All that we had expected of his side had mysteriously disappeared. He would have known by that stage that most of the Scottish press were only there to preside over his funeral rites. It was a pleasant, crisp, southern-hemisphere autumnal day. The mass media were waiting for him on the top of this small hill in the hotel grounds. He came forward rather sheepishly to his chair, and, as he did so, a dog appeared from nowhere and proceeded to frolic with the manager. Ally patted it and it nuzzled his hand. As he sat down, he stroked the dog and said to the packed throng around him, 'Well, at least I've got one friend here today.' Nobody laughed. Here now was a different Ally. He was bitter in a way I never thought imaginable. What had added to his agony was the way some of the press had treated him, because they thought he had signed an exclusive deal with the *Scottish Daily Express* to give them special access for his views to the tune of £25,000. He never actually signed that deal, but when an interview he gave them was billed as 'exclusive', there was a backlash from the other papers, which, he felt long afterwards, had it in for him. Alan Rough felt for Ally then.

'He became a lonely, broken man. You would wander round the hotel and you would suddenly come across him sitting on his own, staring into space. This was his own choice. Nobody was trying to avoid him. He just cut himself off.'

I was glad to leave all that behind and travel to Mendoza further north for what was to prove the final game. The town lay in the very foothills of the Andes and was the centre of the Argentinian wine industry. So, there were immediate consolations arriving there. Leaving aside the fact that, on the first night in our hotel, I caught one of the workers there opening my case and trying to make off with some of my gear, I was glad to get away from the Scottish camp and the misery that surrounded it. I just wanted this wholly draining experience to be over and done with as soon as possible.

On 11 June in the Estadio San Martin, in front of a crowd of 35,000, the Scotland team that walked out to face the Dutch showed one significant change: Graeme Souness was in. Martin Buchan had recovered from injury, as had Bruce Rioch. Tom Forsyth was back in from the start.

The full side was:

Rough,

Kennedy, Donachie, Buchan, Forsyth,

Gemmill, Rioch (*captain*), Souness, Hartford,

Dalglish, Jordan.

I consoled myself with the thought that, since I expected defeat, at least it would be against the Dutch, whom I had long admired for their innovations in football. They were at full strength.

Jongbloed,
Suurbier, Rijsbergen, Poortvliet, Krol (*captain*),
Jansen, Neeskens, René Van de Kerkhof, Rensenbrink,
Willy Van de Kerkhof, Johnny Rep.

I had always liked dealing with the Dutch, on any matter in any context, but I always knew at the same time that, generally speaking, if you brought a group of them together, they would turn disputatious. So it was with their national football team, presided over by their Austrian coach and guru, Ernst Happel, who had gone in the huff with his own media and become an isolated figure, letting his players argue amongst themselves about bonuses, etc. And even before they had left Holland, he had to deal with a problem when Wim van Hanegem, whose talented left foot had mystified Celtic in Milan in 1970, had arrived at Schiphol Airport in full World Cup uniform, but decided he would rather take a taxi and go back home. That still left Happel with nine players from the highly successful 1974 squad with him. Now they only needed to avoid losing by three goals to go through.

There was a sense of grandeur about this game even before it started. It was as if a gigantic ladle had scooped out a segment of the Andes into a paddling pool for some mythical giant from the mountains looming above. It was the most dramatically sited stadium I have ever been in. It was to be a game with a Wagnerian backdrop, and one particular goal that could have been set to the thrum of 'Ride of the Valkyries'. Alan Herron, my co-commentator, and I were certainly on a high platform, along which were our colleagues from all over the world, all probably here to watch the favourites, Holland, take another stride forward in the tournament. But we were both demob happy. Thank God, this was surely the last one. Argentina had so far left us with a sour taste in our mouths. I certainly had tried to cleanse it from my mouth during my stay in Mendoza, by use of the Malbec grape, which has left me with a lifelong taste for the stuff. But it was what was about to happen that made me tipsier.

Back in the studio in London, Jock Stein was part of the pundits' panel. He eventually described the performance of Alan Herron and myself thus, 'It was an amazing transformation. You sounded at first as if you were at a funeral. Then you got slightly more enthusiastic. Then you both sounded as if you were at a wedding. And, at the end, you were almost back to your funeral again.'

Such, truly, were the fluctuations of emotions. How could these same players who had given the appearance in the first two games that they had aged in South America, look so fresh from the start? 'You talked about how you felt you were demob happy,' said Alan Rough. 'I suppose there was a bit of that in us too. We didn't really think we could beat Holland 3–0 as we had been told we had to do. So, yes, this was probably the last. However, there was something extra. We knew we had good players and that we could play good football. Every player in that dressing room before we went out was determined to prove that we were a lot better than what people were saying about us.'

That determination was apparent all over the field. There was no weakness anywhere. Ally had no need to substitute anybody. Note the name of Souness, playing in his first game for Scotland, at the start of a long and distinguished international career. Ally had reservations about him, until he saw him performing in this one with such maturity and self-confidence that it merely exposed the shallowness of thinking and planning that had preceded this whole venture.

But despite all the attacking verve from Scotland, where virtually everyone, but especially Dalglish, seemed to be benefitting from the strong presence of Souness in midfield, it was Holland who scored first. This was after Rioch had struck the Dutch bar with a header from a Souness cross; after the same player had collided with Neeskens, resulting in the Dutchman going off immediately and being taken to hospital; and after Dalglish had the ball in the net, which was ruled out for a foul on a defender by Jordan. Then, ten minutes from half-time, Kennedy gave away possession cheaply in midfield, Johnny Rep charged into the penalty area, collided with both Rough and Kennedy in the area and a penalty was awarded. It was to be historic. Rensenbrink sunk it for the thousandth goal in the history of World Cup finals. But this was the change from the previous games: there was no wilting. Indeed, the Scottish players seemed on turbo charge after that. Only seconds before half-time, Souness again was involved when he sent a long ball to Jordan, who headed it down for Dalglish to lash it home for the equaliser. Yes, in the commentating booth, we were truly getting into the mood for that wedding knees-up.

Alan Rough looks back on that first half with a mixture of pride and regret.

'Somebody sent me a video of the game and, I can tell you, watching it again, we could have been three or four up in that first half. We were really on top of them. This was a great performance.'

The fun and games really start just a minute into the

125

second half when Souness showed his initiative again. He made a run into the box from a Rioch header and, when almost through, was brought down by Rensenbrink. Archie Gemmill stepped forward and calmly put the penalty beyond Jongbloed. 2–1. But I looked at the watch then and it told me we'd only played a few minutes of the second half, so the roof could still fall in on us. Time dragged. God, it dragged. That torturous, treacly movement of time was accentuated by the astonishment of our actually being in the lead. I was trying hard to keep the voice on an even keel, although I was sure its timbre suggested I was like any other Scot in the stadium fascinated by the game, but obsessed by the watch I had beside the television monitor.

At least we were doing more than holding our own. But then came the moment that has a kind of celestial glow to it. With just over twenty minutes to go, Dalglish was tackled by Krol and the ball broke to Archie Gemmill, just outside the penalty area on the right.

What happened next has been featured in a major film, has been staged as a ballet, has been used as an example by motivational speakers within industry in succeeding years and has been recounted countless numbers of times, anywhere in the world Scots have met to talk over the moments that warm their hearts. The wee man simply took off. He slipped and jinked his way past Jensen, the future manager of Celtic, neatly avoided a scything tackle by Poortvliet, nutmegged one of the greatest defenders in world football, Ruud Krol, and delicately chipped the ball away to the right of the goalkeeper, where it nestled with serene bliss in the net. 3–1.

Suddenly, I was aware I was rising. So was every other commentator along the line I could see. They had risen like a chorus line to a conductor's cue. For what we had just witnessed was a narrative with a beginning, a middle and an end. He gathered it, he nursed it forward, he slipped the other legs, then parted with it. It was a brief story, but we responded to it like Gemmill was a teacher telling weans an adventure tale and getting them off their backsides in excitement. Now we were all on our feet completely, with the babble of voices around actually penetrating the headphones I was wearing. It was a goal of impulse and natural ability, which cloaked the fact that it required audacity to deliver it, especially against such renowned defenders. Yes, our voices reaching the panel in the studio suggested the wedding was now at the Dashing White Sergeant stage. Was it raw pride in seeing a Scottish product we could now boast about to the vultures that had surrounded us? Relief after having had to bear so many indignities? These emotions clashed in a pulse that went through me like an arousal I couldn't quite fathom at the time.

Only one more goal and we would go through. But that mood didn't last long. I still cannot account for why Johnny Rep, in the seventy-first minute, was allowed to advance through a hole in midfield without any close challenge and to smite in a superb thirty-yard shot which put an end to our jubilation. 3–2. We knew then it was too much to make up. Damnable goal difference again. Now we were back to that funereal mood, using that hoary old phrase, 'So near, yet so far.' It was the end. Rep had killed us and left us with a cruelly ironic 3–2 win.

Twenty years later, I worked beside Johnny during the French World Cup in 1998 and asked him about the goal.

'I just closed my eyes and hit it,' he said almost blandly. 'Sure, I have scored goals like that before, but not one as well hit. But the idea we planned it that way is nonsense. I thought Scotland were unlucky not to make it that day.'

And then a confession was made years later, in 2016, to Alan Rough about Rep's goal for which, unfairly, he was criticised.

'I had a conversation with Archie Gemmill and he said, "I have to be honest with you. I've never told anybody about this, but that ball hit my heel after he shot." I felt like killing him when I heard that. That's why the ball had a strange flight. It went up first and then dipped. It must have got that direction from Archie's foot. It came down sharp. Honestly, I got a full hand to that. And see when I turned round and saw it in the net, I couldn't believe it. So, I said to Archie, "Why didn't you say that to me all those years ago, it would have taken the heat off me?"' And maybe taken the gloss off Archie's unique goal.

We really hammered the Malbec grape that night, trying to make sense of the whole trip; not just the amazing last performance of Scotland, which did redeem our reputation in world football to a great extent. We thought of all those who may have gained or lost out of the whole experience. Lots had tried to cash in on the act, of course. Francis Quinlan, a lecturer in management studies at Glasgow University, had calculated that £500,000 had been generated by businesses connected to the World Cup effort, even before a ball had been kicked in Argentina. Another business consultant thought that about £300,000 would be generated for the players' pool itself, including an extra resource to be added from the sales of Rod Stewart's World Cup samba song. It lay at sixteen in the hit parade on the day of the Iran game. After that dead-end match there was as much chance of it getting to the Top Ten as Chinese lullabies sung by Mao Tse-tung. Indeed, one Dundee shopkeeper offered them for sale at a penny each, with an offer of a hammer to smash them if anybody wished. Since Rod's office had asked me to add some commentary effects to that record, people thought I had lost out heavily. Not so. I was paid a flat fee. No royalties. Rod is no mug. Nor was Ally. He did cash in hugely on a number of ventures and for that you can hardly blame him. Nor was I ever interested in how much he made out of it all. But did it distract him from his basic duties? It still irked me he had not gone to Peru, although I had enjoyed playing up my role as a shady spy.

It certainly left him open to criticism of such a kind that it was to influence the thinking of the next Scotland manager in a significant decision he had to make about showing how conscientiously he was approaching the next World Cup. In any case, it was simply not in Ally's nature to be anything other than a genial, and harmless, self-publicist who could be heard on occasions singing his own anthem 'We're On The March With Ally's Army', with gusto. And when you consider that Donald Dewar, the newly elected MP for Garscadden, who was to become Scotland's First Minister, was heard to say on the eve of the Scotland–Peru game, 'We can afford to win in Argentina now the SNP is on the run' (Labour just having won a crucial by-election in Hamilton), it was clear politicians had almost unashamedly embraced the notion that the fluctuations on the football field were umbilically related to possible political outcomes.

Indeed, some years later, in a television documentary, Margo MacDonald, who had been beaten in that by-election, thought the World Cup debacle had helped damage that feeling of self-reliance and that it had helped delay the completion of devolution by a couple of decades. This was endorsed by her husband Jim Sillars who, in the same documentary, said of that footballing embarrassment, 'It certainly

129

transmitted itself to the political field. It was a case of 'here we go again'. Are we ever going to be able to do anything right ourselves?' In short, Johnny Rep had stymied the nationalist tide.

He had also made Ally's future look grim. A rumour spread that he had resigned immediately after the Holland game, but that was wishful thinking on the part of his growing number of critics who wanted him sacked immediately, in fact. But he was bullish in his last press conference, insisting that Scotland had only been eliminated by goal difference. It was a point well made. However, the public had turned against him in a way that I think besmirched our reputation as a tolerant people. Like the decision of a restaurateur to put up a public notice in his premises advising people that Ally MacLeod did not eat there. Some of the press were hypocritically vicious too in the ultimate condemnations. And if some of the supporters, who had turned him almost into a cult figure, had got over the barriers in the Cordoba stadium after the Iran match, they might have ripped him apart, such was the hatred being spewed out against him. Of that game, he did make one admission to me. 'I should have played Graeme Souness in that match,' he told me long afterwards. 'If I had, we could have qualified for the final stages. It was a bad mistake on my part.'

People said that he knew little about the opposition, which I think is accurate enough. But Lou Macari makes light of that.

'We place too much emphasis on tactics. Listen, the greatest manager I played under, Jock Stein, never talked tactics to me when he was preparing us. It is man-management that matters. So, I don't think you can hold it against Ally for that. He was much more like Tommy Docherty, who always had

130

the dressing room laughing with his great jokes. Ally was no Doc, but he aimed at having a sense of humour like him. He just wanted the dressing room to be a pleasant place to be in, and it was under him. In any case, if you've got a great set of players you don't need a bloody manager.'

Joe Jordan again emphasises Ally's good nature.

'There could have been a lot of conflicts, but there never were. I can't recall him falling out with a single player, or any of the players with him. '

Alan Rough genuinely liked him.

'He was a nice man. But I think it was the Anglos who didn't understand him. I mean, we used to play rounders before we had a training session. Rounders? The Anglos couldn't grasp what he was getting at. He just wanted us to enjoy what we were doing.'

At the first SFA meeting with him back in Scotland, Ally only survived in his job by a casting vote of chairman Tom Lauchlan after a 3–3 split in the international committee.

Of course, he carries the responsibility for having taken on the role and feeding us with a central fantasy. The idea was sold to the public that we could win the World Cup when there never was a chance of that, and probably never will be, as I was fast learning at that stage. What he had missed with him, to captain the side, was a Billy Bremner. Archie Gemmill might have scored the most famous goal in our history but, throughout, we missed the central drive and captaincy of that flawed 1974 leader: a man who could summon up reserves of strength, not only from within himself, but drag that out of others around him. We would not have lost our two games with that dynamic on hand. What had not changed from 1974 was the SFA failure once again to provide a sensible environment for players to live in together for three or more weeks.

They even tried to put the players into a sleazy hotel, in a dingy alleyway, in Buenos Aires for a night before departure for Scotland, while the officials retired to a ritzy palace down town. Alan Rough observed the reaction,

'Martin Buchan was first off the bus and when he saw where they had put us he said, "I'm not staying in this fucking dump. Lift your bags and come with me." We followed him up to the hotel the SFA were staying in and demanded we got in, the whole lock, stock and barrel of us. And we did.'

In SFA/player relationships, it was the equivalent of the storming of the Winter Palace in Saint Petersburg by the Bolsheviks. Like them, they won.

I had to believe a proud and sensitive man like Ernie Walker would try to avoid that in the future. But one thing puzzled me about him in the aftermath of Argentina that suggested that the trials and tribulations of that time had bitten deeply. A whole sixteen years later, Ally gave an interview to *The Sun* newspaper, sparked off by the news of the Maradona drug scandal in the World Cup in the States in 1994. When asked about his reaction to that, given what had happened to Johnston in Argentina, Ally replied in astonishing terms,

'Everyone thought that if we beat Holland by three goals in our last game – and we were three up at one stage – we'd go through. What they did not know was that FIFA had told us they'd deducted two points from us because Willie Johnston took the banned drug. We [presumably the SFA officials and Ally] decided to keep that news from the rest of the players.'

So, had we all been living a fantasy all these years, thinking that a three-goal victory would qualify us? Intrigued, my researcher, Pat Woods, wrote to Ernie Walker about that time, seeking an explanation. He received a courteous but strange reply.

Dear Mr Woods,

My recollection is that FIFA did deduct two points from Scotland because of Willie Johnston's indiscretion, but there was never any question of keeping this from the players. It is a long time ago now, of course, but I clearly remember that we were all hopping around with excitement during the match with Holland when it looked as though, despite everything, we still had a chance of going through. The news of the deduction of points presumably came to us after the match. In any case, to suggest that there was some kind of plot to keep the players in the dark is rubbish. Like you, I was rather surprised that there was no mention of a deduction of points from Argentina (in the Maradona case) but I must confess that all of my instincts are to try to forget the awful memories of the 1978 World Cup!

Best wishes ...

The fact of the matter is that FIFA deducted no points. The only penalty Scotland suffered was that Johnston was banned for a year from international football, although he never in fact played for his country again. There is no record of deduction of points or anything like that in the FIFA files. One of the commonest outcomes of mental trauma is amnesia. The wounds of Argentina had obviously produced that alternative condition: hallucination.

On the day I left Mendoza, homeward-bound, I bumped into Scottish novelist and Hollywood scriptwriter Alan Sharp at the airport. He offered me what you might say was the final word of a long suffering Scottish footballing addict, when I put to him, consolingly, 'At least we won.'

He growled at me from beneath his wide-brimmed fedora, 'We didn't win. We just discovered a new way of losing.'

He was marked for life, obviously, by this experience. We all were. My own particular mark is still watched by millions around the world. In 1996 Danny Boyle, later to win a director's Oscar and direct the Olympic Opening Ceremony in London, asked me to re-voice my commentary on the Archie Gemmill goal for a film he was making, as the original sound had weakened over the years. He told me he wanted me to hit top C. I did as told, without looking at the script context in which the voice would be used. The film, he told me, was to be called *Trainspotting*. When I watched it for the first time, it suddenly reminded me of that electrifying sensation that passed through me like I had touched a power cable, almost blowing me off that platform, when Gemmill found the net. In the film, which probably only Martians have not yet seen, let me recall that Renton is with his girlfriend. They are having sex. There is the sound of my commentary in the background with occasional brief pictures of the game. As my voice reaches its climax Renton howls, 'I've never felt like that since I saw Archie Gemmill scoring against Holland in Argentina in the World Cup!' He has just reached his orgasm.

His was fictional. Mine was real.

THE 1982 FIFA WORLD CUP

SPAIN

10

ENTRANCE OF A GIANT

It was the kind of evening when it was just bliss to be alive. Seville in June is enough explanation for that. Such a setting can make the outside world feel remote and unimportant. What enhanced this feeling was that we were about to get our first look at Brazil. The new Brazil. The Brazil, we were told, that had brought its old ways back to Spain for this World Cup in 1982. In Germany and Argentina, they had sacrificed style for substance, and seemed to have adopted the role of wanting to defend their masculinity rather than retaining that elastic swagger of 1970. Also, and perhaps more importantly, a new generation of talent had come through. Now we were told the native rhythms were back. Given what we had heard, it was like waiting for a cabaret act to come on. What more could you ask for on that velvety evening? In fact, we got more than we bargained for.

Beside me on the television gantry was the Lisbon Lion captain Billy McNeill, now freelancing as a broadcaster. There were 68,000 in the Ramón Sánchez Pizjuán Stadium on 14 June 1982, the vast majority of whom were only there to see one team. Brazil's opponents were the Soviet Union – or Russia, as everybody called them anyway, and what they shall be referred to as throughout. And, as the game developed, we were slowly beginning to realise that the Russians were giving this much-vaunted Brazilian side a really hard time, and this was a worry to an extent. Scotland were to play both of them in the coming days and, since we thought Brazil were unquestionably favourites to top the group, which also included New Zealand, it would be to our advantage for the South Americans to take points off the others. It did not take long to recognise that Brazil were certainly attractive, elegant, strutting again. Sócrates, in the middle, looking like he had introduced the beachcombing lifestyle to a football field, picking up balls and flicking them away with impeccable passes, with a casual disdain of all around him. Zico, lurking and sparking alternatively. Falcão striding menacingly from midfield. And Eder, a newcomer to us, appearing to possess a left foot of real quality. All in all, they were easy on the eye, but looked as if they knew it, and seemed, for all their obvious flowery talents, to be self-indulgent – an element in this side that was to cost them dearly at a later stage in the tournament. But it was Russia who concerned us.

We had imagined that this game would be a formality for Brazil, but we were increasingly impressed by the work ethic of their opponents, who had actually gone into a lead in the first half, and, deep into the second, were still holding on to it with comparative ease. It was making the group look much more daunting for us. Although Russia's record in the World Cups made a mockery of its geographical girth and the size of its population, this side looked impressive and were clearly as hard as granite. We were pondering those thoughts on the air when, suddenly, there was an interruption. It was the dreaded outside world.

A voice from London said in my earphones, 'In sixty seconds we will be interrupting the broadcast for an important news announcement. We will give you a countdown to stop talking.'

They did, allowing us to sit back, while the play raged on, and heard a typically measured BBC newsreader's voice calmly relate the news: 'The government have announced that the Argentinian forces in the Falklands have unconditionally surrendered.' The Falklands war was over. Now it was not as if Billy and I felt like downing tools in celebration to shout 'Rejoice! Rejoice!', as *that* woman had that night, as neither of us were madly keen on her, but at least the killing had stopped. And it was about to make many feel a little less guilty about coming to a football festival at a time when young Britons were putting their lives at risk in a war in which ultimately 255 were killed, and almost three times that number of Argentinians. No, what came to mind was an argument I had with Jock Stein in San Francisco in the States some months before about the war.

That was going through my mind as I watched Brazil equalise and then win the game in the eighty-ninth minute with a goal by Eder that was as spectacular as any scored in the whole tournament. An argument with Stein that lasted almost a whole day in San Francisco, including when we were munching crab at Fisherman's Wharf, still sticks in the mind. Why in San Francisco? And what did it have to do with us sitting there on a velvety night in Seville?

It all began with a phone call.

It came from a Scottish journalist, Jim Rodger, who had a reputation – much self-promoted – of having the ear of the great and the mighty, asking me to phone Stein in England, where he had only recently taken the manager's post with

Leeds United. It was just after Ally MacLeod had resigned from the Scotland post on 26 September 1978, after vilification in the press and public, which would have been more applicable for the Moors murderer Ian Brady. Ally took a battering after Argentina and it did his health no good. He died, sadly, of Alzheimer's in 2004. Disgusting though all that denigration had been, he knew it was time to go after he had led Scotland to a 3–2 defeat in the Prater Stadium against Austria six days before his departure. It left the SFA in some disarray, since the public expression through the various media outlets was for Jock Stein to be his successor. But he had left Celtic and had eventually moved to Leeds as manager on 21 August only weeks before. Stein going south certainly surprised me since no man was more of a home bird than he. Nevertheless, he had quickly installed himself there, and propitiously struck up good relations with Manny Cussins, the chairman and powerhouse of Leeds United. So, at least on the surface, he gave everyone the impression, including the SFA, that he was at the start of another career at the age of fifty-five.

But as soon as he answered the phone to me, I could tell I would be speaking to an unhappy man. Morose, slowly spoken, husky. I could hear Peter O'Sullivan's voice in the background on television. That didn't surprise me as Stein loved the horses and gambled heavily. I think I was accurate in imagining him lying on his bed romantically dreaming of making a fortune. He then asked me, without any qualms, that if I were going on television that night for network could I suggest something to them. 'Tell London that you can say something about the Scotland job and me,' he said. 'You could say something to the effect that you believe I would be interested in going back to Scotland. You know how to phrase these things. You can't say you've been speaking to me. Just play it like you are confident I would take the job. Make it sound like the SFA are being a bit slow on this.'

So, the man who had managed Celtic to the European Cup triumph had just become my scriptwriter. I leapt at it. So did London. They put me top of the bill on *Sportsnight*, introduced by Harry Carpenter and I think my first line was, 'The SFA only need to lift the phone to Jock Stein in Leeds and they will have their new manager.' The following morning, I turned on the radio for the sports news and heard Stein being interviewed about my comment the night before. 'Archie Macpherson is just flying a kite,' he told the reporter. 'You take all these comments with a pinch of salt. I'm very content doing my job at Leeds.'

The old fox was playing his part with a straight face. On 4 October 1978, just forty-four days after joining Leeds, Stein was appointed to the Scotland post. But life was to be different as national manager. With Celtic, he had taken on a job that demanded political cunning and brilliant manipulation of the media. He dominated Celtic Park. Nothing passed him by. He was now in a different culture. When I saw him for the first time at the SFA offices, he had been housed in what looked like a garret. It was like seeing a king in a broom cupboard. Nor could he control the press as cunningly as he had in a club job, and I think he knew there would be some out there wanting to settle old scores with him, knowing that if you are with the SFA you are a much easier target. But what helped him was his association with the SFA secretary, Ernie Walker. We all looked on this contrasting duo like spectators at a stock car race awaiting the first spectacular collision. To the astonishment of everyone, they in fact developed a yin-yang relationship which helped propel Scotland to another

141

World Cup. In truth, Walker had greater respect for Stein than he had for Ally MacLeod. He certainly didn't dislike Ally, but there was an artifice about him that Walker never really grasped to the full, whereas Stein was an achiever – a great achiever – a man who had won universal respect for creating records. Stein was the monument. Ernie was the tour guide taking us round it.

But the blend didn't guarantee smooth sailing. Scotland failed to qualify for the next European Championships under the pair, but, along the way, turned in some creditable performances. It was generally accepted that Stein was trying to change the whole outlook of how the players approached these games. He was concerned about the 'fiery cross' atmosphere that affected them. He never ruled out passion in football, but too often he felt Scotland had surrendered all reason to emotional charges which lent thrills to the terracings, but which were naïve and unproductive. He wanted them to be more cerebral, with the emphasis on possession and close passing. He wanted, essentially, to modernise them.

It took time before we could acknowledge real progress under his management. What had certainly boosted his popularity with the public was the game at Wembley five months before the World Cup group qualification. A John Robertson penalty in the sixty-fourth minute, sublimely taken, earned a 1–0 victory over England on 23 May 1981. I recall the moment Stein decided that sitting on the bench was no longer for him. I saw him rise and begin to walk round the perimeter, still with his eyes on the game. There were still several minutes remaining with Scotland on that slender lead. It was difficult for me to concentrate on the play without reference to the big man in his very long and slow walk towards the Wembley tunnel, which he eventually reached and stood there like he was watching a practice game. There. In Wembley. Against the Auld Enemy. And leading 1–0. Astonishing. It seemed to make the remaining minutes much longer for the rest of us. It could have been seen as a gesture of faith in his players to see the game out safely. And then the memory came back. He had done exactly the same in 1967 in Lisbon towards the end of that European final when he moved far away from the bench. For all his apparent invulnerability as a strong personality, in these situations, perhaps, it was simply evidence that his nerves were revealing he was a mere mortal who could not settle on his backside under pressure.

You could also have read into it something of his attitude towards this great fixture. It meant a lot to him, but less so than qualifying for the World Cup. He and his side accomplished this on 14 October 1981, with a goalless draw against Northern Ireland, although I seemed to age doing the commentary, as the Irish, desperate to qualify themselves, threw the lot at us. I think it was Alan Rough's finest hour. It was an act of almost singular defiance as the Scottish defence was punctured so often that Scotland's goalkeeper ought to have been chaired from the ground for pulling out an amazing repertoire of saves. But it was enough to take us all to the draw in Madrid on 16 January 1982.

In a country that gave us a literary figure who tilted at windmills, the organisers appropriately delivered a fantasy draw. It was presided over by Sepp Blatter of FIFA, who has certainly become a notorious figure, but to us then was a very genial multilingual person, although offering a charm that seemed to be laid on with a trowel. Some journalists, who were suspicious of him from the start, were not slow to tell us of his profound sociological interests, like being a sponsor of a movement for the return of garters for ladies and the abolition of tights. So, this towering intellect was in charge of the operation which involved balls rolling down transparent tubes. The draw itself was less transparent, despite the fact that, before the event, Blatter spoke to a group of us commentators explaining the simplicity of it all. This he did impressively in several languages. In fact, it was a fiasco.

Scotland was drawn in the Argentina group. Really? Not according to the template that FIFA had handed out previously, which had linked Scotland potentially with Brazil. Barry Davis for BBC London, in the adjacent booth, looked over at me and shrugged, as if I might be able to clarify what had occurred. Like him, I was lost. Suddenly, everything came to a grinding halt and it was clear somebody had blundered. They started again and, this time, Scotland's name was placed beside Brazil. To this day I am not sure what gummed up the works, but I did notice that Blatter handled the embarrassment and the explanation of what had gone wrong with aplomb. You could imagine, there and then, on that stage in Madrid, that here was a man with a Teflon skin and the immense self-confidence of a *Capo di tutti capi*.

'It's a bugger of a draw,' Stein said immediately after to me. 'I didn't want Brazil.' I think he said that without also needing to say that he didn't think we could get anywhere near beating them. And then added with a wry smile, 'I think I would have preferred the first draw.'

Then, in the questioning that was going on after the draw, someone suddenly asked him, out of the blue, what he thought of bull-fighting.

'The bull stands no chance! It's no contest. That's why it's no use.' So, in a few words, he was dismissing the ancient and enduring Iberian obsession for the duel in the sand. He knew fine well about unpredictability in his own sport, like

144

the way Partick Thistle had famously beaten his Celtic in the 1971 Scottish League Cup final. That's what he was getting at, although it also reminded me with a World Cup coming up, that, after suffering a defeat, it was always advisable to give Stein a wide berth.

Now he knew what was in store for Scotland when he began his preparations. He wanted to show he was being meticulous from the outset. He demanded to travel around Spain, even before the draw, to find the best accommodation for his players, given the ghastly mistakes made in the past. Ernie Walker accompanied him on that trip and almost boastfully recounted to me that, during this exhausting trek, he had got one of Scotland's iconic teetotallers to try a sip or two of Rioja. So, the nearest Stein ever came to an alcoholic stupor was in admitting to Walker that he was seeing two of him after a couple of sips. It was back to being a tea jenny after that. All the time he was trying to escape the shadow of Argentina hanging over Scotland and, logically, himself. The campaign there had been a mess in all kinds of ways and he particularly did not want levelled at him the most trenchant of accusations against Ally MacLeod, that he had not done his homework properly. Peru, he had not seen in the flesh. So, when Ernie Walker informed me that Stein was considering travelling all the way to see New Zealand play an Irish League side in a series of games in and around Auckland, it was something we wanted part of. We offered to go with him and make a film documentary of his visit. He agreed. At least for him it would be company on a long haul. But not long after that conversation, the news broke that Argentina had invaded Port Stanley on 2 April 1982 and, in the House of Commons, Maggie had made it apparent she wanted to clear them out. He phoned me with rising doubts, the very night before we were supposed to take off for the Antipodes.

'I don't think we should go,' he said huskily to me. 'The war down there could get nasty and they'll end up cancelling the World Cup, or we'll withdraw. Something's bound to happen. I think it'll be a waste of time to go out there now.'

I had to play this on the assumption that all he was doing at this stage was sounding off his reservations, and that I would just let this bounce off me and that he would be there at the airport. But this is what I really should have said to him on the phone, 'You're right. It is a waste of time, war or no war. You are in your late fifties, we know you are not exactly in the best state of health. We know you have some sort of heart condition that will certainly not be diminished by a horrendously long flight. And why should you bother about what people might say? You are no Ally MacLeod. He was a lovely man, but had no track record like yours. You have a record second to none in interpreting the opposition. You have cups and league flags to prove it. What good are you going to get out of watching New Zealand play friendlies against an Irish League side?'

Of course, I didn't. I hadn't the nerve. And, in any case, unashamedly, I did want to travel to enhance my credentials with BBC London. By the end of the conversation, we knew we were both on our way. Eventually, travel-weary, we stopped off in San Francisco for a night on 3 April 1982, and, although desperate for a respite from war talk, the whole issue blew up again. I had just got into my room and turned on the television when the famous American anchorman Dan Rather's face appeared on the screen with words that went through me like a rapier.

'Good evening. The war in the South Atlantic has taken

146

on a sinister turn with the sinking of SS *Belgrano* and the reported loss of ninety-nine lives.'

Within seconds I heard a hammering on my door and Stein burst in.

'Did you hear that?' he asked. 'C'mon, we're getting out of here back home. Maggie'll nuke them next. I told you it could get right out of hand. Get on the phone and get us a flight back home tomorrow.'

I didn't argue. I thought an overnight sleep might calm him down. It did, but only to an extent, because the next day, going around the city, we heard from a taxi driver taking us around San Francisco that HMS *Sheffield* had been sunk by the Argentine air force. He became morose again.

'I don't think I could face up to this. People are getting killed and we'll be fartin' about in New Zealand with the Maoris.'

We were now in the airport with the two options still open to us. Return or advance. I argued my point that the press knew where he was and, if he turned back now, then they might jump on him at a later date for not following through on his own plans if things turned pear-shaped for him during the World Cup itself. I then told him I was going on without him, if necessary, and would try to make the best of a bad job. I went through to the departure lounge and had a large whisky, for, apart from being largely browned-off with all the indecision, I am not a great flyer. About ten minutes later, he joined me.

'I couldn't let you go on your own,' he said.

We certainly learned about the origin of geysers at Rotorua and the importance of Maori culture in the Land of the Long White Cloud, but from the three games played by the All Whites against a League of Ireland touring side there was precious little to divine, especially from games on rough pitches with rugby markings which the zealots of that sport refused to obliterate. All we could tell was that, technically, they were about the level of a decent junior side in Scotland. Stein did enjoy the reception he got from Scots exiles, including from one Charlie Dempsey, a Scot who had jumped ship as a youth in Auckland, started a joinery business and ended up not only a millionaire, but head of the Oceania Football Association and a prominent FIFA delegate. It was he who almost theatrically abstained from the last round of voting to decide the venue for the 2006 World Cup. His act of abstention had effectively deprived South Africa of winning the bid, which went to Germany, to the disgust of many in world football. I recall him saying to Stein before we left his adopted country, 'Our boys are not good enough yet. It'll be straightforward for you.' Stein, the acme of caution at that moment, reacted only with a bland smile, as if going through his mind again was the thought that New Zealand in Spain would still have a better chance of survival in their sport than bulls would have in theirs.

11

MERRY MALAGA

At the start of the Spanish venture there was a day when it looked like Scotland didn't want to beat England. Seriously. The manager himself led with that perception. Stein had liked to set precedents during his long career as a club manager. Virtually all of them had appealed to his public. But on 29 May 1982 at Hampden, he decided on something that seemed to devalue the fixture that the Scottish public treasured more than any: the game against the Auld Enemy. An 80,529 crowd left him in no doubt how they felt about being beaten by England in the hundredth game between the two, and the last game before Scotland – and England, for that matter – set off for the finals. Paul Mariner for England scored the only goal of the game after thirteen minutes. For a start, the crowd did not get the players they wanted to see in action. They begged to differ from the manager's canny team selection. Aberdeen had won the Scottish Cup the previous Saturday against Rangers 4–1 in extra time. No doubt that game had taken much out of them. However, Willie Miller, Alex McLeish and, particularly, Gordon Strachan were on the crest of a significant new wave of football and desperately wanted to play. The two defenders had lent the Scottish defence great credibility, having conceded only four goals in the eight matches played in all competitions. None of them were selected for this one. The team in fact was:

Alan Rough,

George Burley, Danny McGrain (*captain*), Alan Evans, Alan Hansen, David Narey, Graeme Souness, Asa Hartford, Kenny Dalglish, Alan Brazil, Joe Jordan.

Strachan was kept sitting on the bench, even though the crowd kept chanting his name for inclusion. The mood on the field was so downbeat that you felt the players were only miming their parts. Clearly, Stein had not fomented a passion to beat the English. It was out of all kilter with the public appetite for this fixture. The roar from the press was perhaps greater than the Hampden equivalent that day. Alex Cameron, of the *Daily Record*, who could do sarcasm better than any other in the business, wrote on 31 May, 'Only the pipers played well and they selected themselves ... Scotland were a yard slower on the ball, and this included Kenny Dalglish and Graeme Souness.'

Hugh Taylor, in the *Glasgow Evening Times* the same day, put the boot in as well. 'Robbery! If this was just a warm-up practice game for Spain, how about giving the long-suffering fans at least some of their money back?'

They were sounding as if it were a sacrilege to deliberately play a weakened side against the Auld Enemy.

I could not recall any such level of vitriol being directed towards Stein in the past, certainly not when he was Celtic manager. That single day seemed to suggest that any special immunity he had enjoyed because of his great stature as a club manager had come to an end. In the interview with me, after the match, he kept stressing the need to look forward to Spain, but there was little doubt that the day had affected him. He was brief in his replies, as if he had nothing much to say, and it was clear to me he was desperate to get away. Later, I understood why. He was heading for the dressing room where players were patiently waiting to be told who was going to Spain. Those who witnessed that announcement are still affected by how it was done.

Davie Provan, now an established analyst for Sky, was waiting like the others to find out what lay in store for him. He recalls the scene well.

'The manager walked in and didn't mess about. He wasn't well pleased we had lost to England. And then it came suddenly. All he said was, "We're taking all of you to Spain, except Tommy Burns and Ray Stewart." Just like that. I couldn't believe it. I looked across at Tommy. I knew him well. I thought I saw the red mist coming over his eyes. He had a violent temper. When he lost it, he lost it big time. For a moment I thought he was going to attack Stein. I went right across to him and gripped him. I tell you, everybody in that dressing room was shocked at the abrupt way these two players had been dumped. One sentence and that was it. The whole squad was cringing at the way it was done.'

The late Tommy Burns talked about this to me years later, his bitterness undisguised, about the man who had nurtured him at Celtic Park.

'I had been with Jock Stein during the whole week for these Home Internationals and he had only spoken to me once, just to ask me how I was enjoying the experience. I felt reasonably pleased with myself. Then the few words in the dressing room to everybody. Just that. End of story. No explanation. Nothing. He just walked out. I felt stunned enough at the time. But I have to admit that the passing years have made me angrier about that since I was being denied getting on the greatest footballing platform in the world. I know he was a great manager, but why could he not have had a word about it with me? I'm forty-seven now and I still feel bitter about it.'

Little wonder. It was brutal. And worth recording, because it was also a glimpse into the multi-layered personality of Jock Stein, who could rise to touches of compassion and humanity, as I had witnessed, and descend, just as quickly, to a treatment of players which verged on callous indifference.

These are the men he did take to Spain for a tournament that now had been increased to twenty-four countries.

Alan Rough (Partick Thistle) Age 30/Caps 48, Danny McGrain (Celtic) 32/60, Frank Gray (Leeds United) 27/22, Graeme Souness (Liverpool, **captain**) 29/25, Alan Hansen (Liverpool) 27/14, Willie Miller (Aberdeen) 27/17, Gordon Strachan (Aberdeen) 25/11, Kenny Dalglish (Liverpool) 31/86, Alan Brazil (Ipswich Town) 22/7, John Wark (Ipswich Town) 24/15, John Robertson (Nottingham Forest) 29/21, George Wood (Arsenal) 29/4, Alex McLeish (Aberdeen) 23/15, Davie Narey (Dundee Utd) 26/13, Joe Jordan (A.C. Milan) 30/51, Asa Hartford (Manchester City) 31/49, Allan Evans (Aston Villa) 25/3, Steve Archibald (Spurs) 25/14, Paul Sturrock (Dundee Utd) 25/7, Davie Provan (Celtic) 26/10, George Burley (Ipswich Town) 26/11, Jim Leighton (Aberdeen) 23/0.

It is interesting to note the ages of the key players again, the ones most likely to be first choices. Souness, McGrain,

Dalglish, Jordan, Hartford, Robertson, all in and around the thirty years mark. Maturity and experience was one thing, but they had come out of a long hard domestic season and I am sure that Stein had doubts about some of them being able to step into the extra quota of games over a short period of time in blistering heat. Perhaps that is why we saw evidence of a distant relationship with Kenny Dalglish, who, by the time we had crossed the Pyrenees, never looked a happy figure.

In their acclimatising camp at Penina, just inland from the Portuguese coast, where they were to prepare for a few days before hopping over the border to Spain, it was clear a distinct chilliness had developed between Dalglish and the manager. They had not parted on gloriously amicable terms at Celtic Park. He was left out of one of the friendly matches they played against Torralta, a local side, and I recall him sitting on the sidelines of the small pitch, looking as if he would rather have been tending the East End pub he had just bought in Glasgow. That did not augur well for the finals, for the Scottish support regarded him as a talisman figure. Much of it was to do with personality. Kenny always spoke up about issues and had no fear of taking on Stein on any point. The manager's philosophy was close to benevolent despotism and couldn't accept 'no' for an answer. So, they could be at odds with one another. And yet Stein was concerned about our attack.

'We're not scoring enough goals,' he said to me in his first interview in Penina. 'And at this level you get few opportunities to score. We have to work on this. But, frankly, we've not been good enough in front of goal. Too much elaboration. We've got to be more direct.'

What else could he say, given that in eight matches over

that last year leading up to the World Cup finals, Scotland had scored only seven goals, and in all games since he took over four years previously, they had only averaged one per game. But we had suffered from goal dehydration long before he took up office. We had to go back to that infamous game against Chile in 1977 when they won 4–2 to record the last time Scotland scored more than three goals in a game. So, he had to pick from five recognised strikers: Kenny Dalglish, Joe Jordan, Steve Archibald, Paul Sturrock and Alan Brazil. But Jordan had never shown himself to be prolific, having managed at that stage only nine goals in fifty-one appearances and Dalglish claimed twenty-five out of eighty-six games. Then there were the alternatives: Archibald had scored only one, Sturrock one, and Alan Brazil had yet to score. A miserly bunch in all.

They did score prolifically against Torralta in their two warm-up games – sixteen goals for and one against, which was to provide climatic conditioning more than anything else, and shone no light on how they would line up against New Zealand in Malaga. The other man watching from the touchline on these two evenings was Jim McLean, his assistant, the Dundee United manager. Stein had huge respect for the man he almost shunted into the Rangers job in 1983. He had met Stein in a car park one day before his interview at Ibrox, to seek his last-minute advice on whether he should take the job or not. Stein assured me that, after a long discussion, McLean told him he was heading to Ibrox to take the job, but was astonished to learn from television news later that day that he had actually turned it down. All sorts of reason were aired for that eventually, although Stein's explanation was simplicity itself: cold feet. But, nevertheless, there he was, close to Stein again, and with a football brain that was second to none, although his gentle and discreet presence in the camp was at distinct odds with that of his prowling, smouldering authority at Tannadice, where he regarded the media generally as creatures from another planet.

Very largely, MacLean's presence was a cosmetic ploy, although one that gave the manager, at least, a knowledgeable football man who would listen to him. To be fair to MacLean, Stein rarely took advice from anybody in his career. He certainly did not take it from people in the media, like myself, who repeatedly advocated that Dalglish ought to be brought back to the national side after missing five international games. From 25 February 1981, when he scored the only goal in Tel Aviv to beat Israel in a World Cup qualifier, Dalglish was posted missing until he returned to the side which beat Sweden in another World Cup qualifier on 9 September of that year. During that period, he was helping Liverpool win the European Cup and the English League Cup. Admittedly, he had only scored eight league goals that season; nevertheless, to this day it still puzzles me why Stein spurned him. It is a phase in Dalglish's footballing life that many people have forgotten. Our greatest ever attacking player had been left out in the cold by the man who had helped make him famous.

Although we were all trying hard to take the New Zealanders seriously, for good reasons, we had found it hard to do so after visiting their camp when we had arrived in Spain, to find them lying around the pool and wolfing down chips like any average holiday maker from the UK along this Costa del Sol. You felt this was a new brand of tourism. As I watched them lying back, fully exposed to the sun, I recalled Charlie Dempsey telling us that New

Zealand had one of the highest rates of skin cancer in the world and that he had three operations himself to eradicate it. The 'I don't give a damn' mood seemed to prevail though. We learned nothing from the brief training we were allowed to see. But neither had we before the Iran game in Argentina. Their manager, John Adshead, whom Stein and I had met on our trip to their country, adopted the line of 'poor wee New Zealand', but with the added qualification, 'We are a small footballing nation with mostly amateur players. We may be a bit crude at times and lack certain skills, but we can play a bit as we have proved by reaching this stage, and we want to prove that while we are here.'

This was in marked contrast to the strictures laid down by Stein when his squad arrived in their splendid setting of the sports complex in Sotogrande only several miles from Gibraltar. Stein warned them of the dangers of the sun, which, in Lisbon in 1967, he had seemed to think was as big a danger to his side as the Inter Milan coach, Helenio Herrera himself. Sunbathing was out. With exceptions, as Davie Provan observed.

'We had all been warned about lying in the sun,' he told me. 'It was banned between 10 a.m. and 4 p.m. in the afternoon. I went on to my balcony one day at about one o'clock, the hottest part of the day, and looked along the line of the balconies and there was Graeme Souness lying back in the sun and pouring oil all over himself. And who was sitting beside him? Jock Stein.'

Souness was always an imposing figure and looked a natural leader, whether he was captain or not. In a hotel just outside Seville before playing Spain in a friendly on 24 February that same year, when we lost 3–0, he was at least a half-hour late coming down for an interview with me. As he sauntered down towards us at poolside, as if he had all the time in the world, and with my cameraman on edge to get this done and dusted and back to the studio, Stein beside us, and aware of our urgency, uttered not one word of reprimand. He just said, 'Look at that. Class!' Meaning, of course, that this Liverpool player was brimming with infectious, unruffled self-confidence. There seemed to be an affinity between them born of mutual respect, although Souness was to tell me in a broadcast in later years that the manager never cossetted him in any way, and that kind words directed towards him were actually miserably few. But Stein, publicly at least, liked his swagger: the contrast between his cool demeanour and the punishment he could dole out to opponents when he saw fit. But, for this first game, Stein had appointed Danny McGrain as captain. This was not to last.

The selection had contained one mild surprise: the exclusion of Joe Jordan, who was now playing his football in Serie A with Milan. The reason?

'I think they've picked a team to counter Joe,' Stein told me. 'When we were down there, they kept talking to me about his strength in the air. They might have got it wrong.'

He was referring to Adshead's inclusion of thirty-five-year-old Sam Malcolmson, who had played for Albion Rovers, Airdrie and Queen of the South, a tall powerful man whose main asset was his ability in the air. He was one of three Scots-born players who would face up to us. So what? That was the general mood around the media after seeing Scotland's first team for Spain 1982 at Malaga's La Rosaleda stadium.

Rough,
McGrain (*captain*), Hansen, Evans, Gray,
Strachan, Souness, Wark, Dalglish,
Brazil, Robertson.

So, Kenny was in after all. Brazil was young, bursting with enthusiasm, eager to score his first goal for his country, but his selection was a gamble, considering that players such as the experienced Steve Archibald would be on the bench. But at the back, Stein had selected a man who was about to play the last of his four internationals, Alan Evans. However, if you bring ambitious men together, all of who have the prospect of playing in perhaps a once-in-a-lifetime experience, you are going to have winners and losers, even before a ball is kicked. Willie Miller, who was chosen as one of the eleven members of Scotland's Greatest Team by viewers of the Scottish Television documentary series in 2010, nursed a feeling of grievance.

'Jock went for Alan Evans because he had just helped Aston Villa win the European Cup. And that more than anything was what he wanted to play up with the press. He was the player of the moment. Sure, I was bitterly disappointed. In all the time I played under Jock, only once did I get an explanation from him about selection, and what I had to do on the field. It was a game in the early qualifiers against Sweden. He came to me the day before and told me I would be playing alongside Alex McLeish and he'd be putting Alan Hansen in midfield. Then, would you believe, he came back later and told me Hansen didn't want to play in midfield and I'd have to play there. So, effectively, he had allowed Alan to scupper his plans. That's the only time he ever conversed with me about selection. But that day in Malaga I had to watch from the sidelines and some of our defending wasn't pleasant to see.'

Note the particular mention of Hansen and the hint of Anglo favouritism, to which Miller and others thought Stein was susceptible. You could tell, even from a few words, that Miller and Hansen were hardly drinking buddies. As we shall see, relationships like that do matter.

Davie Provan was also stung badly.

'Before we left Scotland, Jock took me aside and told me that he would play me in the first game against New Zealand. He was also very frank in telling me that he wouldn't pick me for the other two matches. Fair enough, because he explained that he wanted breadth and pace on the wings to attack them in the first game. He said that would destroy them. So, I took part in all the set pieces during training, assuming I was playing. To my amazement, when he read out the team to us, I wasn't included, not even on the bench. I could hardly believe it. To say I was angry is an understatement. When I arrived in the Rosaleda that night, just to watch the game, I had made up my mind that I would go back to Sotogrande, pack my bags and get a flight back home right away. Since I knew I wouldn't be playing in the other games, what was the point of hanging about? However, I slept on it and reluctantly decided to stay.'

By the time they had trundled up one of the busiest roads in the world between Sotogrande and Malaga for the game on 15 June 1982, the official party might easily have imagined that Spain had loaned their musty and humid port city to the Scots. There were huge numbers. It ranked with the kind of tumult that we had witnessed in Liverpool when the whole rigmarole began in 1977, although infinitely more tropical. They crammed themselves into the Estadio La Rosaleda, which, because of its compactness, made the crowd look bigger than the official attendance of just 20,000. FIFA had decided on a late afternoon kick-off when they had assumed the temperature would be less harrowing. But the clothes were clinging to us by kick-off. What certainly was harrowing was the playing of the Scottish anthem before the match. 'God Save The Queen' had been ditched almost personally by Ernie Walker, who had grown fed up listening to it being booed. He had admitted that unease when he told us much earlier, 'They can play "She'll be coming round the mountains when she comes", for all I care, as long as we get a result.' That was a perfectly apolitical view he expressed to try to distance himself from the differing factions who wanted to make merry with the issue. He knew that Frank McElhone, the Under Secretary of State for the Scottish Office had, in the previous year, expressed anxiety over chants of 'If you hate the effing English clap your hands!' that he had heard from Scottish crowds. None of us liked to hear that but, at the time, dismissed it as something associated peculiarly with the terracings, in the spirit of idle banter. On reflection, though, we might have underestimated the number around the country whose chants were less benignly disposed.

So, they played 'Scotland The Brave' for Scotland's opening game in Malaga. I don't know how the recording was made, or by whom, in particular, but either on the stadium sound system or the actual original recording, the throbbing, discordant screeches made you want to hide under a seat. It also went on and on, seemingly interminably, until somebody realised that there might be a crowd break-in if it didn't stop. Billy McNeill and I looked closely at the close-ups of the players on our monitors as they attempted to stand still in the scorching heat, and could see a mix of amusement and irritation on their faces. They were obviously desperate to get going. When they did, the prospects looked better than fair. These were the very calm-looking New Zealand players:

Van Hattum,

Almond, Elrick, Sumner (*captain*), Malcolmson,

Mackay, Cresswell, Boath, Rufer,

Wooddin.

Scotland was simply facing stuffy orthodoxy. There was nothing in the first half that suggested that New Zealand had any versatility in their side. Since they had garnered little from the manager's trip to the other side of the world, it was the professionalism of the Scottish players that enabled them to suss out their weaknesses in several minutes. One player certainly did. Gordon Strachan was about to give us a command performance. Billy McNeill and I lapped him up in commentary like we were seeing a definitive display of traditional inside forward play, the sort of style we think Scotland had copyrighted. He was tirelessly creative. Often, he would make the clumsy-looking New Zealanders look like they were trying to put a lead on a frisky puppy. He would go past them with ease. But approaching twenty minutes gone, there was nothing to show for the grip Scotland had on the game. I thought my own experiences of the previous two World Cups had taught me patience, but I was getting edgy. Total superiority, but nothing to show for it. Then it came. Strachan slipped past three players on the right at speed, like they had been mummified, and chipped it forward to Dalglish, who stroked it past Van Hattum in their goal from a narrow angle. Eighteen minutes gone. Although New

Zealand did have a single break after that, with Rufer, a tall striker, alarmingly going through the middle of the Scottish defence but scooping his shot over the bar, when he ought to have scored, Scotland still dominated. Time for another, you felt. It came eleven minutes later.

Strachan again, from the right, chipped a ball to Brazil, whose shot was parried by Van Hattum for John Wark to poke in the rebound for the second. Two minutes later, Strachan offered us another aspect to his repertoire: the accurate cross. From almost the touchline, he flighted the ball to the onrushing Wark, who headed it with strength to the back of the net. The thought, which went through my head as the first half whistle went with Scotland three up, was that these players were now putting to rest this notion that had developed since the game against Zaire in Germany that a Scotland team couldn't see off inferior opponents and put goals in the bank for any future reckoning. This was the new look. A wobble-free dynamic. Or so it seemed at the time. Although if Billy and I had to consume what seemed like a couple of gallons of *agua sin gas* for survival, awaiting the restart, it left us wondering what kind of state the players would be in down there. We got the answer quickly. Everything had slowed down in the opening few minutes of the half. Why not? They were securely in front; the onus was on their opponents to come at them if they wished. But one move saw the end of Alan Brazil not long after the restart. Dalglish, who had been largely subdued after his opening goal, twisted his way round a defender and slipped a pass to Brazil only six yards from goal. He swept his shot over the bar. It looked amateurish. He was almost immediately substituted by Steve Archibald. Davie Provan noted the error of Brazil's technique.

'The problem was that he didn't turn his body square to the goal. He was always side on to it, which made it difficult to keep the shot down. If he had scored, then we wouldn't have had that scare.'

What scare? They were three up. Put another way, the New Zealanders were offered unexpected Scottish hospitality from an unlikely source, the captain, Danny McGrain. Normally impeccable inside his own penalty area, ten minutes into the second half, he intercepted a cross by Rufer, but his over-delicate pass-back to Rough left the ball in that no man's land of 'Whose ball is it?', and as they hesitated, the ball was seized by Sumner, who poked it into the net. Ten minutes later we were in no mood to joke about the Kiwis when a long ball was played from deep inside their own half which went straight through a woeful gap in the central Scottish defence, leaving Rough exposed. He couldn't prevent Wooddin from scoring their second, simply by seeming to hit it straight through the Scottish keeper to make it 3–2. It was not as if these goals were in any way the result of a New Zealand resurgence. They just seemed to happen. That made it feel worse. There was this ghastly and supremely irrational feeling gripping me again, given the scars I still carried from Germany and Argentina, that we were fated to self-destruct; that we carried some flaw in the national psyche that diminished our taste for victory somehow. Was I seriously thinking those things as the game raged on? I couldn't get it out of my mind. For with the scoreboard showing that scoreline, New Zealand, in their white shirts, began to look frighteningly like Real Madrid for a few moments. The mind stopped playing tricks eight minutes later, thankfully, for with Souness and Gray hovering over a free kick on the edge of the box, John Robertson stepped in and neatly flighted it into the top corner of the net. Seven minutes on, Steve Archibald sent a looping header into the net from a Gordon Strachan corner kick. 5–2. Billy McNeill and I found ourselves shaking hands like we had been reprieved of attempting to explain away another embarrassment to the Scottish public.

Given our previous record in World Cup opening games, the 5–2 victory was a triumph, albeit with a reminder that this was really kids' stuff compared to what now faced us up in Seville against Brazil. The players walked from the field satisfied, to a degree, but in a state of exhaustion, which brought to mind that description of our troops crossing the moorlands in the Falklands, that very week, struggling to reach Port Stanley: they had 'yomped' their way to victory.

12

TOE POKE

Seville was only three days away. Down in the sunny luxury of Sotogrande, the players were in a much better mood than I had ever seen in any of the other World Cup camps. They had won, after all, and were under a manager who was trying to brush off the two-goal scare they had experienced, although forced into being philosophical about it. 'Yes, we are the greatest nation in the world for punishing ourselves at every turn. But we scored good goals. That was the most important thing.' He then went on to tell me about one worry. 'Alan Brazil was in a bad way after the game. He suffers from a chest condition and he could hardly breathe at the end. I'll have to keep my eye on him.'

The drug authorities also had their eyes on Brazil, for after the game he was so dehydrated he couldn't give a sample for the post-match drug test. Because of that, he had to make a double journey between Malaga and Sotogrande well into the small hours of the morning before he could take a test and be cleared. That experience had taken a toll on his physical condition and, because he had looked out of his depth in the Rosaleda anyway, by common consent in the media, he was being discounted for Seville. Not that there were any anxieties about taking on the Brazilians, as Alan Rough reminded me.

'Stein was at his best in the next few days. There was a lot of humour about him. He was good to be about. The banter between him and the players was great. I think it was because winning the game made it so different from our start in Argentina and because the place we were in was superb compared to the shithole in Alta Gracia. And, more importantly, he kept pumping into us that the Brazil game was not the most important match for us. He wasn't telling us in so many words that we couldn't beat them, it was just impressing on us the reality that people were now talking about this probably being the best Brazilian side since 1970. It was the Russia game that we would have to concentrate on. That was the one that we had to win.'

So far, though, the character of this World Cup had been different from the previous two. This time England was involved, which meant their media were much less interested in the Scottish effort. Hardly any of the stars from Fleet Street were about the camp at press conferences, as England were based in the Basque country, far in the north, and had beaten France 3–1 in their opening game, the day after Scotland's match in Malaga, Consequently, their media were in a high state of anticipation that this might be England's year. And, frankly, we were struggling to get any film stories that would interest a network audience, given BBC and ITV's gravitation towards England's efforts at that time. I was at my wits' end trying to come up with something that would be pictorially and editorially interesting for viewers, given the Sargasso Sea of platitudes that you could easily sink in when you asked players, or indeed the manager, about anything at this stage. It was Billy McNeill who unclogged the thinking.

'What about Sean?' he asked me simply one day.

Of course. He could only have meant one particular Sean: 007. He was talking about an acquaintanceship he had built up during the time of Celtic's great runs in Europe. We knew Sean Connery lived somewhere along the coast from where we were in Benalmadena, around Marbella. If we could record him talking about the sport and the country he loved, it would be the ideal way to set us up for Brazil. Any broadcasting channel loves celebrity endorsement. After innumerable phone calls, including to agents in London, we at last tracked him down, and he agreed to give us the pearls of his wisdom. We set off like autograph hunters.

The topless German girl who lay sprawling at the poolside just outside Puerto Banus near Marbella did not seem to mind that 007 was occasionally sneaking a glance at her. We all were. Except that Sean Connery's wife was sitting beside him as well, constantly feeding her poodle and muttering incessantly in French. It was as well the poodle was a distraction because we noted she was unaware of Sean pointedly eyeing the scenery. However, Sean became thoroughly browned off by her interruptions, put down his cutlery with a clatter and snapped, 'Would you shut your effing mouth!' We carried on eating as if nothing had happened.

We were in Toni Dalli's restaurant, being plied with pasta as the restaurateur sang arias and treated Sean like a bishop come to bless his house. As he shook our hands, the first words which came out of his mouth were, 'Are we going to shoot ourselves in the foot again?' It could have come from the mouth of any Scottish fan along the coastline who had watched the New Zealand game, as he had. The great man immediately seemed to be part of that common denomination of support that could not free itself from nagging doubts about a Scotland side, even after a victory. Billy, who has a talent in PR that had been shockingly underused by Celtic at that time, struck up a good rapport immediately, by telling Sean that he was the greatest 007 of all time and that Roger Moore was but a pale imitation of the real thing. The big, tanned and muscular man, who at that stage was going through a quieter phase in his film career, was mightily impressed to be reminded of his halcyon days. But it was the interview that showed how well he summed up what we might call the 'Scottish condition'. For as we were talking to the most famous Scot since time began, it became clear, in his words, that someone who had attained the heights in his career and lived the life of luxury carried with him exactly the same qualms that a punter from Easterhouse, sleeping rough on the beach somewhere on the Costa del Sol, would be mulling over: give us the right stage and we will self-destruct.

I recall his analogy, spoken in a soft tone, that we had just suffered a panic attack. He tried to illustrate what he was getting at. That you walk on to a new bridge and suddenly there is a sag in the middle and a flush of terror begins to rise from your toes. A Hollywood analogy, you would think, but having been on that bridge for a few almost interminable minutes two days before, I knew precisely what he was getting at. And that was the most interesting aspect of the visit: that he was not offering gratuitous support and uttering clichés, but trying in a brief way to unravel that conundrum of recurring incalculable mishaps.

In a sense it was slightly downbeat, but all the more genuine for that matter, and I was impressed. But this ex-Hibernian rookie, who if he had stuck to that profession, could have gone down another route and ended up successfully owning a pub in Easter Road, had obviously suffered occasionally from watching Scotland in the past, and from that scare in Malaga. So, he was one of us, effectively. He talked the same unscripted language as us. On the other hand, as I looked at the palatial surroundings, at the topless girl who proceeded to walk up and down near our table like she was auditioning for a part in a movie, at the reverent way he was treated by everyone, I had to conclude that he had certain things going for him that put him at a slight advantage over that punter from Easterhouse on the beach. But we were pleased we had him on tape being so down to earth. As soon as we had sent all this back, we were told that we were going to have a visitor who wished to chat to us, not about Brazil, but about Scotland. His name was Jimmy Hill.

Hill was, of course, the leading pundit on BBC network at that stage. The summons to meet him was about his need to find out more about Scotland and the tittle-tattle that was surrounding the camp down at Sotogrande, and, of course, about possible team selection, as he would be analysing the game up in Seville. We repaired to a fish restaurant in Torremolinos to courteously fill him in. Although these last three words would have been used in a different manner by many Scots, who disliked him intensely. In fact, Hill was a likeable and charming man socially. And for all the personal reservations I had about him, his work with the players' union in England opened up a new era in player/club relationships and he was a television innovator who introduced pundits' panels to coverage of games and encouraged the use of slo-mo replays. So he had made a considerable contribution, in helping the lot of the professional footballer and offering the best ways to present the game to the public. But he did like talking about himself.

One of his stories was of his relationship with Raquel Welch, and how he had turned down the offer from the glamorous film star to be her European agent. Billy and I were not sure that cast a good light on his judgement. So, the chat lasted well into the night and, with much drink taken, he steadily developed a slightly patronising tone about the Scottish side. This led both of us to send him up, particularly Billy, who said he was definitely going to support his bid for a knighthood, after Jimmy had complained to us about missing that honour in the previous awards lists. What we could not know then was that Hill was about to provoke the most serious breach of relationships between Jock Stein and the BBC, which, up to that point, was one of mutual admiration. The next day we headed for Seville.

It is a deeply religious city of pilgrimage and devotion. It was the place though, where in my view, and appropriately, the Scottish support underwent a conversion that has lasted ever since. Ally's Army had been a phenomenon of blind, unrealistic triumphalism. That night in Seville, the transition to Tartan Army began to take place. On 18 June, the city surrendered to hordes in carnival mood, many of whom, in the carousing that went on, gave the impression they had forgotten what they had come for in the first place. The longest dancing conga line ever seen on the planet, comprising men and women from places of such great cultural similarity as Auchterarder and São Paulo, swung its way around the city centre like a multi-coloured thread in search of a tapestry. The canary yellow of Brazil merged with tartan in an almost tropical profusion of colour. As Seville heat induces skimpiness of dress, there were acres of flesh on show as well. Melanoma was on nobody's mind. The dark days of Wembley, and medieval crowd misbehaviour in London itself, were now being cleansed from the system of Scottish supporters. That evening heralded a new era of Scottish crowd conduct. All this, of course, coincided with an age when English supporters were seriously mimicking the Visigoths. The Scots were sending out a message of deliverance from the past.

And God, it was hot. I have referred previously to conditions that would hinder men from temperate climes giving of their best, even recently in Malaga, but this was like the door of Hades had been opened on us. Take heed of what Alan Rough experienced.

'Honestly, it was the worst ever. In the warm-up I looked at Graeme Souness and John Robertson and, within minutes, I could see their jerseys saturated with sweat like they had been in a pool. I knew this was going to be hell for them. It wasn't the sun. It was just this all-round heat. And then, when the Brazil team came out for the line-up, you couldn't see a bead of sweat on any of them.'

Davie Provan suggests one of the reasons for that.

'I still have a Brazilian jersey from that game that I was presented with afterwards. It was of the finest material; you could hardly feel it when you held it. Our jerseys? You wouldn't believe it. Ours had a lining. A lining. You couldn't make it up.'

Those wearing the jerseys that day were:

Alan Rough,
David Narey, Frank Gray, Willie Miller, Alan Hansen,
Gordon Strachan, Graeme Souness (*captain*), Asa Hartford, John
Robertson,
John Wark, Steve Archibald.

Danny McGrain was out. A great player had made a mistake in that last game and it was clear that Stein had not

171

only blamed him for New Zealand's comeback, but felt he was now past his best. A marvellous professional was again being offered no sentimental leeway by the manager. Davie Narey, who had become the first Dundee United player to be capped when he was picked against Portugal in a qualifying round, was replacing McGrain to add the straight-backed solidity he provided consistently to his club. With Brazil out, Archibald was to start in attack, with Dalglish on the bench, perhaps not surprisingly, since, although he had scored in the opening game, he had faded badly. Alan Rough was attaining his fiftieth cap, a figure reached by only six Scots before that. And brought back to the middle of defence was Willie Miller, who puts another complexion on his selection for that game.

'Of course, I was delighted, but for another reason. Here I was at a World Cup as an Aberdeen player. I looked upon myself as a kind of trailblazer, because it wasn't all that easy for our players to get international recognition. Yes, occasion-ally it did happen, but we felt strongly that if you played for Rangers of Celtic, or if you were an Anglo, you stood a better chance of getting into the side. It took me a while to get there, but I did it.'

It was an echo of what Peter Cormack of Hibernian had said about his non-participation in Germany, and it does indicate how parochial matters still lodged in the minds of some. For Miller, it wasn't a distraction. It was an incentive. It had to be for Brazil were at full strength:

Peres,
Leandro, Oscar, Luizinho, Júnior,
Cerezo, Falcão, Sócrates (*captain*), Eder,
Zico, Serginho.

172

For as much as I wanted Scotland to win this game, I couldn't help feeling that to watch this side play again, as I had in the previous match against Russia, would be something of a treat, and about which I wouldn't mind feeling guilty. I was told the mercury was reaching hundred degrees at kick-off, even though it was 4 p.m. There were just under 50,000 sweltering in the Benito Villamarín stadium, with the Scottish supporters again outnumbering the boisterous South American fans.

The storm cones were about to be raised when Brazil won a corner in only thirty seconds. Scary. But nothing came of it. It was something of a false alarm. For, in the next fifteen minutes, Rough had not had to make a single save. The Brazilians seemed to be at ease with themselves, not indulging in long ball play, of course, but at the same time giving the impression that there was a long time to go and they would take their time about what they had in mind. The man catching the eye was Sócrates again. The tall, slightly bearded figure, strolled around midfield like an elegant dance instructor but sufficiently alert to opportunities to come forward to head an Eder cross just past Rough's left-hand post early on. Scotland, meanwhile, were not exactly chasing shadows. Miller had seemed to add a calming influence to defence. If you have that, you can venture forward more confidently. Souness did get himself into a shooting position as defenders pounced on him, after ten minutes, but, ominously, his touch seemed to lack conviction. He had to watch his spooned shot from the edge of the penalty area sail well over the bar, conveying the thought that Scotland would have to scrap for every morsel of opportunity.

Then, to the surprise of the world waiting for Brazil to begin the process of dismantling those Scottish upstarts,

173

a defender changed the whole tenor of the game. In the eighteenth minute, Souness flighted a ball towards the right, where it was met with a downward header by Wark, into the path of Scotland's right back Davie Narey. If ever there were a moment on a football field that could justify Andy Warhol's statement that 'in the future everybody will be famous for fifteen minutes', it was now upon us. Narey, an unassuming and withdrawn personality, was about to step into the limelight. With several defenders advancing on him, to close him down, and with little time to think, he simply stabbed at the ball, almost like the way Cubillas had taken his free kick against Scotland in Argentina – except the ball was moving when he struck it and never stopped until it had hit the roof of the net.

It was a goal made even more stunning by looking as if it had been pinched from Brazil's own repertoire. The name Narey was being bounced around the globe now in perhaps a myriad of pronunciations. For this was fame, thrust upon him by his act of Scottish audacity. Taking the lead against the swaggering Brazilians? And by a player barely known outside Scottish football ranks, and even then somehow underestimated by many because he didn't wear an Old Firm jersey back home? Even up in our platform, both Billy and I were in raptures, at least for a few minutes, until it dawned on us that such a goal would be a provocation for the Brazilians, forcing Billy to comment, 'I hope we didn't score too early.'

And so it came to pass that Warhol was right, because normal service was resumed after fifteen minutes, when Brazil were awarded a free kick twenty-five yards from goal.

Alan Rough watched his defence take shape for this.

'Andy Roxburgh was one of the coaches with the party.

He would go and watch the opposition. He had watched the Brazilians several times and came back to tell me that Zico wasn't taking free kicks for them any longer. I told him that he was. No, he insisted, that wasn't happening. Forget Zico. There were three of them lined up to take this, including Júnior and Eder. Now maybe my positioning was wrong. But guess who took it?'

It was Zico indeed who stepped forward between the other two, and with impeccable accuracy swept in a curving ball which clipped the inside of the post before it nestled behind the ill-informed Rough. Apart from all Scots around the globe who would never forget that moment, Narey's name, in that allotted time of fifteen minutes, was now buried by the rest of the world as Brazil had assumed their old mantle. So that was it at half-time. Equality. More than we had imagined it would be. So, it might have been a reasonably pleasing interval, were it not for one man who was not actually in the stadium at all, but sitting inside a temporary studio, on the rooftop of multi-storey apartment block looming over the stadium.

Jimmy Hill pontificated from there, aloof, distant, but with no compunction about offering his view on that magical Narey moment. He called it a 'toe-poke'. I recall distinctly Billy spilling his cool drink down his front when he heard that. It wasn't so much the technical description that may or may not have been accurate. It was the tone. This is something impossible to capture in print. It was one of belittlement. How could a man astute enough to have made a success in various businesses so misread what an entire nation would have felt about taking the lead against the favourites for the tournament? Unless, of course, he felt that it was part of his persona to develop this kind of relationship, being aware

175

that banners had been held up by Scots at games in the past, casting doubt on his masculinity. In short, he loved stoking the fires. What he hadn't bargained for was Stein's ultimate reaction.

The second half, frankly, was in many ways a masterclass by the Brazilians. Although their second goal, just after the interval, was the sort you might have seen in any league game, even at the lowest levels. After Sócrates had swept past Narey on the right, and won a corner off Alan Hansen, it was taken by Júnior whose cross was headed in with the greatest simplicity by Oscar. They were now in the lead. Souness, who ought to have been covering him, hardly rose in the air, as if he had the lead weight of humidity on his shoulders. Now their strutting had become more dynamic with Zico, in particular, menacing Scotland by converting his lurking presence into sudden spurts and shots at goal. Now, all patriotism aside, I would not have missed the sixty-fourth minute for all the world. It was exquisite. It was why people loved Brazilian artistry. It was started by the ambling Sócrates feeding Serginho, who then fed Eder on the left. He looked up. Alan Rough properly advanced to the six-yard line to narrow the angle and then clearly remembers what followed.

'You don't want to be beaten at your near post, so you try to defend that, and I was thinking there was no way he could put it across me. But then came the chip. Nowadays, with the kinds of balls we have, some players can do that. But back then you didn't think about that. What a chip. There was nothing I could do about that.'

It was so delicately chipped to the far corner of the net, you felt he had just put the ball through the proverbial eye of the needle. 3–1 and no way back, that was for sure. Although Scotland did not buckle, they were now at walking pace, practically, and made few sorties at goal of any value. The climax came in grand style with the ball played around the Brazilian midfield that was increasingly like pass the parcel, until three minutes from the end when Sócrates, with his back to goal, simply pushed a gentle ball in front of Falcão, who, with his plentiful fair hair making him seen more Nordic than Brazilian, ran from a deep position in midfield and drove a long low shot past Rough, who could hardly be faulted for the excellence in build-up and finish.

The final score of 4–1 was summed up simply by Alex McLeish, who came off the bench to replace Asa Hartford, a defender for a midfield player, with twenty minutes to go, when Stein had decided to shore up the defence and keep the score at a respectable level.

'You know people say the Brazilians had the great advantage over us because of the conditions. But, in all honesty, I think that side would have beaten us under any conditions, they were that good.'

Alan Rough was even more adamant about that.

'You say that the Narey goal was scored too early and that might have provoked them. Listen, they could have beaten us any way they liked and when they liked. They could have seen us off any time.'

The whole day had been like being at a birthday party where the joyful guests make up for the fact that you didn't get the big present you had been hoping for. The Tartan Army had played its part. Soon they were back on the streets. They seemed dazzled rather than despondent. The Brazilians and Spanish wouldn't allow anything else. Only one thing was irking many of them: they were looking for the head of Jimmy Hill. Even in that age, long before the smartphone was invented, word of mouth was proving to be swift and potent among a football crowd, especially in this case, when they had heard of an attempt to slur an iconic goal.

13

007 TAKES AIM

Stein made it clear to us the following morning that if he were to come across Jimmy Hill in his travels around the tournament then it would be something like the *Gunfight at the O.K. Corral* again. He was deeply angered by Hill's comments overall, not just the 'toe-poke' reference. He was right in that respect. In the cold light of dawn, you could say that too much was being made about a two-word expression. But it wasn't simply about that. Placed in the context of the raised emotions of all the Scots – including players and management – seemingly downplaying that morsel of unrestrained joy we had experienced made Hill's description seem inflammatory. It was a misjudgement of mood, rather than simply of words. I suspect it was the same with supporters, who wouldn't have minded had Narey scored off his backside.

Billy and I had a session with Stein in which anti-English sentiment poured out of him, almost as if he had been waiting for some time to let that fly. This I had never heard from him before. Of course, it occurred to me that Scotland had been well beaten by a team playing mostly well within themselves, and Stein never liked being beaten by anybody, at

any time, not even Brazilians, despite his public pronouncement of it being no disgrace. So, like any other manager in
the aftermath of defeat, I suspect he was looking for a way
of deflecting attention from the game; and Hill had given it
to him in spades. He made his feelings known to the BBC,
through myself, that Jimmy Hill would not be welcome in
the Scottish camp. Not that there was any inclination on his
part to come anywhere near any Scot now. And, given my
distaste for blood sports, it is just as well the pair never met
during the rest of the tournament. Nor do I believe that the
BBC would have paid much heed to any complaint about
Hill for, at that time, he was in ascendancy because of his
stature in broadcasting circles and because, despite what
Scots might have thought about him, he commanded a great
deal of respect in footballing circles in the south. There was
only one time I had personal experience of BBC London
doing something that countered Hill's views and that was in
Mexico in 1986, which we will come to. Apart from that, the
following day was certainly not one of remorse, which would
have followed automatically after a World Cup defeat. The
line to the media was quite simple: it had been a privilege
to have contributed to a great game, against a great team ...
Simple stuff that everybody knew would be accepted by the
Scottish support.

Nevertheless, in the four days before the Russia game, a
more sceptical view was growing among the media about
Scotland's position. They had been well beaten in Seville
after all, but hadn't they conceded two sloppy goals against
New Zealand, which, in effect, meant that Russia, who had
beaten New Zealand 3–0, needed only a draw to go through?
It was a similar situation to 1974 in West Germany, when
Yugoslavia required a draw to go through against us in

Frankfurt. We were on the brink again. So, in those days leading up to the game in La Rosaleda, Stein himself became edgy. We were there daily to interview him and take stock of the situation. Our meetings were always taken separately from the press and in that kind of seclusion I was aware of him resembling the Stein of old, of those early Parkhead days, of being extremely sensitive about what the press were saying privately. Who was saying what about him? He kept quizzing Billy and I about that, although we played dumb, knowing that some of the press would be prepared to savage him, if given the slightest excuse.

And everybody was into the guessing game. Who would play in the last chance saloon? Stein had made it clear to us all, in a general conference for all the media, two days before the last group game, that he had not made up his mind about anything, in light of the big names like Danny McGrain and Kenny Dalglish he had left on the bench in Seville, or whether Joe Jordan, Davie Provan or Paul Sturrock would be given a chance.

'It's no sin or a crime if a player's touch has gone or his confidence is wavering,' he told us. 'It happens to everyone at some stage because of one thing or another. But we have players here who have come a long way and they are entitled to a game if they are in touch at the moment. This game against Russia is all important, and that's why reputations won't count when I name the side.'

One recurring discussion amongst us was about central defence. Davie Provan was nevertheless acutely aware of the dilemma in that area.

'Willie Miller and Alan Hansen playing together meant we didn't have an outright centre half. They were both sweepers, in their own way of thinking. Who goes for the ball first?

181

Who's guarding which side? They were both great players, but they never seemed to be at ease with each other.'

Willie Miller didn't demur from that view.

'I have absolutely nothing against Alan Hansen as a person, but it was never the best combination. We were too similar. Alan didn't play his club football with a centre half and he wasn't going to be one, whereas I played with a centre half throughout my career. So, it was difficult to get it right with him. I expected my centre half to be the dominant one and go and challenge for the ball and I would pick up thereafter. That just didn't happen. In my view I would have wanted Alex McLeish beside me, but I don't pick the team. Although I understand why Jock kept picking Alan Hansen, for he was a very good player. But sometimes you've got to think of how a combination will work out.'

Hansen himself made a significant admission in his book, *A Matter Of Opinion*, that he was never an effective tackler. And then went on to be even more self-deprecatory in asserting that determination and aggression were both lacking in his game. Yet he must have been doing something well since in his time at Liverpool he made 621 appearances for the club and had seventeen major club honours to his name, including helping them to win the treble of Championship, European Cup and League Cup two years later in 1984. Let us just say that he was an athlete with intelligence and style, and, on the ball, few defenders were technically better, which more than compensated for any of his admitted weaknesses. But he was notably different in type from the man who felt he should have been first choice in defence.

Alex McLeish kept his own counsel on being left out of a successful partnership that seemed to us to be based importantly on instinct, having played with Miller so often.

'I played thirteen straight games for Scotland at the start of my career, so, sure, I was disappointed I wasn't selected in a starting line-up in Spain, although I did come off the bench in Seville and got twenty minutes of World Cup football. Willie was a great sweeper beside me at any time. Charlie Nicholas used to call him the "head waiter". Jock Stein had said to me when he first picked me, "Just be yourself. You're here because of what you're doing with your club." That sounds simple, but it was the kind of common sense thinking that Jock could apply to situations. It made me feel I wasn't expected to be performing tricks. Just be myself. Unfortunately, he didn't say that to me in Spain.'

Within the camp, Stein did want to show that he was personally relaxed about the Russian game. One night he took Andy Roxburgh and Jim MacLean aside and asked them to write down the team each of them would select. After they had contemplated this for some time, and written them down painstakingly, Stein took their lists and, without even looking at the names, tore up their slips of papers saying, 'Ach, I'll just pick the team myself.'

According to Roxburgh, it was all a bit of a wheeze but, on the other hand, on reflection, he began to think he was letting them know that he was personally shouldering the responsibility for what might happen if the shit really were to hit the fan. If this was a psychological ploy, then it didn't work on Jim McLean, who definitely felt guilty about his role there, and many years later opened up to me about it in an almost theatrical fit of self-laceration.

'I'm still ashamed today of the way I did that job, and ashamed I may have let Jock Stein down after he had shown a great deal of faith in me. Quite honestly, I was a disgrace as an assistant manager.' He said that because he did not realise until it was too late that he had not spoken up when he should have about tactics and team selection. He was too much in awe of the man to take issue with him, and because of his own utter domination of Tannadice, he simply did not know how to handle being a subsidiary. One sentence of his I recall from that last interview with him: 'I would have played Alex McLeish beside Willie Miller.'

But there was another element in play in regards to selection, as Davie Provan recognised.

'There's no doubt about it; Jock was attracted to the Liverpool players: Kenny, Graeme, Alan. They were big time to him. He definitely looked upon them favourably. You could tell he thought they were special.'

Except, on this occasion, with Kenny. That iciness we had noted between them was made manifest when the team was announced. He wasn't even on the bench. When I asked Stein about that, all I got was a terse reply. 'I've picked the strongest team available.' But now we knew who had the responsibility of taking Scotland through.

Alan Rough,
Davie Narey, Frank Gray, Willie Miller, Alan Hansen,
Gordon Strachan, Graeme Souness (*captain*), John Wark,
John Robertson,
Steve Archibald, Joe Jordan.

There was only one change from Seville. Asa Hartford was out. Some of the media were surprised about Joe Jordan being brought back while Kenny was sitting in the stand. Was this something plucked out of thin air since he had missed the first two games? The big striker was playing his club football in Milan at the time. And his inclusion, in fact, did not surprise him.

'I got an injury playing for my club and it took a while to mend. But he played me in two of the home internationals, including the last one against England, out of faith, I suppose. But I wasn't fully match fit and I didn't perform well. Now I actually phoned Jock before signing for Milan to get his advice and to ask him if it would affect my position with the national side. He absolutely assured me that it wouldn't influence him in the slightest. Now he didn't tell me about his plans for me in Spain. Not once. But I think he was waiting for the last game. I would go back in the afternoons for special striker sessions with the coaches, like shooting, movement in the box, all that stuff which I had never done in any national squad before. I kept telling myself, he's not going to all that bother just for me to come here to make up the numbers. I felt I would get a chance in the last game, and I was right.'

The Russian side were bristling with confidence, for that winning Eder goal for Brazil had inflicted on them only their first defeat in twenty-three games. And they had beaten New Zealand with ease 3–0. Their team for Malaga was:

Dasayev,
Sulakvelidze, Bessonov, Chivadze (*captain*), Demyanenko,
Borovsky, Baltacha, Bal, Blokhin,
Gavrilov, Shengelia.

With the collapse of the Berlin Wall still seven years off, to get an interview with any Soviet athlete then was like trying to catch a few words with a golden eagle in the Cairngorms. We were after Oleg Blokhin, their surly superstar whose smile appeared on his face less frequently than that of Halley's Comet in the heavens. We waltzed into a hotel with

185

our camera to sneak up on him, as he lay sprawled out under a canopy, whilst eyeing a group of English ladies, who by their skimpy costumes were certainly not from the Women's Rural Institute, but who were surprisingly sharing the same facilities. But we were marched out again under pressure from four grunting gorillas who clearly did not take kindly to the camera lens of a free society.

The nearest I ever got to Blokhin was when he came to Ibrox in 1987 with Dynamo Kiev and I stood beside him at pitch-side before the game, as he fulminated with another of his officials, in whatever language, pointing to the touchline. Souness had narrowed the pitch to its minimum requirement overnight. It was the Rangers manager's ploy to squeeze his undoubted threat into a manageable corridor. If, overnight, you are forcing anorexia on a pitch, just to thwart one individual, then you know how special a talent the Ukrainian was. Stein had no such option to stifle that threat.

So, we thought we might get some more personal and detailed information on individual players from two large Russian supporters Billy and I met in the bar of our hotel a couple of nights before the game, and who obviously had a few English words. Even a line or two from them, different from the official FIFA handouts, would be invaluable in a commentary. They invited us back to their room where we demolished a bottle of vodka between us whilst plying them with questions about the Russian team formation. They couldn't have been less forthcoming had we been asking them about the deployment of ICBMs around the Urals. By the time we were draining the bottle, it had all degenerated into Billy telling them they were the first KGB men he had ever come across and that, yes, capitalism had a lot to answer for, given the mere pittance he had been earning

when he had lifted the European Cup with Celtic in 1967.
From the glazed looks in their eyes, and their large smile at
Billy's reminiscence, they obviously had thought they had a
budding Leninist in their company. A hangover is all that we
got out of that night and, with it, the inescapable feeling that
we knew little about what was to face us in the next game.

14

THE FICKLE FINGER OF FATE

We came to Malaga's La Rosaleda on 22 June 1982 with a mounting sense of *déjà vu*. Here we go again. In or out over ninety minutes. Our Cup Final. It was a day which seemed to justify the old saying that familiarity breeds contempt, because, for all the somersaulting experiences I had to endure in the previous two World Cups, I didn't really feel any better equipped to face up to this one. This, whatever the outcome, was going to be torture. It was hot again, but after the Seville roasting, it was more bearable. There was a huge march of Scottish supporters from the centre of Malaga to the stadium, amongst which was a group who decided to elevate this meeting to a clash of cultures with a banner reading 'Alcoholism v Communism'. Nobody takes the piss quite like the Tartan Army. In the compact stadium, the swelling sound of the vast Scottish support did lift the spirits. But Stein was as sanguine about their influence as he was when he was manager of Celtic, for, while praising the support, he did say to me once, 'Fans are great. But I've yet to see a fan score a goal for us.' He repeated that to the media in Malaga before the game.

They were in full voice, though. And they had justification

for that because, from the start, Scotland looked composed, neat in their passing, crisp in their tackling and in no way exhibiting any hangover from the Brazil going-over. It was Jordan who had made the first impression with a header from a Robertson cross which went narrowly past. And even though Rough had to make a save at the feet of Blokhin soon after, it was Jordan again who demonstrated the wisdom of Stein's nurturing of the player until the last. Fifteen minutes gone with the ball just outside the Scottish penalty area, Narey intercepted a pass meant for Blokhin and punted it long and deep into the Russian half. Joe Jordan recalls how the goal came about.

'I had a lot of time to think about it because the ball came from well inside our own half and when you are running from almost the halfway line following the flight, you start to think of options, what you're going to do it if comes through to you.'

The Russian defender couldn't control that ball from Narey and allowed Archibald to knock it beyond the defence, leaving Jordan with a one-on-one with the Russian goalkeeper Dasayev, but with still much to do.

'Stevie Archibald was behind me. I knew that, although he never came into my line of vision. So, I couldn't use him to put some doubts in the keeper's head. It was a long run. It wasn't like having a second to think about it. But as soon as I got into the box, I knew exactly what I was going to do. I saw the space at the near post. Most people would think you put it across the keeper. I kept my eye on that space and I think it might have surprised the keeper, because I kept it down and squeezed it in. It was a marvellous feeling.'

It stays vividly in his mind, as it was the tenth and last goal he was to score for his country. At that stage, Scotland looked like an accomplished side, not just because of being one up so soon into the game, but because one man was having a masterly game in midfield. It was Souness's finest hour. There was something in the way he commanded his space that suggested he owed us all something, for not having released this kind of positive talent in the previous games. There was something of Mendoza in his performance. He passed and probed in a way that prompted a surge of freshness throughout the team, which we had feared might wilt in the heat again. The only doubts we experienced as the first half progressed was the attitude of the Eastern European referee from Romania, Nicolae Rainea, who booked him for a tackle that was no worse than any perpetrated by the fierce Russians. Then he simply turned his back on loud appeals for a penalty for what looked like handling in the box by Sergei Baltacha, their very rugged Ukrainian defender. Only a corner came from that, with Jordan heading past. Yet you could not help but feel the tide was with us.

In the past, that feeling of cautious optimism has presaged disaster, so it was necessary to watch the language you used about it. Nevertheless, I felt I was slipping into the comfort zone of commentating when you feel the players are at your command and doing precisely what you wanted them to do. It is a mix of fantasy and reality. Billy, a great admirer of Strachan, was waxing lyrical about one sequence of his when the little man beat three players in the space of the proverbial sixpence and was only foiled from scoring by the Russian goalkeeper sticking out one of his long legs. All this was to the good, particularly as Blokhin was anonymous. No pitch shrinking had been necessary. He just didn't seem up to it. We had heard that he was thinking of joining an Italian club in the decadent West after the World Cup, so perhaps that was on his mind. Occasionally, he would try a long shot from well outside the box, which is sometimes a manifestation of frustration. At that stage, the Scottish defence seemed unflurried, measured, canny. Then it didn't.

With half an hour to go, Souness was still the main prompter, Jordan was the darling of the crowd with his courageous runs against the tough Russian defence and Strachan still darted around like a little firefly. All to the good. Then came the run by Gavrilov, their striker. It started from just outside the penalty area. Suddenly, our defensive legs seemed all aflutter. Who was supposed to be taking Gavrilov on? He reached the penalty spot and shot. Rough got his legs to it but, as the ball rebounded, the Russian captain Chivadze, on the follow-up, swung at it, totally mishit the rebound, but was as surprised as any to see it float like a piece of dandelion fluff up and down into the net. A fluke, by any standards, or a painful reminder that following Scotland was the preference of masochists. Whichever way you looked at it, it was ludicrous.

At that point, a group of Russians just in front of us, and who looked like 'minders', started to bawl and shout and bang the desks in front of them, shaking the whole area. And yes, out of frustration at having just witnessed a streaky goal, and after indicating I wanted them to shut up, but was being ignored, I decided to punch one in the back to make him see sense. He rose. He was about 6ft 8in, or thereabouts. I could see his fists clenching. It was my Checkpoint Charlie moment, even as I was carrying on the commentary. Billy, at that stage, was trying to pretend he wasn't with me. Then another of the Russians interceded, grabbed his mate and tried to calm him down. What influenced the next few moments was not so much a Russian peacemaker, however fortunate enough that one was around, but the loud shout for a penalty from the Scottish crowd. It was when John Wark was fouled by Baltacha in the box. This distracted the pair in front. Having missed the actual incident, I was rescued by the slo-mo replay, which seemed to show both that it was a stone-waller, and that the Eastern European referee would no doubt be having a holiday in a dacha outside Moscow for his efforts. Yes, such thoughts go through your mind. It was all confusion and anger in our media area for that variety of reasons.

Then came the moment in the game which split the crowd. Those who were Scottish saw it like a scene from a horror movie directed by Wes Craven, but to neutrals of a certain generation it was the custard pie moment; that moment when the farce is reduced to its most basic idiom. With only six minutes to go, a long ball was sent from the Russian defence down Scotland's right flank, heading for that touch-line. Harmless. Innocuous. Bland. Call it what you will. It posed no danger. Willie Miller has watched this moment and listened to the commentary often to try to unravel what then happened.

'According to your commentary, I was having a really good game. Now, I was determined that I would be at my best. I honestly didn't think that Alan Hansen would have a particularly good match, so I was doubly determined to do well. I had made up my mind that I would have to make the first tackle, be the centre half if you like, which was not really my kind of game. But I didn't think that Alan was doing it that way, so I had to go for the first touch. That's what I tried to do. So did he. He got that first touch. We bumped into one another.'

Bumped? It was a collision that Laurel and Hardy used to

192

be paid fortunes for. Here were two well-meaning, talented men unable to come to terms with their partner's own sense of worth. Who was to be leader? In that single moment you could see that, for all their respective merits, there we were witnessing, in one blinding moment, opposing mentalities. Hansen felt that the Scottish media heaped the blame on him purely because he was an Anglo and favoured the home Scot and states categorically, 'I cannot accept responsibility for it. I'm not trying to knock Willie, but I'm absolutely convinced that had our positions been reversed – had I been the sweeper – there is no way we would have collided.'

So, what would have happened if Jim MacLean had actually spoken up about this combination? Frankly, Stein wouldn't have taken a blind bit of notice. It was his decision and he wouldn't have budged. For, as they collided, knocking each other off-balance, flat-footed and seemingly stuck to the turf, the ball broke to Shengelia who, unimpeded, ran something like twenty-five yards with the ball, heading for Rough, who was in a quandary.

'My first thought was, do I bring him down and get myself sent off? He could have gone either to the right or left. I decided to wait and, in hindsight, I made the wrong decision. I should have brought him down.'

The Russian rounded Rough and virtually walked the ball over the line, putting Russia one ahead with so little left of the game. Billy and I had given up in commentary, not simply because of the goal, but because of the manner of the debacle, which I knew would be played back as often as a *Tom and Jerry* cartoon. And, indeed, it has been down the years. Of course, Souness did score, with only two minutes left, after winding his way past defenders and then trundling a shot into the net from the edge of the penalty to earn a draw. Such a brilliant effort only exacerbated the feeling that Old Father Time was against us as well. The 2–2 draw saw Scotland out by goal difference for the third successive World Cup.

Alan Rough still laments it.

'This was worse than Argentina, much worse because we felt it's a game we expected to win. We didn't really expect to beat Holland in the final game in '78, although we did. But this one was really doable. It just made it like we'd taken a real beating. And what's more, if we had made it through, we had been promised £500 a man as a bonus and some of us were planning to go to Morocco before the next round. Now it was just back hame.'

Ernie Walker, the SFA secretary, trudged down the stairs at the back of the stand as we made our way to the interview positions, like a man heading for the gallows. His face had the same pallid complexion that I had looked at in Argentina the day he announced the Willie Johnston drug decision. His slow gait was unsteady and stiff, his stare towards the horizon wherein might lie an escape from the sudden fit of madness he had just witnessed.

'It's always too late,' he said to me. 'Only we could have done it that way.'

My interview with Stein was with a man I still greatly admired, even though he had failed. It was something he had clearly feared, perhaps more than at any other time in his career. It was unusual to see him as a defeated figure. The closest I had come to that was the night I had talked to him privately in the hotel in Italy, just hours after Feyenoord had beaten them in the European Cup final in Milan in 1970. Yes, he had looked crestfallen that night, but uttered a kind of philosophical explanation of the outcome, very much like a man who would definitely rebound strongly from

194

that. Not this time. No matter the manner in which we had exited, with the customary hard-luck stories tacked on, he had failed. He did criticise the referee over the claims for two penalties turned down. All this was predictable. I was not alone in identifying the depth of his feelings in Malaga. Ian Archer, in the *Sunday Standard* of 27 June, wrote of Stein's reaction to him immediately after the match: 'Even while engaging in polite conversation, his eyes were fixed on the middle distance. He had been in the same dark places as Willie Ormond and Ally MacLeod. Defeat hurt.'

You have to look for crumbs of comfort amongst the debris, and there were some. Ernie Walker and Stein had set great store by their partnership, believing that given their mutual respect and backing, it would be different this time. In many ways it had been. He had developed a disciplined side whose behaviour on and off the field was impeccable. Stein had handled the press with dignity and without false promises. Gordon Strachan was voted, by the Spanish press, the outstanding player of Group 6, ahead even of the best of the Brazilians. You could, in retrospect, have queried Stein's assertion that the group was the toughest of all, because neither Brazil nor the Soviet Union reached even the semi-finals. But we all knew his warning had been part of his strategy of dampening expectations. Another journalist, Ian Peebles, attempting to scrape the barrel and find some solace, described 1982 in his SFA *Football Annual* as, 'the year Scotland became the half-time champions of the world'. The fact that Scotland had been winning or drawing at half-time in all three games, and had scored first in all of them, was enough to inspire this weirdly creative attempt to pan for gold in a dried-up creek.

You could not assess Scots' overall feelings about their

World Cup experiences in the immediate aftermath of such crushing disappointment. Decades later, you got a better feel. I came across not a single one of them who would rather have stayed at home and missed the experience, whatever fate had to throw at them. And certainly, for the younger and fitter of those in that squad, and even for some of the more experienced who harboured the notion they could thwart the ageing process, the prospect of Mexico in four years' time became an even more desirable goal.

THE 1986 FIFA WORLD CUP

MEXICO

15

THE AVENUE OF THE DEAD

In temperatures that felt like they could liquidise granite, Denis Law and I climbed a pyramid together. The place was Mexico. The year, 1986. A World Cup was going on. As we sat pechin' at the top, the world below shimmered with the heat like we were watching it through a glass prism. But we could make out the shape of the hotel where the Scottish squad for the World Cup was housed. 'Housed' was probably a word that the players would not have used themselves of an environment that suggested they had been illegally imprisoned for doing nothing more offensive than being the last team in the tournament to have arrived in the country. It was dark and dingy, and the rooms were so small they had to be allocated singly, which for players accustomed to 'sharing' was like their first experience of solitary confinement. So, the place was seething with discontent.

So why were we on top of this Pyramid of the Sun which the Aztecs had constructed around the time the Romans were building Hadrian's Wall? Firstly, like Mallory said of climbing Everest, 'because it was there', only a few hundred yards from the hotel. But, secondly, and more importantly, we were letting off some steam, even in the heat. We had been banned from entering the hotel by the SFA. As we sat there surveying the world, I was deeply conscious of how privileged I was to be with a fellow culprit, who just also happened to be one of the most iconic figures in Scottish football history. We had merely been relating stories to the public, from the players, about how the SFA arrangements for them, since they had arrived in the country, had been woeful and the accommodation likely to lead to a revolt. Denis was now on the other side of the divide, reporting regularly, and colourfully, on BBC's network radio. He was proving to be a great companion, for at no stage did you feel he was capitalising on the adoration that followed him, wherever tartan was evident. He was now simply a BBC analyst, going about his business like to the manor born. But there we were together, outsiders, banned from entry. It was a kinship I never dreamed I would have with one of the heroes of our game.

He was now forty-six and had been out of football for twelve years, after finishing his career with Manchester City. He had played his last game for Scotland in Germany in 1974, and was not unaware of the tantalising relationships that existed between the media and the SFA, having been in the middle of the turmoil that characterised Scotland's attempts at preparation for that World Cup. With his blonde mop, his lean figure and his jaunty walk, he seemed little changed from the day I saw him score that signature goal against Czechoslovakia at Hampden in 1962. He loved his new assignments.

'It was great,' he told me. 'Travelling the world without having to kick a ball. And I suppose I got on well with the press because when I felt I had a bad game I just never read the papers. Why punish myself for what they might say

200

about me? So, when somebody had a bad game when I was analysing, I just tended to ignore that without trying to hurt him.' And then he added, with a twinkle in his eye, 'Most of the time.'

Scotland had been the last team to arrive in Mexico for the World Cup finals in 1986 and was now holed up in this faded residence in the middle of an Aztec heritage site dominated by two huge pyramids. With the cruel tragedy of Jock Stein's passing the year before, and familiarity with the cruel strokes of fortune that had dogged Scottish teams in previous World Cups, we chose not to inform anybody in the party that a local historian had told us that the name of the broad ancient road beside them, which stretched into the Aztec city, was called 'The Avenue of The Dead'. We guessed there would be enough problems arising without superstition playing a part. We had enough problems with this media ban. Our familiarity with this scenario stretching back to 1974 simply gave the impression that the SFA liked to dabble in nostalgia.

Outside the gates, before our climb, we stood there trying to spot anybody to get a message inside to Alex Ferguson. Denis was enjoying this, being a man who rarely gave the impression that life was getting on top of him anyway. I would see him a lot during this competition and gained immensely from listening to a man who, whilst he loved his Scottish footballing heritage, never allowed it to muffle his frank opinions. But at that moment we were being denied doing our job. So why had we ended up like this while a World Cup was going on? The explanation is complex, so bear with me.

A new mood had settled on the Scottish camp based on the relationship between Ernie Walker and the interim manager, Alex Ferguson. Jock Stein had died tragically in Cardiff on

201

10 September 1985 near the end of the qualifying game with Wales. You could easily have likened his ending to that of a warrior dying in the field of battle, with the banners he had fought for still flying proudly. And long will I remember the interview I had with one Scottish supporter in the early hours of the morning in the streets of the city when he lamented perhaps for many, 'We'd rather be out of the World Cup and have big Jock back.' That night had thrown Walker and Ferguson together in dramatic circumstances that made a smooth transition to a productive relationship highly problematic.

The SFA secretary had been hugely affected by the death. The pair had become almost like blood brothers. Ernie once told me, almost in a boasting fashion, of how Stein appreciated that bonding, in the most practical way, when one day near Christmas, just after issuing the entire SFA staff with their salary statements for the month, the manager had come to see him. He pointed out that a mistake had been made in his account. That it was more than it should have been. Walker pointed out to him that he had given him a bonus. Stein was taken aback. I remember Walker's words to me at the time: 'Jock just said to me that that was the first time in his entire career that he had an increase in wages without having to fight for it.' On top of that, Walker had become fiercely protective of Stein and, perforce, had to be.

The period between the opening European Championship game against East Germany on 13 October 1982, which Scotland won 2–0, and the final one against them in Halle on 16 November 1983, which they lost 2–1, was disastrous. That victory against the Germans was to be the last. The three defeats and two draws that followed in a group including Belgium and Switzerland was, by any account, a dismal record, so criticisms were becoming more blatant. Then, one evening, we discovered just how essential Walker's protective mantle had to be. We were dining with the SFA, at their invitation, after the draw for the qualifying groups for Mexico. At the table was the president of the association, Tommy Younger, a former international goalkeeper himself. You could say we were all recoiling from the outcome of the draw itself. Before we had left the hall, our group had been dubbed the 'Group of Death'. In Group E, Scotland had drawn Denmark, West Germany and Uruguay. The South Americans and the Germans had won the World Cup four times between them and Denmark were the brilliant newcomers to this stage, having beaten England 1–0 at Wembley to qualify for the European Championships in 1984, where they were knocked out in the semi-final by Spain, after penalties. Sharp intakes of breath were being heard around the Scottish media as we broadcast the facts of that, like we were solemnly warning the Scottish public to get themselves on to a war-footing. After much drink had been taken, Younger's tongue became looser, and more brazen, and without warning, he actually pointed a finger at Stein and said, 'You know, Jock, you have a worse record than Willie Ormond and Ally MacLeod, and they got the sack.'

We stopped eating and held our breaths. Talk like that to Jock? Unheard of. I braced myself for a storm. But it was Walker who broke in quickly, as Stein looked utterly unprepared for such a direct onslaught and I could tell that he simply didn't know how to react under the circumstances. In a previous incarnation he would have had his detractor by the throat. It wasn't so much the inaccuracy of what Younger had said, it was the very temerity. I thought Stein would snap. But the secretary butted in and impressively defused the situation before the table was upturned. Yet, despite his best efforts, Walker could not disguise the fact that, within the SFA, there were significant figures who felt Stein was a spent force and were looking further afield. You would not have required the Jodrell Bank Observatory to identify who was looming up in the horizon as an alternative. Alex Ferguson, at that stage with Aberdeen, had won three Scottish league Championships, four Scottish cups and, of course, had won the European Cup Winners' Cup in 1983. Stein, the man who had effectively got him the job at Aberdeen, had also brought him in as assistant manager for the national side. So, he was already in with the bricks, but not as closely cemented in as he himself wanted to be, because of what he had witnessed under Stein at international level.

For in 1983, during the sequence of poor results, the former Celtic manager, who had the unique experience of steering a club to the pinnacle of European football, told me in a surprising fit of candour, about what he thought of his role as national manager, 'This job's impossible,' he said simply. Stark words, and surprisingly for anything I had known about Stein hitherto, almost defeatist. It was unusual to see a man of that stature virtually at his wits' end. So, Ferguson was aware of the unique difficulties that would confront any manager in the role, and he was ambitious. This bright upstart of Scottish football, who had shattered the Old Firm hegemony and won respect throughout Europe for his triumphs there, had little intention of putting his future career into an area where events could occur, over which he would have no control – like the continual clash between club and country, and the growing awareness that players placed more emphasis on cash than on national loyalty. Ferguson had witnessed all that and didn't really harbour any serious ambitions for the Scotland job. You had to listen to him at close quarters to grasp his vitality, his desire to get to the top anywhere in club football. Before he distanced himself from me, after an incident between us when he felt I had been unfair in criticising his goalkeeper Jim Leighton playing for Scotland once, I had many an intimate conversation with him, particularly in the boot room at Pittodrie. It was there he loved a blether, and gossiped about everybody and everything. It was there he told me about rejecting Rangers' surreptitious offer to become their manager in the eighties because, even as an ex-Ranger, he couldn't agree with their 'What school did you go to?' recruitment policy at the time. And it was there he told me in an interview, 'I'll be here at Aberdeen for years. It's nice to have been asked to manage Scotland on a temporary basis, but make no mistake, I'll be staying here.' But he did add, 'I think I'm too young to be full-time in that national job. Maybe in a few years' time. You never know.' You could also say, make no mistake, that despite his talk of undying loyalty to Pittodrie, this was a man bristling with the kind of ambition that made you think these confines were getting too parochial for him. Nonetheless, Alex Ferguson was appointed on a temporary basis on 4 November 1985.

He had managed Scotland's progress to reach Mexico by way of the play-offs, defeating Australia of the Oceania group, over two legs, firstly with their 2–0 win at Hampden on 20 November 1985, with goals by Davie Cooper and Frank McAvennie. The return game, I missed out on, because of what Ferguson had said himself before the match at Hampden in his interview with me. 'I need at least a two-goal lead to go down there. If it's less than that, then we could be up against it. With all that travelling and a different climate you just never know.'

In achieving that 2–0 lead, BBC Scotland decided against sending me all that way for what they thought would be a foregone conclusion. I could hardly contest that, since I went along with the hard fact that the Socceroos, although physically very strong, would have to face determined Scottish defending and their guileless attack would find that difficult to break down. There was another factor that we could hardly ignore, that as club manager at Aberdeen, Ferguson had never blown a two-goal lead in any game. In these circumstances, the lead looked resilient enough. In fact, the game turned out to be a dull goalless draw but, being covered live by Channel 4, it was watched by a huge audience in Scotland.

But the whole trip had its incidents, which cost one player dearly. A local Melbourne newspaper had commented on the fact that Scotland supporters had barracked the great tennis player John McEnroe throughout his match in the Australian Open, which was being played in the run-up to the game. The SFA were fortunate that there did not seem to be an investigative zeal among the journalists there, or else they might have discovered it was actually some of the Scotland players themselves who had been taunting the American and had been enjoying a few beers, making hay while the sun literally shone. The problem was that it went on after the sun had disappeared below the horizon, and the curfew hour of midnight was breached by several players. But it was one naïve young man who was caught *in flagrante delicto*, and as a result would never see Mexico.

He was Mo Johnston. He was a healthy boy with lusty habits, like many aspiring young players. Except he was less discreet than most, especially within an hotel policed by SFA snoopers, who as men probably envied Mo his ability to pull southern hemisphere ladies, but had to adopt a high moral tone, and reported this to Ferguson, who put Johnston out of the reckoning for the World Cup. Highly talented on the field, mercurial, the kind of loose cannon on the field to produce the unlikely when you needed it, as he was to prove for Scotland in the future, his very youthfulness could have been an asset, at the very least, in coming off the bench as an impact player. Stein had given him his first cap against Wales on 28 February, when he came on as a sub and scored a goal twelve minutes from the end to help Scotland to a 2–1 victory at Hampden. But, importantly, he was also a kindred spirit of Kenny Dalglish, who was one of the few players who would actually have no qualms in standing up forthright to Stein and state his opinions. Johnston and he collaborated on one occasion, to inflict acute embarrassment on their manager, as Alan Rough recounts.

'We were down at Turnberry, prior to a qualifying game, and the manager got all the players together to make a suggestion to them about a deal with a company that would swell the players' pool money. It was with the Melrose Tea Company. Well, he spelled out the commercial deal and thought it was as good as we could get. However, Kenny piped up and objected. He said he thought we would get a better deal if we waited until we had actually qualified, then we could demand better terms. Jock was not amused and argued his point. Suddenly, wee Mo raised his hand and piped up, "I agree with Kenny. I think we should wait." Stein nearly blew a gasket. "How many World Cups have you been to, ya little shit?" And then went out and slammed the door. He came back in after our discussion when we told him we were sticking with Kenny and would wait till we qualified. He went out and slammed the door again. But when we went back into the foyer of the hotel where the press had assembled, there was a 6ft cardboard cut-out of the figure of Jock Stein with a cup of Melrose's tea in his hand. The manager had already done the deal. Or thought he had. No wonder he was fuming. The whole thing was just left in limbo until we did qualify. All this happening in front of the media. Mo had the nerve to stick out his neck against the big man.'

So that precocious spirit, which backed Dalglish to lead a players' mini-revolt, had also got Johnston into trouble in Australia, and meant he would not appear in a Scotland team until picked by a different Scotland manager in a European Qualifying game against Bulgaria eight internationals later.

The week beginning Saturday, 3 May 1986 cast a shadow over Scotland's preparations for Mexico which mirrored, in a way, the danger of an approaching nuclear dust cloud which was threatening to move across Europe towards Scotland from the nuclear disaster of Chernobyl, that had occurred only a week before. At the epicentre of the footballing events, which produced considerable fall-out, was Kenny Dalglish. On the Sunday of that weekend, he played in a testimonial game at Hampden between an Anglo-Scots side managed by Tommy Docherty, and home-Scots managed by Ferguson. This was only twenty-four hours after scoring the goal as player-manager of Liverpool, against Chelsea, to win the First Division Championship in England. Ian Paul of the *Glasgow Herald* summed up his current position neatly. 'It was a fair old conclusion to a season that has seen him become the first Scot to collect a hundred caps; a season during which he has been feted, wined and dined for a testimonial year and one which will be extended to Mexico next month where he will be much a part of Scotland's World Cup plans. In one fell swoop he has managed what Bill Shankly, Joe Fagan and Bob Paisley could not, the league and cup double.'

Now he was King Kenny. The first time I had seen him, he had been carrying a hamper as a youngster in Malpensa airport, Milan, in the aftermath of Celtic's defeat against Feyenoord in 1970. Stein simply said to me of this anonymous youngster, 'He's gonna be some player.' Purely fortuitously, we spent some time together in his early career with Celtic when we were both on holiday in Menorca where he was staying with Jock Stein's close bookie friend, Tony Queen. He was just a lad who liked to play kick-about with my sons, and was able to see the funny/horrific side of playfully pushing my wife into the apartment pool, little knowing that she couldn't swim, or worse, had just been at the hairdressers. She survived, forgave him, and perhaps for the only time I can recall, I saw a sheepish and slightly embarrassed Kenny, as compared to the thrawn character who stood his corner against even the mighty Stein. There was another face I saw that night in Milan, which sticks in the memory. Alex Ferguson, the ex-Rangers player, then with Falkirk, was sitting amidst a swarm of Celtic supporters, giving an early indication of his ambition in football, having taken the trouble to travel to watch his great rivals in a European Cup final. Since then, I watched their burgeoning careers running along parallel lines, until that particular week when these paths would firstly converge then separate in a manner that has left lingering doubts about their relationship to this very day.

For events were crowding in on the World Cup squad announcement. The day before the much-publicised Dalglish testimonial game, the Scottish League season had ended in an unprecedented drama. Dundee beat Hearts 2–0 at Dens Park on 3 May, when a draw would have been sufficient to have earned the latter their first league title in twenty-six years. Meanwhile, Celtic had run over St. Mirren at Love Street by 5–0 and won the league instead. Over and above that, there was some public discussion about why people should go to a testimonial match for a man who was certainly not on benefits. The statements issued by Dalglish, that a considerable amount of the proceeds would go to charity, did not convince even some Celtic supporters, who refrained from attending. In fact, 25,000, turned up. So, the World Cup had been pushed into the background by the media, who were concentrating on the astonishing Celtic win, Dalglish's dubious testimonial, and Souness's bold statements about turning Rangers into a force once again. On Thursday, 8 May, Ferguson wanted his squad announcement that day to push even the Chernobyl threat into the background. He succeeded, but not in the way he had originally intended. There was a noted omission amongst these following names.

Jim Leighton (Aberdeen) Age 27/Caps 26, Richard Gough (Dundee United) 24/23, Maurice Malpas (Dundee Utd) 23/10, Graeme Souness (Sampdoria, **captain**) 33/52, Alex McLeish (Aberdeen) 27/43, Willie Miller (Aberdeen) 31/48, Gordon Strachan (Manchester Utd) 29/34, Roy Aitken (Celtic) 27/20, Eamonn Bannon (Dundee Utd) 28/9, Jim Bett (Aberdeen) 26/17, Paul McStay (Celtic) 21/14, Andy Goram (Oldham Athletic) 22/3, Steve Nicol (Liverpool) 24/8, Davie Narey (Dundee Utd) 29/28, Arthur Albiston (Manchester Utd) 28/13, Frank McAvennie (West Ham Utd) 26/2, Steve Archibald (Barcelona) 29/26, Graeme Sharp (Everton) 25/6, Charlie Nicholas (Arsenal) 24/15, Paul Sturrock (Dundee Utd) 29/17, Davie Cooper (Rangers) 30/14, Alan Rough (Hibernian) 34/53.

As I read through the list, my first reaction was that there had been a mistake. I could see the heads all down, looking through this with the same sense of slight mystification. For Alan Hansen's name was missing. There were divided opinions within the Scottish media about him. Some saw him as a talented individual who played consistently at the highest club level, already had World Cup mileage on his trip meter and, furthermore, his name on a team sheet would impress any world-class opposition. Others almost dismissed him as some kind of dilettante who looked as if he was slumming when he had a Scottish jersey on. Myself, I thought he ought to have been a shoe-in for a place in the squad. So, almost immediately, Ferguson had to try to explain his thinking to us. When I interviewed him, he was at pains to tell me how agonising it had been to make that decision.

'I spoke to Alan and, to his credit, he took it well and wished me and the lads the best of luck. It was hard, but you have to make choices. That's it.'

Not quite. There was anger afoot.

16

FERGIE'S FOCUS

Managers never expect universal acclamation when they have to make selections. That is one of the ageless norms of football that ultimately determine the character and strength of the leader. So, Ferguson would have been well prepared for reactions to his announcement of the squad for Mexico. They came in different forms. Of the first one, with no disrespect to the player, the Scotland manager would simply have let it flow over his head without blinking. It came from David Speedie, the Chelsea striker, who had been left out and sounded almost murderous in telling the *Evening Times* (Glasgow edition), 'I've been made to look like a fool. I just can't believe that telephone call from the Scotland boss. I feel totally humiliated. Ferguson assured me six weeks ago that I was going to Mexico and now he's gone back on his word.'

A manager's word in football, we have already seen from previous World Cups, is as dependable as the Scottish weather, so Speedie's outburst did not arouse much controversy. The other reaction was almost sinisterly muted, for Alan Hansen kept his counsel to himself. He knew there would be sympathy for him in some quarters, although subsequently he was to confess he believed there was historical bias against him and other Anglos in the Scottish media. He had also been made aware that both the *Sunday Post* and the *Sunday Mail*, on the weekend before the announcement, had projected a list of players to be selected and that he was in neither of their predictions. When he referred this to his close friend Dalglish, he was assured that there was no way Fergie would leave him out of the pool. Of course, there had been much discussion about the central defensive partnership of Miller and Hansen, which had led to the mix-up in Malaga. And, as we could tell from Jim McLean's views on the matter, he would have gone with the Aberdeen pairing in the very last game in Spain. So, even within the Scottish camp, there were opposing views on that area. It is equally true that English journalists, who watched Hansen in weekly action for Liverpool, were incredulous that a lanky, traditional centre half figure such as McLeish could be preferred to the elegant Hansen, which gave rise, particularly in the south, to suggestions of favouritism for Ferguson's own Aberdeen players. A man well placed to comment on that was Charlie Nicholas, whose inclusion, as an almost forgotten Arsenal player, was like a lifeline to a man needing a revamp of his career.

'This was a massive surprise to me. It was really weird. He was one of the finest I had played against. I thought he was one of our truly world-class players. Remember, I played against him for Arsenal. In fact, when you think of it, I was in limbo for a long period when Jock was in charge. He never once came to see me playing for Arsenal. He just relied on reports. Don Howe was playing me just behind the two strikers and I wasn't scoring the goals that people were expecting. I'll be honest, I think if I had stayed at Celtic, or gone to Liverpool where Jock Stein really wanted me to go, or to Manchester United, I would have got more caps. But somehow Arsenal under Don Howe didn't seem to make the impression on football people as other clubs did. But Fergie brought me back for a game in Israel just five months before the World Cup, which we won 1–0. And he and Walter Smith kind of marked my card that I was in with a chance of getting to Mexico. So, I was delighted to make it. But I fully expected Hansen to be going as well, and I was astounded that Hansen wasn't included. He had everything. He was a footballing defender, not an outright centre back. But so what? Many a great team has played without a standout centre half. But, at the same time, I don't think Fergie would have picked players out of favouritism.'

Frank McAvennie, one of the English First division's top goal scorers with West Ham at that time, stressed the value of Hansen's intelligence on the field. 'He wasn't the hardest player to play against physically, but he was intelligent. That's what made it difficult for you. He knew how to position himself and when to pounce. To not select him was baffling.'

What certainly was not more widely known was that Stein had become utterly frustrated at the number of times Hansen had called off from games, including the crucial one against Wales in the decider in Cardiff, so perhaps the Liverpool player was one of the reasons for his 'impossible job' pronouncement. A mood had hardened among the Scottish coaching staff, which included Craig Brown and Andy Roxburgh, that Hansen had not been fully committed to the cause. The fact that he was only ever capped twenty-six times for Scotland against Miller's sixty-five and McLeish's seventy-seven, does indicate a lack of belief in him at international level, in contrast to his outstanding club form.

214

He flew through the air with the greatest of ease, that daring young Joe Jordan stamping our passports for Germany on that historic evening of 26 September 1973.

How did it get away? Billy Bremner's anguish after THE MISS against Brazil in Frankfurt provoked both sympathy and personal criticism.

Jock Stein, here in Frankfurt with David Coleman, was truly the *éminence grise* for the Scottish squad in Germany in 1974.

Daily Record

SCOTLAND'S BIGGEST DAILY SALE

4p   Tuesday, June 25,   No. 24,518

FAN-TASTIC!

That's what our World Cup team think of the fans—and the welcome home

Back sooner than they would have wished from Germany, but undefeated. The triumphalism of the fans at Glasgow Airport sowed the seeds of the delusions to follow in Argentina.

'Football is not a matter of life and death, it is more serious than that.' So said the Shanks. Ally Macleod lived out that belief in Argentina.

Before it all went wrong. The Scottish fans ran the full gamut of emotions and enchanted the Argentinians.

Cool Cubillas. Mobbed by his colleagues for his free-kick goal, the moment that signified our entrance into the vale of sorrows.

The loneliness of the long-distance footballer. Willie Johnston travelled halfway round the world to discover that medicinal pills can lead to expulsion.

When Gemmill's famous shot eventually hit the net, the world's commentators, assembled top-right, rose in unison in unprecedented acclamation.

Billy McNeill, my co-commentator, in the
Estadio Ramón Sánchez Pizjuán on
14 June 1982, just before the most dramatic
interruption to a live BBC broadcast.

In 1982, a tired Jock Stein
learned something of Maori
culture, but nothing new about
New Zealand football.

The Tartan Army's
philosophical
approach to taking
on the Russians in
Malaga in 1982.

© TRINITY MIRROR/MIRRORPIX/ALAMY STOCK PHOTO

'So, Jimmy Hill, what
was that you said
about Davy Narey's
goal against the
Brazilians?'

Mark the date and place.
Seville, 18 June 1982.
The day the Tartan Army
was truly born.

In Malaga, Gordon
Strachan bamboozled
the New Zealanders
and flummoxed the
Russians, for which
the Spanish press
voted him the group's
outstanding player.

Hansen and Miller line
up to face Russia. Their
eventual mishap together
was like not knowing
whether to laugh or cry.

Injured Charlie Nicholas' broadcasting debut in Querétero, Mexico, 1986, which caused a contractual storm. In the middle of the group, Jimmy Hill argues with BBC producers that having Charlie and me replace him to introduce the broadcast was a breach of his contract. He lost.

Getting a leg over. This is the image beloved by the Tartan Army for a man big enough to score against West Germany in Querétero but too wee to beat the hoardings.

Kung Fu was obviously in the Uruguayan coaching manual as Paul Sturrock discovered in Mexico in the last game in 1986.

Even our goalkeeper, Jim Leighton, was a spectator to the Brazilian Müller's goal, which sent us home from Italy in 1990.

Lottery winner? No. Ally McCoist responding to the goal v Norway in 1989, which helped qualify us, but with the nerves stretched to the limit.

The new Paris fashion show. Dressed in a manner that the French believed was a renewing of the Auld Alliance, Scotland looked *soigné* just before Ronaldo and Co appeared in 1998.

The Scottish captain couldn't disguise the pain he was suffering in the dead end that was St-Étienne.

Time to go home.

Ah, well! Wha's like us!

But there is little doubt that Dalglish wanted Hansen to be included and had tried to persuade Ferguson, wrangling with him lengthily on the telephone. He was rebuffed, as he should have been, by a manager wishing to protect the integrity of his independent thinking. It is known that Dalglish pointedly took a bottle of champagne round to Hansen's house as a token of support on the day of the announcement. Then the bombshell.

On Monday, 12 May, after Dalglish had become the first player-manager to lift the FA Cup in the final against Liverpool, he withdrew from the Scotland squad. He had consulted a specialist about his troubling knee and had been informed it needed a complete rest. He had previously told the *Daily Record* on 31 December the previous year, 'Frankly, I would go to Mexico with a broken leg. But if I'm not playing for Liverpool, you won't see me there.' I remember my own mother being stunned by his sudden withdrawal, so you can imagine what was going through Ferguson's mind. But, what, in fact, was actually going through his mind? His public words to the media gave the impression of a man restraining himself from what he really felt.

'It is terrible news that he has had to be withdrawn. It came out of the blue. He was so vital to our plans and has had such a fabulous season that we hoped his touch would continue for us in Mexico.'

But Ferguson did add pointedly, 'We can only feel sympathy for Kenny.'

Link 'came out of the blue' with 'has had such a fabulous season' and you feel a sense of personal let-down as a subtext, which many of us felt lingered for many a long day. To people close to him in the business, Ferguson was incandescent with rage. To them he sounded like he had been betrayed. As for his Hansen decision, in his autobiography of 1999, Ferguson reminds us of Hansen's minimal explanation of a knee problem and sudden departure from training on the eve of the Wembley game against England on 23 April 1986 and the anger Stein felt at his call-off from that crucial game in Cardiff. He goes so far as to claim that Stein was so angered by that, that had he lived and been in charge, Hansen would not have been on the flight to Mexico. That speaks of justification for his own personal decision. He also echoes Dalglish's denunciation of those who claimed he had pulled out of Mexico to snub Ferguson, reiterating Dalglish's comment that those doing so were impugning the integrity of the surgeon who had advised him not to go.

As a consequence, there was hardly a cheer heard in any street throughout the land when it was announced that Steve Archibald was to replace him. The Spurs player had only scored four goals for his country, the last of which had been in the previous World Cup against New Zealand. What was interesting to those who knew something about the inside of Pittodrie, is that Archibald had a tempestuous relationship with his manager before moving south. Just before he left for Spurs, he suddenly admitted to me in a *Grandstand, Football Focus* interview one day, that in wishing to show his disgust with Ferguson he had walked into the manager's office armed with a football, intending to do damage to a man he was becoming to hate, and kicked it at Ferguson behind the desk. Apparently, he missed. That would not have surprised those who harboured doubts about his striking abilities at the exalted level of a World Cup.

But despite the major disappointment of Dalglish falling out and failing to achieve a record four appearances in World Cups for a British player, Scotland did not limp towards Mexico. No party led by Ferguson could ever be accused of having negative thoughts, even though the SFA had provisionally booked flights back home at the end of the qualifying round, no less. And even some players, like the youngest, Paul McStay, had booked summer holidays starting well before the quarter-finals. Given our past record, this ca'canny approach was not too surprising. Nevertheless, everybody around Ferguson was imbued with the spirit of enthusiastic endeavour. Whatever future lay in store for him, he made it clear he was going to give it his best shot. That attitude was to prove infectious.

Roy Aitken, Celtic's captain, still recalls the effervescence of training at 7,000 ft in Santa Fe, New Mexico, their first stop on the long passage to Mexico itself.

'Fergie was brilliant. He seemed to do everything right. He had built up a good background team: Andy Roxburgh, Craig Brown, Archie Knox – they all knitted well. The variety he brought to the training methods, the way he talked to the players, the sense of fun he introduced – all that added to the great atmosphere. When we had that long spell of altitude training in Santa Fe, we felt we could not have been better prepared for the finals.'

Craig Brown, who was at that time part-time manager of Clyde, but a rising star in coaching circles and would eventually manage Scotland to considerable effect, was keen to be involved in preparations, but was also given friendly advice by Ferguson about that. 'He told me not to indulge in any fancy coaching methods when I was taking a group. Keep it simple. If you present them with anything fancy, they'll just resent it and it won't be effective.' Frank McAvennie, who was to come into conflict with Ferguson eventually, pointed to the relaxing side of the experience.

'It was the best holiday I've ever been on. I say that because it was all about bonding and we had a great time. There were new faces about and we could get to know them and what they were like. That's what I took out of this area. Although, as you know, it was a bit of a cowboy town.'

But their residence was palatial. The hotel was only forty-five minutes from the site of where the first atomic bomb was exploded at Los Alamos. The desert air and the luxuriousness of their living quarters had clearly induced a sense of well-being, which was in stark contrast to the harrowing season most of the players had come through. The media were sharing this accommodation with the players, leading to a plethora of interviews on offer with very accessible men, which lent to the impression that a new, healthy and productive relationship had been developed between players and media. Those of us who had been through it all before still nursed the feeling that, when the sounds of battle would commence in the real world, it wouldn't last. We were right, of course. But, meanwhile, we grabbed all that we could while the going was good. Particularly sought after was Souness, obviously because of his role as captain. But more, much more. He was the newly installed player-manager of Rangers. Indeed, as the squad was settling into their new dudes-ranch existence in this desert area, the Scottish captain had been dealing with club matters, as an offer of £650,000 had been made that very week, back in Scotland, by Rangers, for one of the Scottish squad, Richard Gough. Coupled with the fact that Souness had not joined the squad at their Glasgow base before departure, but with special dispensation had been allowed to catch up with them in London, the impression was being given that he would be accorded special treatment and that it was possible that Rangers business would blur his focus on Scotland. Charlie Nicholas refutes that.

'He was focussed all right. I had been sharing a room with Graeme in the build-up to the World Cup. It was an education. I thought I was stylish, but he put me to shame. A porter would come up and hang everything up for him in the wardrobe. It was all colour co-ordinated, would you believe. And here I was, no socks, wearing an earring. It was a weird combination. He was the original Champagne Charlie and I was supposed to be his successor, the young bubbles. But, and here's the important aspect, he was the fittest player I had ever come across. I mean he was a great physical athlete. Strength everywhere. And a mental toughness. He wanted Scotland to do well in that World Cup, no doubt about that whatsoever.'

There was another interpretation. Maurice Malpas had experience of Souness's newly acquired Rangers complex.

'Graeme picked our brains, although we couldn't realise it at the time. Andy Roxburgh, one of Fergie's assistants, had come up with the suggestion that the whole squad should be split into groups and that we would do our training in those groups, and go out to dinner together so that we would become a bit more intimate with one another. Souness was in my group. Now I didn't really know what was happening back in club football in Scotland, and I had no idea of the job he now had. But every time we sat at dinner, he grilled me about Jim McLean and about Scottish football, about players, about current form. He really would want to know as much as I could tell him. I couldn't understand why he was so interested in Scottish football. It was later I realised what it was all about, for he had never played in Scotland and wanted to know everything in a kind of crash course.'

Even after only a few days into the Santa Fe preparations, everybody knew what Souness's future would be after

Mexico. And he was not slow in laying down a template for his, and Rangers' future, in a way that almost took the breath away. He made his first declaration of intent on a hill overlooking the Sante Fe prairie stretching beyond us and bleaching in the sun. Our problem was that Souness was being politically coy. Of course, we wanted to know his Rangers plans, World Cup or no World Cup, but he refused to speak about Rangers on camera. Off camera, he let fly with breathtaking candour about what he intended to do.

He was speaking to someone who grew up in the Glaswegian orthodoxy of the Old Firm culture. So, to hear Souness speak about signing Catholics, or not caring if Celtic beat Rangers four times in a season, so long as Rangers won the league, was like hearing someone refute the law of gravity. Some of my colleagues wondered how a man, hell-bent on revolution within an institution that had been resistant to change for a century, could be fully committed to a national team wishing to improve its World Cup record. On my part, I took away the impression of a fully self-assured man who was taking life in his stride, whatever pitfalls might lie ahead. Never at any stage in his career, outwith his later illnesses, was I aware of Souness not enjoying life, and I felt that his cool, effortless self-confidence could do no harm to those around him suffering any World Cup qualms. But he wasn't the only man with alternative thoughts in his mind, as Charlie Nicholas reveals.

'I had been sworn to secrecy at Highbury, but I had been told that Arsenal were interested in Fergie. So, one day at training, I whispered that to him. He not only admitted that Arsenal had talked to him, but even asked me what I thought of the club. I told him it was a great club and I was excited at the prospect of this dynamic man coming to Highbury. I told him the club probably needed a shake-up, perhaps including me, and that it would be a great move for anybody. I asked him if he would be taking Walter Smith, if he decided to make the move. But he told me that Souness had got him for his assistant at Ibrox. That was news to me. Can you imagine? I was discovering all this was going on in the background while we were getting ready for a World Cup.'

So, the apparent tranquillity of the Santa Fe training camp was in fact riddled with the intrigue of men whose personal ambitions were certainly not being put on hold just for a World Cup. But there was another factor creeping into the mood after five days there: impatience. So, the arranged practice of two twenty-minute sessions against Billy Bingham's Northern Ireland side in Albuquerque, forty miles away, was a welcome relief, especially as the onlookers were impressed with Charlie Nicholas, who scored with two brilliant twenty-yard drives in the two sessions, which ended diplomatically in draws. From the look on Ferguson's face when I talked to him afterwards, I could have put a safe bet on the fact that Nicholas would be in the starting eleven against Denmark, even with ten days still to go.

After that, you felt that everybody now wanted to get on with it and take on the next leg of our journey to Los Angeles. So, as a summary of the mood for BBC's *Grandstand*, they required me to enter that comical parallel universe that television reserves for reporters from time to time, and had me dress up in a sombrero, then sit upon a horse out in the desert, with the music of Ennio Morricone for *The Good, the Bad and the Ugly* to be played in the background, and to be seen disappearing over the horizon towards Mexico, as it would appear. Yes, ridiculous, I know. I thought of Willie Ormond on his camel prior to Germany as I did it, except that, unlike

Willie, as I went over the hill out of sight, I fell off the horse, fortunately not on camera, because the animal's ears picked up the clang of the ranch triangle, calling on all and sundry for their chuck, and bolted. It did not escape the notice of Murray Ritchie of the *Glasgow Herald*, who wrote of this sequence, 'We must acknowledge the contribution of Archie Macpherson, whose new preoccupation with gimmickry was a feature of the build-up. From New Mexico, Archie set off on horseback for the Aztec stadium, his final command to the steed being "Whoa!" Please, can someone take him aside and explain.'

Pointedly, the following day I took my physical and critical bruising on to a seat of a plane to La La Land; for the whole journey the plane rocked and rolled in stormy conditions, which felt in fact like we were on a bucking bronco. Los Angeles was, of course, at sea level, which was what Ferguson had to explain at a press conference on arrival and, hearing that other countries were curious, if not downright critical, of the fact that Scotland would be the last team to arrive in Mexico, even after the opening ceremony and opening game, he told the *Glasgow Herald*, 'The least of my worries is about what other countries think about us. In fact, I'm sure they would rather be in our position. To get the full benefit of training at altitude we had to come down to sea-level again and last night's training session showed how well the squad's fitness has come on after spending fifteen days up at Santa Fe. Others may complain about us being last into Mexico, but our programme has been carefully mapped out and everything has gone according to plan.'

The passage through LA was equally smooth. The Hollywood Kickers, whose name is more appropriate for the chorus line from *42nd Street* than a football team, and Los Angeles Heat, the stronger side, were disposed of 4–0 and

3–0 respectively, to a background of the inevitable Scottish support which had come from a' the airts to lend their customary optimism. Included among them was, of course, Rod Stewart, domiciled in LA, who went out of his way to apologise to goalkeeper Alan Rough for having criticised him for his last performance against England at Wembley in which Scotland lost 2–1, saying it wouldn't be worthwhile going to Mexico if he was in goal. He was apologetic, saying he would certainly be there to watch the games, even if Rough was playing, but would only fly in and out for them, as he didn't like that country much. This time, prudently, he had not put a World Cup song on disc. Rough had taken the criticism well, and explained to me why he was with the squad at all.

'I was the third-choice goalkeeper this time, behind Jim Leighton and Andy Goram, and I didn't expect to play. What's more, I got selected in a strange way. I was down at Turnberry before one of our games. It was before Jock died. He called me over and asked me how I was getting on being back in the squad after being out for a while. Then he said, "Do you know why you're here? I'll tell you. I was in the house one night thinking over things, wondering who I should bring in as a third goalkeeper. I mentioned it to Jean, my wife. She just piped up and said, *I like Alan Rough, why not him?* So that's why you're here." When you think of it, I might just have been the first player picked for a squad by Jock's wife.'

Rough accepted Stewart's apology and, with the rest of the squad, left the contrite singer behind and headed for Mexico City.

17

SLUMS AND SLAMS

If LA could be described as a dream factory, then the city we then arrived in gave the impression it was the product of someone's nightmarish imagination. Crowded, noisy, smelly, dilapidated cars bumper to bumper in congested streets – and that was in the fashionable middle of the city where our hotel was. We had split off from the squad who were making their way to their own residence, which was to be described later by Charlie Nicholas as 'a prison'. For the rest of our stay in the centre, we were to witness an astonishing ritual. Thousands of Mexicans would congregate in the square around the hotel to sing and dance in celebration of their national side, every single day. And every single day, almost on the dot, at 4 p.m., the heavens would open. The monsoons were of biblical proportions, but did not deter the celebrations, thoroughly drenched though they became. The crowd knew what they were letting themselves in for. But it seemed to sum up the spirit of defiance of these most genial people who had suffered all kinds of hardships, including the disastrous earthquake which had hit the city only eight months previously. By simply being there, it made you feel you were lending some kind of support to the spirit of consensus that had transformed a football tournament into a symbol of national survival.

But there was another side to the city. It changed my view of this tournament. If the centre of the city was far from appealing, then it was a veritable Shangri-La compared to the neighbourhood that housed the stadium where Scotland would play their first and last game. They called it Neza-hualcóyotl, or, thankfully, Neza for short. It was a stinking slum area, which we were told had a population of about one million. There were beggars everywhere. Ragged bundles in the streets would turn out, on closer inspection, to be mothers with kids, wrapped together to shelter from the frequent monsoons. The appalling and obvious misery underscored the disgrace of bringing a World Cup to a country so burdened by unrelenting poverty. In fact, to make matters worse, their currency, the peso, plunged during the tournament. If you combine that with the persistent clammy heat, and the altitude problems, it would have seemed to any ordinary mortal that it was something of a mystery why Mexico had been chosen at all.

'Corruption,' was one of the words Ernie Walker quietly used to me when I quizzed him about it eventually in the FIFA hotel, the Camino Real, in the centre of the city. Although Ernie was justifiably to rise in stature within FIFA, and particularly UEFA, he expressed mistrust of Sepp Blatter from the first time he ever mentioned his name to me, and he hated João Havelange, the then FIFA president, with a venge-ance. These were the earliest warnings I ever heard about the unethical, incestuous nature of the structure of FIFA, which in later years was to collapse under the weight of its own dubious morality. Walker talked me through the process like he was explaining the plot of a novel of international power politics. The competition had been thrust on the largely downtrodden Mexican population in a shady deal involving Televisa, the Mexican television company whose directors were close friends of Havelange, after Colombia, who should have hosted the finals, had to pull out because of terrorist activity in the country, and perhaps for the more compelling reason that they were impoverished. So, they simply took it to another impoverished country in a barefaced sleight of hand by men who were about as philanthropic as the pirates of the Caribbean. It seemed I was hearing firm confirmation that television was now shaping the game to suit its own needs, and from domestic football, right up to this exalted level, the so-called people's game would largely be structured around the fine print of a television contract.

Ernie then told me he had been backing every effort to take the finals to the USA; the Americans felt they had an ace in their pack in Henry Kissinger, formerly an advisor to President Nixon and advocate of the hard-line policy that caused the trampling-over of countries in South East Asia, but now a born-again peaceful football ambassador. Armed with a ninety-page document in support of the bid, as opposed to Mexico's ten-page document, and with the support of the American congress and Pelé no less, at a special congress in Stockholm in May 1983 Kissinger thought that the vote in favour of the States was inevitable. He was to discover that the combination of Televisa and Havelange was to prove even more resilient than the Vietcong were to Kissinger. Mexico won the vote unanimously, which prompted Kissinger's retort, 'The politics of soccer make me nostalgic for the politics of the Middle East.'

I recall Walker saying to me, as we sipped our coffees, 'I'll be working bloody hard to get the finals to the States sometime.' Indeed, respect for him grew within FIFA; because he was seen as a measured man of sensible ideas and drew respect from that anti-Blatter faction, he had enough support to become one of the triumvirate that effectively chose the USA for the finals in 1994, which he sadly missed because of his prostate cancer. In the city, in the context of his FIFA identity, he seemed a more relaxed man than the figure we had to deal with out at the Scottish hotel, which was reached by a hair-raising drive through the demented streets and roads of the area. For rumours were rife that the Scottish players were in the spirit of revolt.

The hotel indeed gave the impression that the Scottish players were entombed. It was dark and dismal and cramped-looking, with furniture that looked as if it had been installed by the Spanish conquistadors centuries before. Sun outside, Dracula's lair inside. I didn't require to be told what the players thought about it, but it is worth paying attention to Charlie Nicholas, who perhaps in recalling his hedonistic lifestyle rooming with Souness, can still hardly believe it.

'You were in a cell by yourself. Honestly, the bed looked more like a bench and you had to put your mattress down on it like they do in a prison. There was barely any furniture to store things. This single room idea only causes problems. So, what we had to do to counter monotony was to meet in Jim Steel's room – Steelie, as we called him. He was a masseur and just one of the great guys in the game. He would get us all together in his room and let us blether away to each other and give us massages. And coming from all the other clubs, it was great to hear about club life in other places. Then, unfortunately, we had to go back to our cells.'

It sounded a very familiar refrain to me. And as for passing the time solo, Maurice Malpas was not amused.

'My bed was a mattress on a bench. That was it. And for company, I had a television set the size of a postage stamp. Everything was in Spanish and there was more snow on the screen than anything else. Don't underestimate how frustrated you can become about these things, especially when we heard the Danes were living in the lap of luxury and had their wives and their girlfriends with them, drinking beers at the poolside and all that. No wonder we started to complain.'

So, later, we took ourselves off to the Danish camp with the camera and, indeed, it was like the Marbella Club compared to the Pyramids Hotel, and, over and above that, the Danes, who all speak English, could not have been more accommodating. There were females about, whom we assumed were family, and it was all slightly surreal compared to the Avenue of the Dead. Sepp Piontek, their manager, certainly gave us a convincing paean of praise for Scottish football, adding the usual stuff about their pride, their fighting spirit, their great support – all out of the good book of diplomatic niceties. But at the end I vividly recall him saying, 'But no Dalglish?' Quite. I couldn't tell if it was a question to me or just an assertion, but I brought the interview to an end without getting into the labyrinth of explanation.

Ferguson was a personal antidote to the miserable environment. He could not have been more accommodating, even though he must have been incensed about the fact that it took half an hour along these risky roads just to get to their training facilities. It was only later that his ire really spiralled. But, initially, he concentrated purely on talking me through his squad, with particular mention of his strikers, and gave a large hint that Charlie Nicholas would start in the first game. 'He's been great. He's hit form at the right time for us.' But even more interestingly, he told the *Glasgow Herald*, 'Souness has got to make a mark in this World Cup. With all his talent and qualities of leadership, he must create an influence on our side that will get us off to a good start. He has been a good captain for us in the past, and now I expect him to show it at the highest level.'

Was this a deliberate public challenge? Did he fear that the thirty-three-year-old might not be up to it after all? It was interesting to note what Alan Rough said about the long build-up to the finals and the relationship between that pair.

'At every team meeting it would be Graeme that would put his hand up to be heard about something. He wanted to know this or that. It was very noticeable. I don't think Fergie was all that pleased, but you could tell that Graeme wanted the squad to notice what he had to say. He was now a manager himself, of course.'

So, armed with my now familiar sensibilities, fear of losing, and the gnawing feeling of needing a stiff drink to cope with it all, but desisting (well, until afterwards when I made up for lost time), I sat myself down in the commentary position in the Estadio Neza on 4 June 1986. Alone. My former commentating colleague, Billy McNeill, was now with the opposition, ITV. Probably for more money. ITV was thriving at that period, but we were still able to have a word about the teams, just after they had been handed to us.

SCOTLAND
Jim Leighton,
Richard Gough, Alex McLeish, Willie Miller, Maurice Malpas,
Gordon Strachan, Roy Aitken, Graeme Souness (*captain*), Steve Nicol,
Charlie Nicholas, Paul Sturrock.

DENMARK

Rasmussen,

Busk, Morten Olsen (*captain*), Nielsen, Jens Jørn Bertelsen,

Lerby, Jesper Olsen, Arnesen, Laudrup,

Berggreen, Elkjær-Larsen.

All I can recall Billy saying to me now was, 'I thought they might have given Frank a go.' By that he meant McAvennie, the West Ham player who was one of the most colourful personalities in the pack. The player himself was incensed at not being the first-choice striker.

'Remember, I was the leading goal scorer in Europe at the time and going head to head with Gary Lineker for the Golden Globe award. He eventually won it by one goal on me because he took and scored more penalties than I did. And, what's more, if there were two players born to play with one another in attack, it was Charlie Nicholas and me. We were just made for one another. So, I was fuming. And I told him to his face that he might be the manager, but I completely disagreed with his choice. No disrespect to Luggy (Sturrock), but I was on fire. Fergie and me never spoke to one another for years after Mexico.'

Myself, I knew that Ferguson had a great respect for Paul Sturrock, and I wasn't particularly fussed about the selection, because the side was very much what we thought it would be. There was a healthy presence of Scots in the 18,000 crowd in the neat, tidy stadium, which was a virtual oasis amidst the squalor of the surrounding area. Somehow, it did not seem like a World Cup environment. My memories of the huge Scottish following in Spain, with the energising fillip it gave everyone, from players to media, made this scene in a small Mexican stadium appear to be more that of a provincial cup tie. In Spain, we had truly felt, from the first game, a sense of grandeur about the World Cup. This now seemed humdrum by comparison. We were also watching Denmark playing their first-ever World Cup game, and didn't they want to show it.

In the first few minutes or so, Scotland saw little of the ball. There was this early impression of the Danes trying to show off in a kind of way. They clipped the ball about like they were trying to emulate a pin-ball machine, and created two half-chances in the first few minutes which immediately displayed the calm, but decisive, nature of Willie Miller in the centre of defence, with those kind of snappy interventions that always reminded me of the action of a gin-trap, as he took ball crisply before man, but let him know in no uncertain terms that he would be around for the rest of the afternoon. This immediately suggested solidity. By comparison, Nicholas and Sturrock were turning the Danish defenders and making them look vulnerable. Their defence was built around the veteran Morten Olsen, their captain, who would eventually go on to manage the national side. He was canny, considered, intelligent, but not quick on his feet. That is something that Nicholas knew about in advance and wanted to exploit. That thinking would lead to an incident that would fundamentally alter the complexion of the game and, perhaps, even the outcome of the whole tournament for Scotland.

You could tell that Nicholas was troubling this defence, even from the earliest stages. He had been having special coaching sessions with Walter Smith in Santa Fe, alerting him to how he received and controlled passes. He almost scored the first goal of the game at the climax of a move that turned the Danish defence inside out. Nichol on the left feeding a high ball to Gough on the right, a header from him which found the chest of Nicholas. Now came class. He controlled the ball on his chest while dipping his shoulder and putting his opponent on the wrong foot, but his beautifully controlled shot was blocked on the six-yard line. Artistry foiled, but it was a warning to the Danes of what might befall them if they didn't take care of Nicholas. They eventually did, but in a manner that seemed more out of Scandi noir than Hans Christian Andersen.

Before Nicholas got the heavy treatment near the end of the game, they had tried it on Gordon Strachan, who was slammed heavily to the turf by that Scouse-accented and muscular Søren Lerby, which ought to have brought some action by the Hungarian referee, Lajos Nemeth. There being none, encouragement was being dangled in front of the eyes of some individuals in their ranks. Roy Aitken, who could look after himself on any field, was then crudely hacked by Elkjær-Larsen. We were taken aback by this, largely because, as fellow Europeans, we thought their style would be completely within our own province. There was an element of provocation in their play, which I'm sure none of the Scottish players had expected. However, I have to separate the wheat from the chaff. For there were skilful Danish players on the field as well. Altogether, they gave the impression they were playing with the economy of effort, looking almost casual at times, then bursting forward with skill, particularly from the feet of the young Michael Laudrup, in that effortless but gliding action that he was came so easily from him.

The Scottish defence looked calm and assured though, and the Miller-McLeish duo at the centre of it was coping capably with the occasional foray, and even allowing

Gough's attacking verve at right back to be loosened, as it was midway through the first half when he raced into the box to take a superb pass from Strachan, but from ten yards could only hook the ball over the bar under pressure for a central defender. To this day Gough recalls it as perhaps the best chance Scotland had in the game.

'I did well to get past their defence, but it was the bounce of the ball that beat me. I think the defender had got a touch to the ball and it came up high at me. I was also kind of side-on to the goal, which meant I got underneath it. But I knew from then on that I could go at them. The miss actually encouraged me. It didn't get me down.'

Scotland's defence looked solid. The Hansen controversy seemed distant, but threat there always was from Preben Elkjær-Larsen, who by the end of the tournament was to win the Bronze Ball as the third best player in the competition, and you could tell he was a man intent on making amends for his penalty miss against Spain in the semi-final of the European Championships in 1984, which knocked them out. He had blistering pace, but by half-time a kind of stalemate had developed and, indeed, we could hardly complain about the way Scotland had negotiated that first period. It had been competitive enough, but without arousing much emotion. But where was Souness? The captain was there all right, but thinking back to that day, I can understand the problem we had with him. In my mind was the image of the way he burst on the international scene in Mendoza eight years previously, and then gave us a master-class in midfield play in Spain against the Russians. The fact is, we knew what he was capable of, but he was now thirty-three. We were, perhaps, overlooking that. It wasn't as if he was inept, but his influence was not as discernible as we had expected. But, consolingly,

233

I looked at my notes and saw that, notably, Leighton in the Scotland goal had not had one save to make in that half.

You felt, in the second, that the Danes were becoming more dangerous, and, several times, Miller produced magnificent tackles to deny Elkjær-Larsen and Jesper Olsen when both looked about to score. But, ironically, the great Aberdeen defender was at the centre of the breakthrough when, in the fifty-seventh minute, Arnesen in midfield sent a ball though the middle for Elkjær-Larsen, who was tackled by Miller near the edge of the penalty area, but the ball simply rebounded from Miller's legs into the path of the Danish striker, who just managed to keep his balance and slant the ball past Leighton, off the inside of the post, into the net. There were elements of that Russian untidy equaliser in Malaga about it, which aroused the same anguish, but it was heartening to see Scotland's immediate positive response, which saw them find the net eventually. As Roy Aitken explains. 'It was 1–0 to them, but I felt we still had a great chance. So, I took a ball through, volleyed it and saw it crash behind their goalkeeper. You can imagine how I felt, seeing that hit the net. I felt that was it, the momentum would shift our way. Then, somebody pointed out the linesman on the far side had his flag up for offside against Charlie Nicholas. I couldn't believe it. Charlie was on the touchline, nowhere near the goal. In no way was he interfering with play. Nowadays that goal would have counted. It didn't then though, and that certainly dumped us.'

But not wholly. Nicholas, enraged by that, surged towards goal with only ten minutes left, with revenge in mind. I remember it well, seeing him make a beeline for goal with only one defender and the goalkeeper in front of him. At last I felt that real tingle of expectation. It was then that the moment came which was so crucially handicapping for the entire Scottish effort in Mexico, as Charlie himself now describes.

'I had bypassed Berggreen. I had taken him out. At least I thought I had. I had one defender left. Morten Olsen. He was a very creative centre back, but he wasn't fast and I knew I could take him for speed. I could go past him in a heartbeat. I still had about thirty yards to go, but because of the way he had turned his body, I knew I would get the ball to my left foot when I passed him, because although I was predominately right-footed, I always finished better with my left. Then, suddenly something from the back hit me. I know now it was Berggreen. I couldn't see it happening, but I felt it all right. I hit the ground, trying to catch breath and the pain was intense. It was brutal. He raked his foot down my leg. It tore my ankle ligaments. Sometimes in professional football you take one for the team, and that's what Berggreen had done. He did it for the team. He took a risk and got away with it. And me? I couldn't play on.'

Alex McLeish agrees with me that it was a pivotal moment for Scotland's entire tournament.

'It was an assault and it was astonishing that Berggreen only got a yellow. We worried that Charlie would be out for the rest of the tournament, and the annoying thing was that he had been back to his best. In that form there was always a goal in Charlie. I felt it was tragic for him and us.'

Klaus Berggreen later boasted to Danish journalists, 'I did it for Denmark!' Thus providing immediate sympathy for Samuel Johnson's remark, 'Patriotism is the last refuge of a scoundrel.' For Scotland, having used both of their substitutes previously, with McAvennie and Bannon replacing the exhausted Sturrock and Strachan, were now down to ten men and the cause was lost. Once again, a very decent performance had been negated by a single streaky goal.

That 1–0 defeat did not extinguish the light of optimism in the manager's eyes, for he was far from negative with me immediately after the game, when he emphasised the positives, rightly praising his Aberdeen defenders and believing that Richard Gough had had his best ever game for his country. But he also had to acknowledge he would have a problem fielding a strike force against West Germany with Nicholas certainly out and Sturrock looking as if he had drained the life out of himself and might not recover in time. However, it is worth recalling the thoughts of Maurice Malpas, who hardly put a foot wrong in the game. I value his assessment because he had played his club football under Jim McLean, who, although being disliked by many in the media, for many valid reasons, nevertheless was an advocate of purist football. Of the Danes, he said, 'Technically, they were better than us. Scotland traditionally played to intimidate teams. I don't mean playing dirty. I just mean we were physical and put great effort into our games. We never stood back and let people play; we were always in their face. To be honest, nine times out of ten, the other teams were better than us technically.'

Yet, without in the least rejecting that view, what was equally true was that I never experienced any sense of an inferiority complex within a Scottish squad. And truly, we knew they would be right in the faces of West Germany next.

18

TEST OF ENDURANCE

It would be a big ask for Scotland. I had been an admirer of the whole ethos of German football since they had taken on one of the best teams ever, the Magyars of the 1954 World Cup, and disposed of them through assiduous preparation and technical efficiency on the field. All this stemmed from their great belief in a coaching system, from kids at school upwards, during the years when we were faffing about with doubts about that wee establishment down in Largs. It showed in their style, and still does, to this day. And, of course, let us not forget, they were much bigger than us, even in their designation as West Germany then. So, it was vital Ferguson got his team selection absolutely fit for purpose. It caused much discussion among the media.

Some of them were newcomers to the World Cup and looked like they were suffering the shock of just having been robbed of all their goods and chattels. I sympathised with them, since it had taken a long time to work my 1978 Cordoba depression out of the system. But I relished the antidote of argument, and there were many angry men around the table, offering views on team selection, attitude, refereeing and substitutions. Hardly anything was missed. But the most vigorous debate centred around Souness. My good friend, and excellent journalist, the late Alan Davidson, who, like me, was a great admirer of the new Rangers player-manager, emerged from the din with a notion that you could hardly ignore. He put it more succinctly when he wrote his article that following day for the *Evening Times (Glasgow)* with the same thoughts, 'Fine player and dominant figure that he is, Souness tends to overawe the rest of the team and I believe that others should take on more responsibility.'

I could hardly disagree with that and you had to wonder what was now going through Ferguson's mind about him. What I now know is that perhaps there had been some long-term planning about Souness's involvement in Mexico. That is certainly what Frank McAvennie believes.

'I spent some time with Graeme in Santa Fe. We would talk about football in Scotland and England. And then one day, out of the blue, he told me that he would be dropped for one of the games in the finals. Souness being dropped? I could scarcely believe it. He was the true superstar in the side. But that's what he told me. Long before we reached Mexico. It was unbelievable.'

The following day, we risked life and limb again in the crazy car journey to the pyramids area to get an insight into Ferguson's mind about this and other matters. But when we got there, we were met by security guards who told us that all press, but particularly broadcasters, were to be banned from entering until further notice and that no interviews were to be allowed. We were told that unfair comments had been made about this dowdy, depressing hotel, in the Scottish newspapers, which had gone to town on its inadequacies. That accounted for the press-ban, perhaps not surprisingly, given the SFA's previous sensitivity to adverse comment on their frequent inability to recognise a doss house when they saw one. But broadcasters? Where had we crossed the line? The issue was about a phone. There was only one in the hotel. Getting access to it was like fighting for the conch on that island where the boys almost turned into cannibals. The reaction wasn't quite as bad as that, but it certainly intensified the feeling amongst the players who, when they really should have been luxuriating in the World Cup atmosphere, in fact, felt marooned. So, the players rightly complained, but to nil effect. Charlie Nicholas remembers the farcical outcome.

'I was a single man at the time, so it didn't bother me all that much. But I felt sorry for the married men who really needed to keep in touch with family and kids.'

One such was Maurice Malpas.

'My wife was pregnant at the time and I needed to know how she was progressing. I was desperate to know. But the only time I really got to speak to her was when Dick Donnelly, a Dundee journalist, took me up to the press box after one of the games to use his phone. That was the first time I had spoken to her in days. She was OK, but we were all angry about that.'

What then transpired is that a television reporter had set up a special line inside the hotel for his company, but allowed one of the players to use it to tell the world about this dilapidation. When the word got round the squad about this, a queue developed for that precious phone, and they subsequently ran up a bill that must have been the equivalent of ET's call back home. All of them phoning loved ones, of course, but also painting a picture of misery and boredom and slamming the SFA for a failure in planning. When this reached the ears of Ernie Walker, he went ballistic and had the line dismantled. Hence the ban on broadcasters.

Which brings me back to Denis Law, me and the ban.

He was with us at the gates when we were shut out. It was bizarre. Frankly, he was greatly amused. He is not one of nature's moaners and, from experience, had probably prepared himself for something like this occurring. As we talked about how we might surmount this problem, we were suddenly alerted to the sight of a figure striding out determinedly towards the barrier. It was Alex Ferguson no less. He made straight towards us.

'That bloody man won't stop me from talking,' was his first comment, before we set the cameras rolling. It more than hinted at a breakdown in personal relationships between him and the SFA secretary. I was not surprised. Ferguson was in no mood to succumb to the normal SFA strictures for a job that was only going to last until they exited the tournament. Although the manager sounded vitriolic, I have to say that none of the players I have talked to noticed any friction between the pair. They were probably too busy thinking about matches they had to play and, equally, how to survive in the house of horrors. He was complimentary about his players when he did the interview, and expressed confidence in their spirit for the Germany game in four days' time. Although the sentence I do remember was, 'Charlie's injury really upsets me. He was top of his form.' He was obviously worried about who he would play up front now. He greeted Denis like a hero, before sloping back into grief.

Denis, himself, was always straight with his views. He thought little had been learned by the SFA from the other World Cups in knowing how to handle men cooped up together for weeks. He talked about the German side, which he fancied strongly, to go far. Does that mean we had no chance? Denis never ever dismissed Scotland out of hand.

Of course there was a chance. So, it was almost therapeutic for me to listen to his optimism. He lifted me from a kind of mid-course World Cup blues to whetting my appetite for the German match. And the need to interview the man planning our downfall: Franz Beckenbauer.

I had conversed with him twice before. I had gone to New York on holiday and wangled my way into the New York Cosmos stadium, using a BBC identity card, and walked on to the pitch to talk to him, as he walked off at half-time. The Cosmos were playing against Seattle Sounders, for whom the Scottish international Tommy Hutchinson was principal midfielder. The fact that five men were sent off in that game was interesting enough in itself. But I wanted a quote about the prospects for American soccer from him for a column I was writing. He stopped, sweating profusely, and politely stood for a couple of minutes, providing exactly what I wanted. Here was a toff, if ever there was one. A real spud. That's the feeling I had leaving the stadium then. This was reinforced years later when, as German manager, he came to Hampden prior to the finals to spy on Scotland. Jock Stein had arranged for him to make a special presentation on the pitch. The Scotland manager had asked Alan Hart, then Head of BBC Sport, if they would provide a trophy to be presented by Beckenbauer to Archie Gemmill for having scored the outstanding goal in the 1978 World Cup. He did so gracefully, and late at night, in his hotel, he gave me an interview about European football in general. He was lucid, informative and had a kind of doctor's bedside manner about him.

But we were in for a shock. It was a very different Beckenbauer I was to meet at the German hotel on the outskirts of the steamy town of Querétaro, where the next game was

241

to be played. The building was vast and high ceilinged, suggesting it may have been a monastery in a previous existence. But it was the Ritz compared to the Scottish abode. He had called a press conference, which we were permitted to attend, but not to film, since the procedure was to be entirely in German. Had we done so, we would have had to asterisk some of the subtitles because the Kaiser was on the attack. It was not a bawling match, more a lecture peppered with sizzling contempt. Spitting fury. It seemed so out of character. A colleague from German television was kind enough to translate and revealed that a story had appeared in a German newspaper claiming that some of the players in his squad in their pre-World Cup training camps had secreted prostitutes into their rooms. He lashed into the assembled press, then rose, and pulling on a classy self-control, came straight to our position in an adjacent room, sat down, took deep breaths, as if to compose himself, then talked to us in perfectly enunciated English.

'What can you do when you have such vultures surrounding you?' he remarked, after explaining the issue in detail. 'They just print lies, you know. Do they really want us to win?' It could have been an SFA official speaking to me in Argentina. So, it wasn't all smooth sailing for the Germans after all. There was some satisfaction to be taken from that, although in my interview with him, I gathered the feeling he wouldn't be having sleepless nights about us. They also had something to prove to the obvious growing cynicism of their own press, for they had gone a goal down to Uruguay in their opening game in only four minutes, and only equalised with six minutes remaining through Klaus Allofs to make it 1–1. Beware a backlash, is what Ferguson emphasised to us the day before the game. He wasn't fooled. He knew the Germans sometimes started tournaments cannily. Now they could flex their muscles. Not only that, but they were so meticulous in their preparation that they would resort to surveillance that John le Carré might have written about. Beckenbauer sent Bertie Vogts to see if he could get into a Scotland training session to find out if Strachan was fit or not. He couldn't, of course, especially as he was wearing a Germany jersey. But he saw Coca-Cola men unloading barrels of the stuff into the ground. He asked one of the workers if he could swap jerseys. So, wearing a Coca-Cola uniform, he did slip into the training session and reported back. He noted Strachan was fit and that there would be no Charlie Nicholas.

So, on 8 June 1986, we arrived in the city of Querétaro, which, in the local indigenous dialect, means 'The Place Where The Ball Is Played', and entered the Estadio Corregidora, which felt like we had joined the municipal Turkish baths. I have referred previously to adverse climatic conditions in World Cups, particularly in Seville in Spain in 1982, but that was temperate compared to this. Standing in the queue to go through the security check, the humidity bore down on us like heavy weights being placed on our shoulders. God knows what it was going to be like on the pitch. Then came the team announcements. Ferguson had made three changes. Sturrock's ankle injury ruled him out, Eamonn Bannon, who could run like a gazelle, was brought in, Steve Archibald, as expected, replaced Charlie Nicholas, and, significantly, David Narey replaced Alex McLeish, who had been excellent against Denmark but who had been laid low by a malady of ancient origin – Montezuma's Revenge, a sickness that requires you to have a pail handy.

'I think I drank some tap water and that was that,' he told me. 'Stupid, I know. I had to go to bed, feeling really ill. Then the manager came to me and said. "How are you feeling? You cannae let me down now." He really was making a big appeal to me. So, the morning before the game, I agreed to do a fitness test. He put me through it with the ball, running, heading, all of that, but I had to hold my hand up and tell him I just wasn't fit enough to make it. I watched the game on television in my room, but hoped I would be fit for the last game. Which I was. But the manager refused to bring me back. I was gutted. I fell out with him over that.' McLeish played conscientiously for his country seventy-seven times and in all of that time received only one yellow card. He was a model of stable consistency and was understandably incandescent at what he perceived to be a snub.

So, the team selected was:

Leighton,
Gough, Miller, Narey, Malpas,
Bannon, Aitken, Strachan, Souness (*captain*),
Nicol, Archibald.

We read through the West German side with increasing apprehension, given the vast experience contained within:

Schumacher (*captain*),
Briegel, Förster, Eder, Berthold,
Augenthaler, Magath, Matthäus, Littbarski,
Allofs, Völler.

Yes, they had lost the final in Spain. But they had been over the entire course. They were hardened and captained by Schumacher, who believed in the blitzkrieg principle, even as a goalkeeper, when he flattened Patrick Battiston of

France with a Battle of the Bulge assault in the finals in Spain in 1982. Although highly questionable, it showed a certain kind of leadership, especially as he got off with it. And, at the heart of the side, the imperishable Lothar Matthaüs, the personification of dedicated, technically empowered German football, captain of the World Champions in 1974 and their most capped player ever, of whom Diego Maradona wrote in his book *I Am The Diego*, 'he is the best rival I've ever had. I guess that's enough to define him.' The rest, around Matthaüs, were no slouches either.

But there was personal consolation for me. I had a co-commentator this time. Step forward Charles Nicholas. That terrible tackle he had sustained against Denmark proved that it is an ill wind that blows nobody any good. His injury left him surplus to requirements and I stepped in and got Ferguson to sanction his use. So, the man who would become widely known through Sky Television made his network television debut here. I stress network, meaning UK-wide, because a couple of hours before kick-off, the producer told me that, not only would we be sharing the commentary for Scottish viewers, but that he and I would introduce BBC London's coverage of the game, direct from the broadcasting platform before the game itself. They were giving Scotland its full place in the sun on this occasion, much to my amazement. Or were they? About half an hour later, the same man came to me and said there was a pause on that arrangement. We had to wait for a final decision. It was puzzling and frankly unsettling before this major event. We hung around for another hour, kicking our heels, wondering what the hell was going on. Then we were told that we would definitely be introducing the programme. It wasn't until later that that same producer whispered in my ear that the hold-up was because Jimmy Hill, who all the time had been standing close to us behind the main stand, had taken the trouble to phone his agent in London to query whether my usurping him for that particular start-of-programme introduction was a breach of his contract. I don't know what was said to whom eventually, but, knowing some of my London colleagues well, including the strong Scottish editorial element there, I'm sure some brusque language was used to rebuff the objection. So, Charlie and I climbed to meet our destiny, as it were.

The pace was not electric. It was busy, but you could sense that the intense heat and the effect of altitude, with the city being 6,000 feet above sea level, that this was going to be brutal. You could feel the players were aware of this. The play came in quick spurts, with what looked like welcome respite in between. That did not mean less action near goal, but there was nothing exhilarating about this. This would be a trial of perseverance and durability. Indeed, after about ten minutes, I began to hope that the newspaper story about the German players consorting with prostitutes might be right after all and that, like a flock of Delilahs, they had shorn some of the players of their strength. Not Felix Magath and Lothar Matthäus in midfield, though, they were the controllers. In only three minutes, they were to produce a move between them, finishing with Allofs looking as if he would score with a header, but which produced the first of a string of amazing saves from Jim Leighton, who probably defended that day as well as any Scottish goalkeeper I had seen. However, I have previously referenced the row I was to have in the future with Ferguson. It was about Leighton. That day, after the brilliant save, he failed to cut out a corner and allowed Rudi Völler to head against the post. For all Leighton's shot-stopping brilliance, I always felt he was vulnerable to the cross ball, as he was in that instant and said so then, and repeated that months later in another game for Scotland, which provoked Ferguson into reaching for his hairdryer to defend his goalkeeper.

Scotland, though, were not passive. Particularly Strachan. In the earlier stages of the game, he looked as if he were thoroughly enjoying himself. It was like Spain. His neat dribbling and quick spurts were disturbing their attempt in midfield to appear composed and balanced. In drawing attention to himself, it opened up gaps and allowed others to stride forward, like full back Malpas, who came in on a Strachan-inspired dash, but shot over the bar though from twenty yards. It was encouraging though, especially as the mood was latched onto by Bannon shortly after, who took a pass from Archibald and fired in a shot which was brilliantly tipped over the bar by Schumacher. But, to be honest, the first goal came as a surprise. Not that Scotland hadn't threatened, but approaching the twenty-minute mark, the German defence did look intact, from goal outwards. The move started from the deep, where Nicol was in possession. It went to Gough, then quickly to Aitken, who had been beavering away in midfield, mostly as a spoiler, but with a great sense of awareness. He split their defence with an astute through-pass, which was seized upon by Strachan who, from an acute angle, fired the ball past Schumacher. At first it looked like the wee man would jump the waist-high advertising hoardings, to join the exuberant Scottish support behind that goal. But, in fact, he only managed to get one leg over, to use a phrase, and stuck as he was there, it looked like his Devon Loch moment, but with a triumphant smile on his face.

It was the next eight minutes that was to anger Ferguson.

Scotland could not keep the ball effectively to hold on to their lead and, with alarming predictability and Teutonic efficiency, the Germans created a text-book goal – a triangular movement involving, inevitably, Magath, with the preliminary run, the pass to the outside to Matthäus and the cut-back from the goal line to Völler, who actually kneed the ball in from only a couple of yards. We noticed towards the end of the half Pierre Littbarski, no slouch he, leaving Souness behind in a short spurt that made the Scottish captain's legs look like they had been cemented to the ground. Ominous. Willie Miller recalls what was going through his mind at the interval with the score 1–1. 'Even at club level, I found German teams were damned difficult to beat. They were superb technically, of course, but they also had this great physical determination and strength to back it up. For all that I was pleased so far with the game, I knew we would be up against it in the second half.'

So would their bodies, in the fight against the conditions. On the television platform, Charlie Nicholas and I swallowed water like it was life affirming. So our principal thinking was, who would succumb first to the fiendish conditions? What we didn't know was that there was more than water being provided in the Scottish dressing room, as Maurice Malpas acknowledges, 'I remember some of the players coming in and getting oxygen. It gave them something cool to breathe, that's all. It was refreshing to get that in their lungs, but when you walked down the tunnel again, you could feel yourself beginning to breathe in all that horrible humidity again.'

All the brave men went at it once more, but only four minutes into the second half the game took an unhealthy turn for Scotland, with a German counter that fitted the habitual historical pattern of Scotland conceding entirely preventable goals. Miller and Narey moved to tackle Allofs in the penalty area, but the ball broke cruelly from the top of Narey's boot, right into the path of the German striker, who gratefully accepted the gift from ten yards. Now 2–1 down, I had to credit Scotland for not folding and repeatedly mounting moves against the Germans, even though, as Richard Gough admits, it was now torture. 'I lost eight pounds during that game. That is a helluva lot. I always look after myself and keep fit, even now long retired from football, but that was the worst effect I've ever had in a game. But we had to keep going, although, to be honest, I just felt that the Germans always had enough in them to beat us no matter what we did.'

Scotland now seemed to be faced with a team of giants, who far from looking like having a rest from naughty hotel pranks, seemed as if they had come straight from a health farm. What a difference a single goal can make. Leighton had to be immense after that, and was. Shots from Allofs and Litbarski might have beaten another keeper. It kept Scotland alive. And not without their opportunities, as a result of bringing on Frank McAvennie who, with thirty minutes to go, but with little chance to settle in, missed a chance after Bannon got his head to a Strachan corner. The ball broke to the substitute, but he couldn't compose himself quickly enough to take advantage. 'I just wasn't on the field long enough,' he told me. 'Honestly, I wasn't getting the right chance. That was two substitutions for me and I just couldn't get going in the time I was given. It just made me all the angrier.'

Scotland's best chance thereafter came when the rampant Richard Gough came all the way from the back to follow a cross from substitute Davie Cooper, out-jumped the German defence, but could only watch his header skim the top of the bar. The game was now like watching a slow-motion replay. Souness not only looked on his last legs, but actually seemed on the point of exhaustion. Clearly, he had been affected by how much of the game had passed him by. As the players trudged off the field with the Germans victorious, I asked Nicholas, 'Is it conceivable that Fergie will drop Graeme for the last game? He just doesn't look fit.' The injured striker, who had now learned through his television experience when to be perfectly candid, was much more diplomatic then. 'Graeme's a great player,' he replied. 'How do you drop great players?' That dilemma was staring us all in the face now.

19

ASSAULT AND BATTERY

But before grappling with that, there was a curious aftermath to that game which brought us back to a basic reality. Pierre Littbarski and Strachan were kept behind for the statutory drug test, and given the aftermath of the Willie Johnston affair in Argentina, the BBC insisted I stay on for the results, just in case. As an illustration of the torturous dehydration everybody suffered that day, even though they drank water constantly, bottle after bottle, neither of them could pee for nearly an hour and a half. In what I am sure was a breach of every regulation in the book, we ended up joining them at a table, somebody produced a pack of cards from somewhere, and into a game of brag we went as we waited for nature to come to the aid of two little men who, off the field, looked like choirboys who had just sneaked away from evensong. Strachan managed to pee first. 'Scotland one, West Germany nil,' he said, as he exited the test room, punching the air after the all-clear. Of all his renowned one-liners, that is the one I most prefer.

With the Danes having thrashed Uruguay 6–1, it meant we needed to win the last game against the South Americans to progress. Ferguson's anguished statement after the game made all the pages of the press. 'We cut our own throats!' He was specifically speaking about the team's inability to gain possession and hold on to their lead for more than that meagre four minutes. There was more to it than that, but there was no denying that tiny passage altered the game. All the mutterings that then circulated amongst the media was like hearing the tinkling of that out-of-tune piano in the very familiar last-chance saloon again. Souness was central to the tequila-fuelled arguments amongst the media about his immediate future. Truly, a player I had long admired had looked fatigued beyond recovery to me. My view was that he had run the race bravely, but enough was enough. Others disagreed. That was just part of the conjecture over the next few days, although Charlie Nicholas, who was close to Souness then, paints an unforgettable picture of commitment and exhaustion. 'Immediately after the game I left the commentary platform and went down to the interview area, and met him and then went for a couple of beers with him. He had lost a whole stone in weight. He was the fittest guy in our group by a distance. But you could see his ribcage for the next two days. It was unbelievable what he had taken out of himself.'

The end for Souness then? The debate had started. We weren't aware of the full extent of that as we returned to the Adams Family hotel, the day before the Uruguay game, where we were now permitted access for interviews. Indeed, Ferguson was bullish. There was not a shred of pessimism in his appearance, and in the eager way he talked about his side. After all, his team had played creditably well in both games. The press had reflected disappointment, but had certainly not indulged in the kind of assaults we had experienced in other World Cups. He was particularly enthusiastic about the recovery from injury of Charlie Nicholas, since only one goal had been scored and that by a midfield player. As always, here was a Scotland manager worried about the dearth of goals and hoped that, with Sturrock recovering as well, that the two, who had started so brightly against Denmark, would make a pair again. He would not reveal anything about selection and when I asked him about Souness, it was a case of a 'wait and see' kind of answer. This was a man raring to go. A one-goal victory in the next game would be sufficient for him to better all the managers who had preceded him and you could tell he was aware of that tantalising prospect. But his captain presented him with a problem. All the coaches gave their views on his possible selection.

Walter Smith argued for him. Craig Brown and Andy Roxburgh, like me, thought he shouldn't be picked – that he just wouldn't be up to it any longer. We do know that, before Ferguson made his final decision, that he, Walter Smith, and Souness himself, talked about this and agreed that it would be something of a humiliation for the team-captain to be a substitute on the bench. It had to be either in or out completely. The manager understood that, and took the trouble on the eve of the game to go to Souness's pigeonhole, or room as it was called, to tell him to his face that he was to be dropped for the first time in his career. The captain, who had taken an aversion to Mexican food, and had existed on Mars Bars, glucose and water drinks, losing almost two stone overall in the period, took it well, at least outwardly. Others didn't.

With so much on his mind, it was not so surprising that Ferguson admitted this to Jim Reynolds of the *Glasgow Herald*. 'I only slept for an hour last night. I was tossing and turning all night going over all the possibilities. Everyone in the squad is fit for selection but I have to decide whether or not Uruguay will try to beat us or play for a draw that would see them go through.'

The sleepless night produced this team:

Leighton,
Gough, Albiston, Narey, Miller (*captain*),
Strachan, Aitken, McStay, Nicol,
Sturrock, Sharp.

So Souness was out and the youngest player in the squad, Paul McStay, was in. So was Arthur Albiston, for his first game, at the expense of Maurice Malpas, who so far had been faultless. Graeme Sharp was also in for his first game, principally for his physical presence in what was expected to be a combative game. This was a selection that provoked a wild argument between the manager and the usurped Steve Archibald. But to say Scotland expected a rough time was an exaggeration. For, as I write out the Uruguayan side, I can't help but feel now that I am listing the names of men sought after by Wells Fargo for Wild West crimes ...

Alvez,
Gutiérrez, Acevedo, Diogo, Batista,
Ramos, Barrios (*captain*), Pereira, Santín,
Cabrera, Francescoli.

There was one notable exception. From the start to seven minutes from the end, when he was substituted, having run himself into the ground, one man stood head and shoulders above everybody else on the field. Enzo Francescoli. It was a cruel irony to watch this man's elegant skill in contrast to the

254

thugs around him in the same colours. His control and close dribbling for a spearheading striker, left up by himself in a 4-4-1 formation, after the sending-off, you could only admire. He wasn't slow to hand it out himself, but primarily we saw in him the style that ought to have brought credit to their side. But that image was eclipsed by ill-disguised brutality.

We were back in the modest Estadio Neza on 13 June 1986, with the crowd around 20,000, where it was obvious that the neutrals were backing Scotland, to judge by the welcome they received. It was only fifty-six seconds into the game when we understood why there was no continental sympathy and that perhaps the Uruguayans' reputation had preceded them. It took one tackle to reveal that. José Batista picked out Gordon Strachan like a drunk man looking for a fight. He scythed him down. In commentary, I had scarcely drawn breath and found it hard to believe that such an assault could be so blatant and so soon. Batista had sunk his boot into the midfielder's leg in front of a world audience. Even a referee like the Frenchman Quiniou, whom we knew could be tactfully blind to some incidents on the field if it suited him career-wise, had little option but to send him off in a World Cup finals record time for a dismissal. Walter Smith, on the sidelines, recognised the inevitable pattern that followed. 'The trouble is they then dragged us into a battle we shouldn't have got involved in. We got caught up in this aggression. There were running battles going on all over the pitch. We couldn't get out of this. They had dragged us down to their level and that suited them. I don't think I have ever watched so many fouls in an international game.' So, the South Americans were down to ten men for the second game in succession, having lost Bossio early on in the game against Denmark, for a savage foul on Laudrup of Denmark.

You could therefore say that playing with ten men came naturally to them.

So, a particular target was Strachan, who had just been hailed by Beckenbauer as the outstanding player in Queré-taro. He was repeatedly hit with tackles that brought some free kicks, but also confirmed the view that Quiniou had decided there would be no more reds, having got his obvious publicity already. I began to worry, as the challenges rained down on virtually all the Scottish players, but particularly Strachan, that, in an emergency, would an ambulance be able to negotiate these damned crowded streets to a hospital? Roy Aitken was also aware of their added theatrical qualities. 'I'll always remember how they fell down, feigning injury, lying as if dead at times, kicking the ball out of the field, dwelling over free kicks and goal-kicks, clipping our heels, pulling our hair from the back, spitting on us, punching us off the ball. A lot of crudeness. But it was the starting and the stopping so much that spoiled the rhythm of the game. If you look back at the records I think you would find that the ball was only in actual play a third of the time. It was a charade. The worst thing that happened to us was that man being sent off at the start.'

It was more than a charade. It was the usual *danse macabre* for us. This feeling certainly started to surface in the eighteenth minute when Scotland contrived to recreate that Bremner 'miss' in Germany in 1974 when his legs seemed to freeze in front of the Brazilian goal. Roy Aitken was not just an observer to this, but the man who had made the final pass. To this day he is still incredulous about what happened. 'I got to the goal line and I saw Stevie Nicol coming in toward goal, so I cut it back to him. Now I know Stevie could finish all right, and he could really hit a ball. But I could barely believe it. He just seemed to fluff it. All he needed to do was just hit it cleanly. He didn't. It was the outstanding chance in the game.'

This excellent solid midfield player, whilst not a striker, had scored thirty-seven goals in his Liverpool career. I think he was beaten by seeing it as that simple. That is the only reason I can think of. He only pawed at it as a result. The soft shot was easily taken by their goalkeeper. In the entire ninety minutes, it stood out as the single most glaring chance on either side. A sense of foreboding began to seep in again, particularly watching the Uruguayan officials at half-time almost swamping and harassing the referee and his officials as they made their way off the pitch. Ominously, they took no action against them. The first half had seen little in the way of any breakthrough. Francescoli had shown his brilliance with some dazzling runs but was being met by Willie Miller in his best vigilant form. It is difficult to recall either keeper called to stretch himself to any extent.

The second half was patterned the same way, with acts of perhaps unavoidable retaliation by Narey and Nichol, earning them bookings. And yes, there was a certain change of rhythm when Nicholas and Davie Cooper came on in a double substitution with twenty minutes to go, which led to more enterprise and Narey crashing a shot narrowly over the bar after taking a pass from Cooper's talented left foot. However, easy though it is to state it now, I never felt we would score that day, after the Nicol miss.

An ugly no-scoring draw had produced that same sense of World Cup desolation that I had now come to know as 'Airport Time Again'. The Uruguayans had been vicious and, regrettably, got away with using every nefarious trick in the book to survive to the end. But, whatever the unacceptable nature of the game, the cruel fact remained that Scotland had lost to ten men. Perhaps any other manager would have been savaged for that result, but the ugliness of the game superimposed a plausible excuse on the outcome and made us, in the immediate aftermath, overlook views on selection. Paul McStay had looked overwhelmed. Graeme Sharp looked surprisingly meek. Sturrock had not looked completely fit. Davie Cooper had come on too late. Nicholas was not fully match-fit. Only our defence rated high marks. And our midfield, in all, lacked substance. Then came a contentious press conference, which had all the dignity of a cockfight. The Uruguayan coach, Omar Barras, had called the early sending-off of Batista as 'murder by the referee', which set the tone of the proceedings. The Uruguayan press were mouthing things loudly in Spanish, which seemed like calls to arms. As we were hardly in a fraternal mood then, we were up for anything that might ensue. And then there was Ernie Walker. If ever a man looked like he was about to discard his erstwhile diplomatic demeanour, throw off his jacket and ask Barras to step outside, it was him.

I had seen Walker in the aftermaths of disappointments in all previous World Cups, with a face that had looked ashen and weary. That day, when he came to the cameras in the press area, he was quivering, shaking, rage pulsating from every pore. This is exactly, word for word, what he said to us: 'We found ourselves on the fields with cheats and cowards. We were associated with the scum of world football and if anybody thinks that had anything to do with football then that's news to me.'

I emphasise the 'exact' words, because it was the word 'scum' which caught the eye and ear, and was placed into all sorts of contexts by the various news outlets making it even more lurid than in its first airing. Hardly any Scot in that press room recoiled at his statement, and indeed almost felt like applauding. Yet, for years later, Walker would almost implore me not to run that interview again, or even mention that statement in any of my interviews with him, because, on reflection, even though he might have been speaking for all of us at the time, it clearly embarrassed him afterwards, and as an ambitious figure within UEFA and FIFA, he plainly did not want a highly emotional statement, in post-match furore, to become associated with his own preferred persona of the cool, calculating man.

Ferguson rightly ranted about the Uruguayans. I sensed though, not just anger, but a kind of relief that he was about to ditch the task that his great mentor had called 'impossible'. 'As a nation they seem to have no respect for anyone. That was a debacle out there. I know we are out of the World Cup but honestly I am glad to be going home because this is no way to play football.'

He knew, too, there would now be questions about his selection for the last game, since even to this day some of the main protagonists in the matter have split views.

'Stunned,' Nicholas told me how he felt when the team was eventually read out to them. 'I could hardly believe it. I think it was the only real mistake Sir Alex made in the whole tournament. I think if Souness had played we would have got through.' Richard Gough echoed that, 'Here was our captain, our leader and he wasn't going to be there. I felt uncomfortable about that. I just felt something vital would be missing. But I also felt sorry for the manager. It was a tough one for him to make.'

Maurice Malpas understood that, but was still surprised. 'I think he should have been there. Easy enough to say that after the event. But there was something missing, as I could see.'

Frank McAvennie still insists Souness knew what was coming. 'I think he knew he wouldn't play in all three games, as I told you. He should have been there. That last game was about how to take on bullies. He would have sorted some out.'

But Craig Brown put it another way. 'I agreed with the manager that Graeme, even in the friendly game in LA had looked leg-heavy, and especially when we got back to altitude in Mexico. He just wasn't the Souness of dominance in midfield. And I am sure that even the Prozone system, which can measure a player's work on the ball, would have shown that he wasn't putting in the shift that he normally would do. For the average midfielder, it should be about 1,100 metres in a game. I don't think he was near that level. So, yes, I went along with the decision to drop him. I think it was the correct one.'

Alex McLeish's disappointment about that was compounded by the fact that he didn't play either.

'I thought Souness should have played, but I was more concerned about myself. I was fit enough after that sickness, but the manager made it clear he wouldn't replace Davie Narey for me, although I would have been playing alongside my club-mate Willie, which the manager had always heaped praise on. We fell out big time over that.'

Perhaps Paul Sturrock summed it up well, 'It wouldn't have mattered who we fielded. We got the shit kicked out of us anyway.'

There was a growing sympathy for Souness immediately afterwards, among most of the media. But then he did something which annoyed those same people, and I suppose I was responsible for it. He decided to give me an exclusive interview, later that evening, in which he announced that he was retiring from international football and that he would be devoting all his energies to Rangers. None of the press knew about this. When it was eventually broadcast, Alan Ferguson, the SFA commercial consultant, witnessed the reaction among the press.

'At the airport for the flight home, he and I got pelters. The press wanted to know why he had given the BBC an exclusive on this and left them out. It then was a fractious flight home, with a lot of bickering about them failing to get this story. And, of course, it was an important one. So, relationships were strained.'

Alan Herron still wanted to get this story back to his newspaper, the *Sunday Mail*, but when he tried to enter the players' lounge at the airport, he had to argue with the SFA official for some time before he was allowed in. When he eventually gained entry, he spotted Souness and McAvennie sitting together. 'I asked him a straightforward question, the obvious one: "How did you feel about being dropped by Fergie?" "Over the bloody moon," he replied, with heavy emphasis on the sarcasm, and then added forcibly, "And I'll tell you something else, I will never play for Scotland again."' Herron rushed to get a phone and discovered there was none available in the airport. He went outside to a local pharmacy and was able to phone back to his newspaper in Glasgow, but discovered that both the sports editor and his assistant were in the pub and nobody would take a message to them. So this story, with Souness's explosive quote, was completely missed by his newspaper.

Alex Ferguson was on that same flight back and was now free to pursue his own dreams and become the most successful manager in British football history, after an experience that barely scratched his reputation, even though his team could only score one goal and gain one point. He officially quit on 15 June. I thought he was exciting and refreshing to be with, and had gone along with virtually all his decisions, not that he would have cared one way or the other, even though I now admit that Souness could have made a difference in the Neza. He had been given solid support by the SFA, in supporting the need for altitude training, and laying on conditions that ought to have helped eventually, although you wonder if the science behind that had really worked out, given the horrendous toll that was taken on their bodies in Querétaro. Certainly, the hotel conditions gave rise to the feeling among the players of lack of consideration of their basic needs, and it bred resentment, no matter the valid reasons for being there. It was just such an alarmingly familiar scenario which they must have known would breed cynicism among the media reporting these scenes.

But it was the man retiring from international football who would provide the most significant legacy from Mexico for the Scottish domestic environment. For he was heading to implement a transformation in the club game that would be as supportive for any Scotland team in the future as the Dutch Elm disease would be to a forest. Even on the day he was to play his last game for Scotland in Querétaro, Souness was huddled with Walter Smith and Alan Ferguson in a corner of the hotel, in full view of Alex Ferguson, sorting out the transfer to Rangers of goalkeeper Chris Woods, who was in Mexico, but with the England squad. It was the start of a revolution, even before the World Cup had ended for him. His foreign and English imports would radically change the domestic game, particularly promoted eventually by a man in David Murray, who introduced market values to the game, which paid scant attention to the long-term development and nurturing of native talent. But paradoxically, many critics of that policy, took it upon themselves to adopt it in different degrees, but most notably by Rangers' great rivals Celtic who, more than twenty years later, had as many foreign players on their books as any other club in the entire European continent. So, Mexico was not just about another World Cup disappointment for Scotland. Souness's actions were pointing to a change in the direction that football would take thereafter, as club football gravitated towards the importance of the European club tournaments, with the riches which could flow from that. That momentum would pull many of the urban masses of the Old Firm, most notably Rangers fans, away from the traditional regular support for a Scottish team, as well as clearly stunting the growth of potential Scottish talent. Mexico was bequeathing to any future manager of the national side a condition that could turn out to be as troublesome as Montezuma's Revenge.

THE 1990 FIFA WORLD CUP

ITALY

20

THE YOUNG PRINCE?

As headlines go, 'Andy Who?' was a tabloid classic of its time. In two words it contained an accurate reflection of public bemusement, revealed a newspaper's own perplexity, and was laden with that insensitivity which was the trademark of a journalism that was by nature confrontational. It was published in the *Daily Record* on 17 July 1986. It referred specifically to the surprise appointment of Andy Roxburgh as the new manager of Scotland to replace Alex Ferguson, who was off to plough his own fertile furrow, and, knowing him at the time, would rather have taken a post as the Muckle Flugga lighthouse-keeper than go anywhere near the SFA again. Those two words, splashed in a newspaper, hung around Roxburgh's neck for some considerable time, and in that sense, for lasting impact, I would rank it with the memorable, although utterly tasteless, 'Gotcha' of *The Sun* newspaper on the sinking of the SS *Belgrano* in 1982.

I could detect barely a ripple of enthusiasm anywhere for the SFA's choice. Even Craig Brown, his colleague and friend, was surprised by this decision. Like many in my trade, I had been advocating Billy McNeill for the post. His pedigree as player and as manager, on both sides of the border, seemed like he had been particularly crafted for the job. The only other name to be mentioned in the same breath as McNeill was Jim McLean, the Dundee United supremo, whose track record could hardly be ignored. However, McLean's name surfaced with a certain reluctance among us because, although he was highly regarded as a superb football tactician, his abjectly miserable sense of public relations, which seemed to stem from the bleakness of a huge inferiority complex demonstrating he felt the whole world was against him, made him unappealing to many.

So, McNeill at that stage seemed to be favourite, backed up by newspaper support from the likes of Alex Cameron of the *Daily Record* when he wrote, the morning before the appointment, 'If the SFA don't approach McNeill then it will be the one serious failure in Ernie Walker's highly progressive reign as secretary.' Away from the main centres of opinion, in the provinces, Iain Scott, who was to become sports editor of the *Glasgow Herald* and sports news editor of the *Daily Record*, was one of the few who actually enthused about Roxburgh's appointment.

'I was working for the local newspaper and I spoke out in favour of him getting the job, although a lot of journalists didn't. It seemed refreshing. Although, I have to be honest, after a while I began to change my opinion.'

Walker must have anticipated all of this and made an official statement to us, after the appointment, which included the following, 'Andy is a bigger name outside Scotland at the moment but that will change soon. Top countries such as Italy and Holland often send for him because of his knowledge of the game.' But he also went out of his way to meet some of us privately, to expound his views on the decision. He took me aside in the Grosvenor Hotel in Glasgow one afternoon and went through a lengthy explanation of what lay at the root of this selection. Broadly speaking, as he described the kinds of battle-hardened managers they had opted for in the past, it was like listening to a variation of the Beauty and the Beast tale, in that he wanted to end the era of the hairy monster and present us instead with the spotless young prince. And, many months later, when Alan Davidson and I were in his office enjoying Walker's hospitality, and aware of the politicking that could go on within the international selection committee, we asked him candidly who really had engineered this appointment? 'I did,' he said, simply and almost proudly, which to us at the time underlined two factors: the sway that the SFA secretary now held over the association and the fact that this was very much an unprecedented personal endorsement. So, two reputations were at stake, not just one.

But Walker was not some isolated figure plucking some new ideology out of thin air. Outside the general media reaction were men with solid achievements in the game who wholly backed this move. Alex Smith, one of the few managers to have won the Scottish Cup twice, with different clubs, St. Mirren in 1987 and Aberdeen in 1990, and the best man at the wedding of his lifelong friend and youth team-mate Billy Bremner, was at the heart of the movement to convert minds to the value of coaching qualifications, even though he came himself only from the school of hard knocks, from which he and his dear friend had emerged successfully. He knew Roxburgh was not going to have an easy ride.

'His coaching skills were brilliant, but I knew there would be opposition to him because of the long-standing prejudice against the SFA coaching courses at Largs, where he was in command. Do you know that until about the early eighties, the two biggest clubs in the land, Rangers and Celtic, never sent any of the players or trainers to these courses? Jock Stein felt his club didn't need coaches. And if you've won a European Cup and a whole series of titles and cups, who could argue against that? But the Old Firm were, in fact, blanking out the way the game was developing around the world. But I can tell you when views began to alter. When Jock became Scotland manager, he appointed Andy to help him in Spain in '82 to analyse other teams and help out with the logistics involved in all the day-to-day running of the camps, and he was impressed with what he got from the man. But what added to that, and really altered Jock's view on the Largs set-up, was the day he came down there to hear a lecture given by a Michael Fordham, a lecturer from Bradford University, about the mechanics of football management, and heard a variety of managers gathered there putting in their views, as they actually acted out a model of the daily workings of a club. Jock was absolutely transfixed. He was supposed to stay for a couple of hours. In fact, he stayed for a couple of days. After that, there was a flood of players from all round the country, and Europe, coming down to Largs for their coaching badges, including players from the Old Firm. Andy was at the root of all that.'

There were many, of course, who could easily have answered that 'Andy Who?' query, for we had known him since he had taken Scotland's Under 18 team to win the European Championship title in Finland in 1982. And then a year later we had travelled to Mexico with him and watched him nurse that same squad into the quarter-finals of FIFA's World Championship. It truly was an emotional moment to see him guide his team to a victory over the host nation, in the Azteca, in front of a crowd of 86,582 through a solitary goal by the young Stevie Clarke. And I recall his press conference, after being beaten 1–0 by Poland in the quarter-final, which coolly emphasised the pride he had in his young charges for having got that far in the tournament. So, he had made a positive mark with many of us; a former headmaster in his element among young footballers. And that was that. When people spoke in those terms about his previous achievements, it was almost like damning him with faint praise. That was his particular scene. Ours was ours, with the big boys, the real pros. This was our conventional line of thinking on a man who would find it difficult to avoid the tag of schoolteacher and who had played with Partick Thistle and Falkirk in a modest fashion compared to other more accomplished players in Scottish football.

So, I certainly had my doubts about this elevation. There was an air of the 'lad o' pairts' about him. Someone who had come through the ranks to the top against the odds. But, at that time, it was difficult imagining him with the whiff of cordite in his nostrils, taking on some of the tougher hombres who populated dressing rooms in senior football. Indeed, the impression the more cynical held was that the SFA had opted for a kind of in-house nepotism, since part of the SFA hierarchy at the time was the ebullient Jack Steedman of Clydebank, Roxburgh's uncle. But that kind of reasoning was a kind of debasing talk o' the steamie.

There certainly was little talk about the value of coaching, and certainly scant significance attached to Roxburgh's great success with the younger national sides as a platform for promotion. The reaction was generally about personalities. So, unsurprisingly, the Scottish public were not in a high state of excitement about his elevation and only 35,000 turned up to watch Roxburgh's debut game at Hampden, on 10 September 1986, where the opposition were Bulgaria in the first match of the European Championship qualifiers. There is no need for a spoiler alert on what follows.

It was probably the worst international game I have ever seen. Perhaps the passing of time has added a kind of cynicism to the recollections because, admittedly, I had been a McNeill advocate, a hairy monster fellow traveller in Walker's terms, and I had to subdue the temptation to say to the Scottish public, 'I told you so!'

In a sense, at the end of the goalless draw, with barely a shot at goal of merit in the entire game, the crowd did it for me, by chanting, 'What a load of rubbish!' It was a visceral chant I had never heard at Hampden before. So, when I went to the press conference afterwards, I thought Roxburgh would be blown away. He wasn't. I found myself admiring the articulate way he conceded the reality of that evening. No bland clichés. Ironically, his articulate response, delving into the specific ingredients of the game, like a motor mechanic talking about a breakdown to those who wouldn't know a spark plug from a crankshaft, was actually interpreted by the detractors as proof of their assertions that he was not fit for purpose. 'A load of fanny,' I heard one journalist say as we left the room. And that was it. They were classifying him as a smart-ass technocrat who didn't have it in him to inspire the experienced players he had fielded that night; Davie Cooper, Paul McStay, Gordon Strachan, Richard Gough, just to mention a few of those players who had simply plumbed the depths.

But that view was far from universal. Firstly, came an endorsement from the man who had been expelled from the Mexico venture in 1986 for his alleged nocturnal escapades in Australia. Mo Johnston, the man who was to instigate one of the most controversial periods in Scottish football history by turning his back on his genetic inclination towards green and white and taking on a new hue at Ibrox, who now resides in the less turbulent and congenial climate of Florida, looks back on Roxburgh with great affection for bringing him in from the cold.

'So back in 1989 I get this phone call from a man who introduces himself as "Andy". Honestly, I didn't know who this Andy was, as I was playing in France for Nantes. Honestly. Well, he introduced himself and right at the start said to me "I want to make you my first striker, not just to be in the squad, but my first choice. I've been watching you playing and I like your personality, I'm very impressed." I told him frankly that, because of how I thought I had been treated back home, I wasn't really interested. I just wanted away from all that junk that was talked about me. Well, that didn't put him off. He flew over to see me in Nantes. We went for a long dinner and, listening to him, during it, I realised he was not only the man for me, but for Scotland as well. And I tell you, to this day, I still talk to the man.'

Still, from that first drab game against Bulgaria, to the Rous Cup match against Brazil at Hampden on 26 May 1987, which the visitors won 2–0, Scotland recorded only one win out of seven under Roxburgh, and that victory was against the meekest of the meek, Luxembourg, at Hampden. So, everything seemed drearily familiar, in fact, in the inevitability of Scotland failing to qualify for the European finals. And make no mistake, at that stage, the prospect of reaching another World Cup in Italy in four years' time seemed as remote as Liechtenstein putting a man on the moon. In fact, it took that whole period to work the dire pessimism out of our system. It started with a visit to a sunny Mediterra-

273

nean island that put some badly needed vitamin D into our system.

Cyprus on 8 February 1989, in the town of Limassol, is a day never to be forgotten. Everything we interpret in football and the significance of games in a series is highly subjective. For me, this game was key to Roxburgh's very survival and, hence, one of the most important in the qualifying group, despite the assumption that it would be a formality, or perhaps even because of that assumption. Limassol was the place that could have broken him completely. This game contained all that was still uncertain about his appointment, but, in contrast, the unyielding determination of this man to do things his own way. For, if you had to go by the undercurrent of conversations among the media and the constant griping from some of the public on radio, or on the pages of newspapers, you would have imagined there was always a feeling of imminent revolt within his squad. But, in talking to those who had long experience of working with Roxburgh, there was in fact almost unanimity of respect. Take Roy Aitken of Celtic, whom he eventually appointed captain, and who was one of those players who had come through the mill with him as a stalwart of the U21 side, and was accustomed both to his personality and his methods. He still recognises the different values Roxburgh added to the side.

'His preparation was astonishing. He was the first Scotland manager to use video to good effect. Certainly, Sir Alex had brought a colleague, Brian Hendry, from Aberdeen to Mexico in 1986 to use video in preparation for games, but nothing to the extent that Andy used it. You could easily claim he was the first manager to fully exploit the video camera. In the past, you had to rely on the coach to use his memory to get through to the players. Now they recorded training. Free kicks, corner kicks, all the formations for set pieces. It was all there for us to see. What he did is now common practice around the world of football. Now, of course, there were players and people on the outside who thought his ideas of keeping group harmony, singing songs, watching what we ate, was all kind of school-boyish.'

Anybody studying the match analysis sheet that assistant manager Craig Brown compiled after the Costa Rica game, at Italia90, can see how diligent he and Roxburgh were, well before the introduction of commercially produced and extremely expensive analysis systems used throughout the world now.

Outside of stats, Pat Nevin, who was nurtured in the youth system under Roxburgh, certainly recalls the efforts at bonding, of harmony, of tuneful patriotism.

'He hated "Scotland the Brave". He wanted "Flower of Scotland" to be sung instead. He kept telling us about how passionate the rugby people were singing it at Murrayfield. At the time I didn't know the words, but he had us all singing it before games, eventually with the youths. Now, to some people, that might have sounded kind of naff. But, I tell you, I thought it was a great idea – it got you going. However, in general, there was one thing that I felt was a weakness. It was not in his nature to ask his teams to come out and have a go, to be adventurous. He didn't seem to have that in him.'

Those who did think the bonding stuff was all naff, and there were many around me who did, conveniently over-looked the fact, as they ridiculed it, that the Celtic players did exactly that in the tunnel before they walked on to the pitch in Lisbon in 1967. They sang the club song lustily. Inter ultimately did not consider the men they faced that day had used a school-boyish ploy. And nobody in the media thought that singing was naff that day.

However, on the other side, Alan Rough was one of those who baulked, not to say blanched, at this.

'I just couldn't take to him. I remember in the team bus we were making jokes about Mars Bars. When I think of Andy I think of the Mars Bar.'

Rough is referring to Roxburgh's fondness for advocating the Mars Bar as either the totemic sweet that it is, or as the source of a quick energy burst. Allan Herron of the *Sunday Mail*, himself an admirer of Roxburgh, was perhaps the first outsider to witness this predilection.

'I was in Monaco with the youth side, which Andy was managing. They were in the final of a tournament. We were in this very high-standard hotel and one night we sat down to dinner. The headwaiter then announced that we would all be getting pig trotters for the main course. Andy recoiled. "The boys are not having that stuff." He then left the dining room, went upstairs and came back armed with Mars Bars. So, while I sat having my pig trotters, that night the boys had Mars Bars and peas.'

So, the tabloid press, and some of the experienced players, were less interested in his innovatory thinking on football and more on what they thought were simply faddish irrelevancies. Hugh Keevins, making his way up the journalistic ladder at the time before becoming established at the *Daily Record* and Radio Clyde, welcomed his entry on to the cliché-ridden managerial stage.

'I can't remember a single funny thing Andy ever said. He was just so proper. He was articulate. He couldn't be more helpful and never stood in your way. And he didn't swear. He was entirely different and civilised, and some people just couldn't get that. But perhaps he tried too hard to be correct and be that bit different. I remember when we were in Sweden for the European Championships and, at his first press conference, he started off by saying, "Well, here we are in *Goteberg*," like the Swedes would pronounce it. Twenty-five years later I still wince at that. We were in Gothenburg, as anybody else might have said. He didn't need to appear always to be so correct.'

But Cyprus was special. It was there that Roxburgh did push his preparations to a new level. It was based on what is now known as Aggregated Multiple Gains, or AMG. Psychobabble? Not if you're up to date with coaching, it isn't. For some coaches it's Holy Writ. In simple terms it means that, at the highest level of sport, the difference between winning and losing is down to a single-minded and meticulous focus on little things; minor details that most people might overlook. It was the guiding philosophy of the great British cycling coach Dave Brailsford, whose record in the area was second to none, leaving aside some later medical controversies later attached to him.

In that context, the minor detail, for the preparation for this match, which others might have overlooked, but Roxburgh didn't, was how a stopwatch operates. Time and tide waits for no man, and this was uppermost in his mind.

Firstly, he sent Craig Brown out to Limassol to spend some time there, the week before the game, to study their football. Brown ended up being asked to take training sessions with the local club. It was like sending someone to judge the psyche of sun-drenched players. Roxburgh himself had watched the Cyprus–France match on 22 October 1988, which ended 1–1, and noticed that the Cypriots did not go about things with undue haste. Wasting time seemed to be in their coaching manual.

With all that in mind, Scotland arrived on that island

backed by a media forecasting an easy win. When would we ever learn? For if it hadn't been for the combination of two Old Firm players showing the true grit that came from the many encounters playing against each other, we could have fallen into a pit from which we might not have emerged. Oh, and there was the other thing: the stopwatch. And how it played a part in Roxburgh's game plan. It wasn't his. It was the referee's.

21

A LAST GASP

This was the team the manager decided to play that day:

Leighton,
Gough, Malpas, Narey, McLeish,
Nicol, McStay, Aitken (*captain*), McClair,
Speedie, Johnston.

The pitch was hard, the day was hot, the crowd were fanatical, and with Mo Johnston scoring in only nine minutes when he fastened on to a sloppy pass back by a Cypriot defender, I recall relaxing and waiting for more. But, when I looked at my own watch some time later and found it was fifty-four minutes into the game and had just watched the Cypriots score a second goal to go into a 2–1 lead, that leaden feeling of old – of unintended consequences harming us – began to seep into me. Certainly, I sobered up a little when the continually adventurous Richard Gough scored with a slightly deflected equaliser from eighteen yards seven minutes later. Thereafter, as desperation clearly set in on the park, and the Scottish bench was acting like it was in the first throes of a mental breakdown, the watch by my side seemed almost to be mocking me, as time slipped away.

Craig Brown was painfully aware of that.

'Andy had watched Cyprus playing in their other games, particularly against France, and he noted that they were masters of time-wasting. Even their ball boys were complicit, taking an eternity to put the ball back on to the field. And, true to form, that was happening in front of our very eyes. The players were delaying everything, rolling about on the ground, feigning injury, just stopping the whole flow of play. Time-wasting was just part of their game plan. So, even before the game, Andy had warned the East German referee, Siegfried Kirschen, about this. And I am definitely sure that he got to him at half-time, as well, to stress their time-wasting.'

I could scarcely believe what was happening. The watch was telling me that, with the score at 2–2, we were into five minutes of stoppage time. And the game was still churning on, with Scotland's frantic efforts looking more desperate, but unrewarding. So, there I was, watching what appeared to be a lost cause, and the stats I had kept stored up, but thought I would never have to use, were staring me in the face. Cyprus had played 105 games, won seven, drawn thirteen and lost eighty-five, scored forty-nine and conceded 305. Stats to choke on at that juncture. Then came the cavalry to the rescue, in the shape of two players with the stamp of Old Firm determination about them. Celtic's captain, Roy Aitken, found himself with the ball at his feet after the whistle had gone for a free kick as he realised the final whistle would sound soon, but conscious of the fact that the referee seemed to be adding time to the game.

'Now, I knew that we were well over the time. I could tell

that and, of course, I was pushing forward. Then the referee awarded a free kick to us, out near the corner flag. I just grabbed the ball, put it down and sent in as good a cross as I could.'

Rangers captain, Richard Gough, was prowling in the box and just happened to be as good in the air as any player in world football.

'I thought big Roy was a great player. But I always felt that his best position was central defender and not the kind of holding midfield position he played for Scotland. But the great thing about him is he would never give up. Neither would I. We just kept pounding on. I have to say, when his cross came over, my header for the winner was one of the best I had ever made. The right jump, the right contact. I knew then we had made it.'

So did the Scottish bench, at 3–2, in one of the most extended internationals ever played. The actual overtime ranged in various calculations from seven to nine minutes, so it is no wonder the bench went berserk. However relieved I felt personally about this at the time, I could scarcely credit the ecstatic reaction of Roxburgh and his colleagues on the sidelines, who reacted as if the World Cup itself had been won. It seemed spectacularly excessive. This was Cyprus after all. Not the Olympic stadium in Rome, remember. In retrospect, though, to be absolutely fair, this was a perfectly human reaction to a rescue from impending disaster, and, whatever the quality of the opposition, they had attained a result. But what we couldn't know at the time was what happened in the dressing room, when Craig Brown went to talk to the players.

'I went in there to point out to them that they had to be thankful for how Andy had correctly influenced the referee.

If he hadn't done that, then we would have ended up with maybe only a couple of minutes added. But he had correctly pointed out that the referee had to quantify how much time was being wasted by them. And they were blatant about it, rolling about the pitch as if they were dying, the ball boys taking an eternity to collect loose balls. It was ridiculous. Well, the referee did take all that into account and deserves credit for it.'

Now there was no way anyone in the media could know how accurate this all was, but it was certainly surprising that an East German referee, coming from a sporting ethos which was generally rigid and formal, could have been so compliant as to pay heed to the warnings of a foreign football manager. However, there were some in that dressing room who didn't take kindly to Brown's endorsement of Roxburgh's manoeuvres. One was Stevie Nicol of Liverpool, who obviously disliked Roxburgh and couldn't approve of what he thought were his headmasterish bonding ideas, and certainly took umbrage at what he thought was Brown implying that the manager had won the Cyprus game for them. It was surprising that he would take exception to Brown, as he was an Ayrshire friend of Stevie through Willie McLean, who nurtured him at Ayr United before selling him for a club record fee to Liverpool. But, Nichol later made it clear in his autobiography that he was offended by Brown's appreciation of that reasoning, and facetiously reminded the public that he could have sworn Gough scored the winning goal, not Roxburgh.

Yes, but seven minutes into stoppage time! It was a comment that incensed Brown, as he knew it was being taken out of context by a man who had a list of grievances to make about the manager anyway, ranging from allowing supporters into watching training sessions, to insisting on card games on long trips, and that, under his leadership, the SFA put considerations for the likes of accommodation for officials before that of the players. If he was ever to meet up with Martin Buchan and listen to his tales of Argentina, he would realise that it wasn't Roxburgh who first instigated the SFA's insensitive hierarchical arrangements. And, as Brown also points out about Nicol, he missed one of the easiest and perhaps most crucial of chances against Uruguay in 1986, the inference being that players ought to be cautious about dispensing criticism.

But the most startling paradox of all was embodied in the figure of Richard Gough, who had scored two goals, including that dramatic winner. He himself was aware of the irony.

'I wasn't getting on at all well with Mr Roxburgh at the time. We had had our disagreements and he did show that at the end. When he talked to the press afterwards, all he said about the goal was that it was a great cross from Roy Aitken. He didn't mention me.'

The press were generally aware of that animosity. Gough was now part of a Rangers team laying the foundations for their eventual nine-in-a-row run. Under the powerful personality of Graeme Souness, he clearly saw the football world through different lenses. And as Rangers were then the dominant force in Scottish football, led by a man of powerful personality, perhaps Gough found it awkward to make the transition to Roxburgh's measured mentality and who, at that time, was playing him at right back. At Rangers, he was a leader who played centre back, his favoured position. So, he was the proverbial square peg in a round hole as far as the Scotland manager was concerned, although Gough denies the other allegation that was sometimes aired about his apparent unease with Roxburgh.

'I was captain of Rangers. Roy Aitken was captain of Scotland. That never arose as an issue with me. I had great respect for Roy. He was captain and that was that. But yes, I preferred playing central defence and that is where I wanted to play for Scotland.'

Roxburgh was fully aware, though, that whatever misgivings he had about Gough as a nonconformist, his quality of play was indispensable to their progress at World Cup level. And, indeed, Gough got a better press after Cyprus than Roxburgh did, even though he had successfully pressurised the referee. As Alan Davidson wrote in the Glasgow *Evening Times*, 'The Swiss precision of a stopwatch couldn't camouflage the frailties,' but went on to say of Gough, 'His leap and timing to get on the end of Roy Aitken's free kick was classic.' And the *Glasgow Herald* encapsulated the general mood with, 'Fans suffer as Scots flirt with lasting shame', although, on its front page, it highlighted what occurred after the game. 'Scots Victory Provokes Riot'. Not among the Scottish press, of course, although some had begun to feel like that, but among the locals who didn't take too kindly to the East German referee's concept of the passing of time. They threw stones and bottles at the players coming off the field and had to be forced back from the stadium front doors by security police, as they tried to invade the dressing room area, where sat a shivering East German referee, who, by that stage, was beginning to think that life on this side of the Berlin Wall was not so attractive after all. Roxburgh himself was equally perplexed, and baffled that the media were almost ridiculing his claims of his Svengali-like control over the referee. Roy Aitken defends him stoutly.

'If you're going to credit Alex Ferguson and Jock Stein with a psychological approach to putting one over the opposition, then you've got to credit Andy as well. For look what happened in Gothenburg when Aberdeen were in the Cup-Winners final. Fergie had invited Jock as a guest. The night before the game, Jock took Fergie aside and gave him a bottle of whisky and told him to let Real get on the training pitch first. And then said, "When Di Stefano comes off the pitch, present him with the whisky as a gift from Aberdeen. He'll go away thinking you're just a wee team from Scotland not worth bothering about. That you're inferior to them. They'll start thinking it's going to be easy." I tell you, don't dismiss the tiniest details. They all might add up to something.'

And they say the world of quantum physics is difficult to comprehend! Mind games have their own mysteries. But against his critics, Roxburgh was armed with robust statistics. For Scotland, under him, now had five points from a possible six and were in a strong position to qualify from their group, particularly if they were to beat France in their next game at Hampden on 8 March 1989. Despite being managed by the great Michel Platini, the French had been underperforming. They had flair without punch; style without substance. They had gained only three points from three games. They needed to win in Glasgow, although they were plagued by injuries that had taken some experienced men out of the reckoning. In keeping with the importance of the occasion and the significance of this fixture, Roxburgh had chosen Gleneagles Hotel for their base for this game, which in itself drew criticism for a decision of unnecessary extravagance on the SFA's part. Those who had travelled with Scotland around the world and had experienced some of the Fawlty Towers the players had been housed in abroad applauded this decision, though, as a sign of elevated thinking. If rich golfers could stay there, so could professional footballers. But they had an initial problem on the day of the game: the weather. Rain moved in from the Atlantic with a vengeance.

Nobody gave that much of a thought at first, until the afternoon they set out for Glasgow from the hotel. They were not far down the road when they came across a huge traffic jam. An accident had occurred which might possibly have been caused by flooding. Whatever, they were stuck, jammed in, with little prospect of a breakthrough. Time dragged on as they sat there with the gnawing thought that they could be in big trouble getting to Hampden in time. Panic began to set in. Nowadays you can hardly see a pro without his ear to a phone of sorts. This was long before the age of the ubiquitous SIM card. They were perplexed. Then came the solution: Roy Aitken suddenly remembered he was technologically ahead of his colleagues.

'We were all really starting to worry about this when something occurred to me. I don't know why I hadn't thought of it at first. Maybe because I wasn't accustomed to that kind of thinking. But I remembered I had a phone. It was one of the first mobiles. It was as big as a brick with an antenna sticking from it. But where was it? I realised I had left it in my own luggage in the compartment under the bus. I remember the scramble I had to get out of the bus and get into the luggage compartment. It was frantic. Everybody was on edge. Then I got it. The first thing was to phone for the police to come and help us. We got through, but waited and waited with hardly any movement in the traffic. Then they came. From then on we got a police escort all the way to Hampden.'

The Scottish international team, about to play against their toughest opponents, arrived at the stadium exactly thirty minutes before kick-off. No time for a proper warm-up. No time for a decent calm team talk. No time to sample the atmosphere. Straight into it. And they went for the French from the start like men possessed, watched by a relieved Craig Brown on the bench.

'It was astonishing the way they leapt into the game. They had no time to think about what they were about to do. They were all over the French from the very start. It seemed to be counter to everything we believe in for preparation for a match. It is to their great credit that they responded to the emergency facing them. It was a great performance.'

The players were:

Leighton,
Gough, Malpas, Gillespie, McLeish (*captain*),
Nicol, McStay, Aitken, Ferguson,
McCoist, Johnston.

Mo Johnston, who was to arise from a muddy pitch as the hero on a horrendously wet and windy night, felt that the late arrival was actually to his benefit.

'I would never stretch all that much before a game anyway. I would deal with the hamstrings first then just kick the ball about. That was it. So, all the fuss about getting there late didn't affect me.'

His two goals, the first revealing the quickness of thought to tame the ball with one foot then sweep it away with the other, surrounded by thrusting legs, and the second with a header assisted by the inability of their keeper, Joel Bats, to deal with a ball like a piece of slippery soap, underlined the value of the mutual admiration relationship that had developed between Roxburgh and striker. Never had that *haute cuisine* French meal with a footballer meant so much to a manager. For, on the other hand, the French had played some immaculate football and met a resilient Scottish goalkeeper in Leighton, leading to Platini telling us afterwards, 'In all the years I have been playing and watching France away from home, I have never seen us have so many chances to score. But we did not, and I cannot understand why.' Neither could I, for I thought the lavish praise heaped on the side by the Scottish press for this performance was as excessive as the cynicism they had applied to the stopwatch affair in Cyprus. I was in the minority, to be honest. We had, nevertheless, beaten the side we imagined might be our biggest stumbling block, and the predominant thought was that, even with three games left, after beating Cyprus 2–1 at Hampden in the return game the following month, we were effectively through. After all, we were now top of the group unbeaten, although in that last disappointing and frustrating Cyprus game, the crowd went home only satisfied that the 50,081 attendance had boosted the coffers of the Hillsborough Disaster Fund.

We were top of the pile. It looked good. Almost inevitable. A single point was all that was required to qualify, with three games to acquire it. There was predictable hype about that. A cinch. Then a 3–1 defeat in Yugoslavia on 6 September, which contained perhaps the neatest and briefest example of our tendency to self-destruct, with two own goals, one by Nicol in the first half and Gillespie in the second, felt like the screaming of brakes on our momentum. Then losing 3–0 in Paris a month later to France, who played the last half hour with only ten men, reminded us Scots, borne on the wave of burgeoning confidence once again, that there were only two things certain in life: death and taxes, as Benjamin Franklin once said.

The evening of 15 November 1989 at Hampden, against

Norway, will be remembered, with little real affection, for two goals of wildly contrasting effect on our emotions. The first, only a minute before half-time suggested we could look out our Italian phrase books. But the man who scored the first remembers both goals and talks about them like he is talking about a near-death experience. His name, Ally McCoist.

'I remember it like yesterday,' he told me, sounding like a man who had been shorn of the cares of management at Ibrox and was back to his basic, ebullient self. 'My goal was one of my best. There was a long clearance from Maurice Malpas, over the top of the Norwegian defence. I just gambled and got on to it. Erland Johnsen couldn't catch me. The keeper was the big Spurs man Erik Thorstvedt, and I could see he thought he was going to get to the ball. But I got to it just in front of him and lobbed him. I knew we were on a collision course and that was what it had to be. And when we did, all I can remember was watching to see if the ball would bounce up and go over the bar or into the net. It felt like an eternity before I knew it was in the net.'

Listening to him talk about what was a magnificently taken opportunity cast the mind back to those other moments that effectively propelled us into the other World Cups. Joe Jordan's goal against Czechoslovakia at Hampden in 1973. Kenny Dalglish's clinching second goal in the game against Wales at Anfield in 1977. John Robertson's penalty for Scotland's second goal against Sweden at Hampden in 1981 and Davie Cooper's penalty in Cardiff in 1985 – all still reverberate with the sense of conclusion, of triumph, of ascendency. McCoist's goal, on the other hand, in retrospect, is almost squeezed out of the recollections by the absurdity of the ending, which we watched in a state of disbelief and shock – rather like, as an innocent bystander, coming across someone jumping off a bridge when you could do nothing to stop them, and all in slow motion. For Norway scored, not only in the final minute, to make it 1–1, but with a ludicrous goal that simply compounded the agony of the spectacle. Johnsen, their defender, drove the ball goalward from all of forty yards. Leighton seemed mesmerised by its flight and, to the astonishment of even the Norwegian defender, the ball eluded the keeper and ended, as if in afterthought, in the net. McCoist, like all his teammates, froze at the sight.

'I couldn't believe it. Honestly, Jim should have saved the shot. I know we only needed the point. But just think, if they scored again we were out. Can you imagine? I thought, we could be facing the worst of all Scotland's debacles. That's what went through my mind at the time. Then I thought of the referee. How much time was left?' There were 63,987 on the terracings and ten other Scottish players were thinking exactly the same, as Hampden collectively seemed to hold its breath. Afterwards, Alex McLeish admitted the same to me in a much quainter way, 'I was just praying the referee wouldn't add on any "Cyprus time".'

He didn't need to. The game was stopped two minutes into stoppage time. Hardly anybody gave pause for thought. After all, we had qualified. But it had taken Scotland three games to muster that one point, and they still almost botched it. Then, on 16 May 1990, only a few weeks before the opening World Cup game, Scotland were beaten 3–1 by Egypt in a friendly at Pittodrie. The fact that they had scored three own goals in a couple of games suggested that Hannibal crossing the Alps with his elephants had a less harrowing time reaching Italy than Roxburgh had with his less predictable humans.

22

DOMESTIC DILEMMAS

When you walk into the Stadio Luigi Ferraris in Genoa, you feel very much at home. It's not vast. Intimate. Modern. Pleasing on the eye. Enclosed within the bustling, crowded, noisy city, as if it was a comfort zone. You felt you could reach out and touch the players. It reminded me of the original Dortmund stadium of 1974. On the afternoon of 11 June 1990, watching Andy Roxburgh walk on to the field an hour or so before kick-off to an affectionate response from the large Scottish contingent in the 30,867 crowd, who did not seem to have been muted by the drinks ban which had been implemented throughout the city on the day of the game, he looked as if kick-off couldn't come quickly enough for him.

Within the media areas, there was certainly admiration for the man's achievement in reaching this point. But it ranged, dishearteningly in many ways, from the grudging to the simply respectful. Nobody had been carried away to the point of adulation. Looking back to his predecessors in the same role, I still felt around me a reluctance to fully buy into the prospect of his achieving a first for us in qualifying for the later stages. The importance and the imminence of the occasion simply concentrated minds on the uniqueness of a man who, at this exalted level, had not only a great deal to prove about himself, but also had to justify Ernie Walker's revolutionary decision to create a new mould of management. It was almost as if he was still seen by many as a trialist rather than a fully fledged figure of authority.

He certainly could claim to have special affection for the city. Roxburgh told me long before the opening game that, when he had been a special assistant to Jock Stein, they had travelled together to Genoa to see Graeme Souness play for Sampdoria. When their car reached the city centre, Stein had turned to him and asked him if he would like to take over his job from him some time in the future, as he, Stein, could not go on forever. He admitted he was flattered by that suggestion, but had put it to the back of his mind. Now here he was in the same city, suddenly seized by the immensity of his task and bemused by the quirks of historical coincidence. In practical terms, he had to make only one adjustment from his ideal squad he had based his planning on. In Malta on 28 May for a warm-up game that produced a hugely underwhelming 2–1 victory, Davie Cooper received an injury in training which put him out of the reckoning. At the time, given the resources he had at his disposal, it was not considered crippling, but, in light of subsequent events, the man of mercurial one-footed talent was to be badly missed. When I talked to Gary McAllister, the future Scotland captain, about the World Cup in France, he deviated for a moment to talk about that injury.

'Do not underestimate the loss to the squad of Davie. His skill would have been a standout at this level. I would have just loved to have seen him in action. What a shame.'

Here is the squad which reached the portals of the splendiferous Hotel Bristol sitting on a hill in the middle of the Italian Riviera town, Rapallo, their base for the tournament.

Jim Leighton (Manchester United) Age 31/Caps 55, Alex McLeish (Aberdeen) 31/69, Roy Aitken (Newcastle Utd, **captain**) 31/53, Richard Gough (Rangers) 28/49, Paul McStay (Celtic) 25/46, Maurice Malpas (Dundee Utd) 27/34, Mo Johnston (Rangers) 27/33, Jim Bett (Aberdeen) 30/24, Ally McCoist (Rangers) 27/23, Murdo MacLeod (Borussia Dortmund) 31/14, Gary Gillespie (Liverpool) 29/ 11, Andy Goram (Hibernian) 26/9, Gordon Durie (Chelsea) 24/6, Alan McInally (Bayern Munich) 27/7, Craig Levein (Hearts) 25/5, Stuart McCall (Everton) 25/5, Stewart McKimmie (Aberdeen) 27/ 4, John Collins (Hibernian) 22/4, Dave McPherson (Hearts) 26/ 4, Gary McAllister (Leicester City) 25/3, Robert Fleck (Norwich City) 24/1, Bryan Gunn (Norwich City) 26/1.

On 6 June, it was heartening to see the smartly suited squad enter the luxurious Bristol Hotel in Rapallo on the Italian Riviera, which had been designed for the industrial oligarchs of Milan and Turin, to ease the pain of making so much money, and doing so in some splendour. Roxburgh was now under the closest scrutiny he had ever experienced from the moment he had stepped on Italian soil. So were the players; all of whom must have been aware that, in the past, the media had reported, and also plundered, even the slightest deviation from the norm.

'Perfecto,' the wine-waiter replied when I asked him how he felt the Scottish players were behaving in this opulent setting, with only days to go now to the opening game with Costa Rica, who would be playing for the first time in the finals. In the World Cup draw in Rome in the Palazzetto

293

dello Sport on 9 December 1989, Scotland had been drawn with the Central Americans, Sweden and, once again, Brazil. The entirely predictable thinking was that if we could beat the highly competent Swedes and perhaps scrape something against Brazil, which we had achieved in Frankfurt in 1974, then we'd go through, with the emphasis on the Sweden game. Hardly anybody I knew at the time thought any differently. Costa Rica? They had qualified out of the Confederation of North, Central American and Caribbean Association Football (CONCACAF) group on goal difference from the USA. A pool of mediocrity, as we thought, and we started to look up exotic facts about the country to slip in colourfully, when appropriate. I gleaned that they exported many bananas, so I kept that up my sleeve, as in the belittling phrase 'Banana Republic'. But, more tellingly, those words never came anywhere near being used in that opening game.

The players were no strangers to the area. Months before, Roxburgh, in typical thoroughness, had taken the entire squad out to Rapallo to give them a feel for their surroundings; the hotel, the town, the training facilities. He even arranged for them to go to the local Genoa derby match between Sampdoria and Genoa to be introduced to the crowd. They were led by Joe Jordan, who had been appointed SFA Liaison Officer. Jordan did his duty for his country that day with his competent use of the Italian he had picked up by playing in that country. He milked it to such an extent that the Scotland players, introduced to the crowd, one by one, were no longer aliens to the locals, but most probably had their backing from then on. AMG, as they say in coaching circles.

At the head of the party was the new Chief Executive of the SFA, Jim Farry. He had requested exclusivity in the Bristol for the entire period of the first group game, and had naturally been turned down since, had the hotel agreed, it might have ended up in litigation for them with Fiat executives for breach of promise, given their penchant for the quiet weekend there, illicit or otherwise. So Scotland had to share the facilities with a public who were certainly not from the great unwashed, and where this waiter I had been quizzing was more often engaged in dropping ice cubes into tall cocktail glasses than pulling tall pints. Elegant figures could be seen draping themselves about the glittering pool in contrast to hairy legs in training shorts lopping through thickly carpeted corridors. Civilised, you would agree. Except for those of us sensitised to the weaknesses of footballers in past World Cups, who were as resistant to certain temptations as iron filings are to a magnet, this possible clash of cultures seemed like a kind of shotgun wedding that could end in tears.

Then there was the fact that Farry, in his efforts to cultivate a good relationship with the fans, who knew very little about him, except that the press had placed great emphasis on the fact that his first job in life had been as a gardener, in an unprecedented decision, opened up an office for the Tartan Army inside the hotel. It had allowed them to pop in and mix with the players whenever convenient. Brave, to the point of being foolhardy, given that we had seen, as far back as Argentina, that fans are as fickle as the Scottish weather.

However, that was the old cynicism surfacing again. For, on the evidence to hand, it appeared, from all that we could see and hear, that on this occasion the SFA had got it exactly right. This locale made some of the other World Cup bases seem like gulags. So, the new man Farry seemed to be eager to please and accommodating to everyone in front of a scrutinising media, aware that Ernie Walker would be a hard act to follow. At that juncture, Farry was immensely communicative with the media. In later career, when the cares of office seemed to overwhelm him, he adopted the persona of the hard-faced apparatchik, which, for some reason, he thought suited the post. At a Football Awards dinner some years later, I watched him at the top table as Andy Cameron, the Scottish comedian, had the punters rolling in the aisles with his quick-fire, witty repartee. Not one twitch of amusement appeared on Farry's face throughout, which resembled one of these immoveable facades at Mount Rushmore. For the life of me, I couldn't understand why, since, in coming across him after he had retired, I found him to be a warm and engaging personality.

Hugh Keevins, who interviewed him frequently, agrees. 'That hard public face was completely different in private. He could be the most charming and amusing of men.'

As for Roxburgh, you thought that he had reached his nirvana. In his adoration of Italy as one of the sacred areas of football, and delight at the genial nature of the people around this area, it made his pious pronouncements on this environment sound like a pilgrim about to embark on the Stations of the Cross. He had cause to be complimentary. The Rapallo town council had spent £300,000 (a substantial amount in 1990) on relaying the pitch in the training area close to the hotel, so delighted were they to have the Scots among them.

Because of this, those players who had been over the World Cup course before, like Roy Aitken, were kindly disposed to the manager and his efforts to establish the right kind of creature comforts.

'Andy loved a meeting. We used to say that he would call a meeting to discuss having another meeting. But hey, it broke up the day. And let's not forget the choice of this hotel was down to Andy and nobody else. You'll remember Mexico. We were in bloody cells. I had to while away the time on my single cell with my headphones on. It was soul destroying. Now we were in a place with the best atmosphere, the best food, the best accommodation. It was up to us now.'

But the media were falling into a pre-opening game rut. Headlines of note were few. Our interviews with players and manager sounded like retreads of those from 1974. We were trapped in cliché canyon, albeit painlessly, since the Italian Riviera has time-honoured ways to soothe even the savage breast. But then we heard news that was almost like being touched by a cattle prod, such was the tedium of repetitive press conferences. Wallace Mercer was about to invade Rapallo.

Even in the midst of preparations for the biggest sporting tournament in the world, that news made us feel like kids being told the circus was coming to town. The owner of Hearts was a self-confident successful entrepreneur who had improved the status of his club, but could have been called, at the time, football's chief exponent of megaphone diplomacy, with a booming style that greatly pleased newspaper editors. Find Wallace and you would find a great quote. His coming to the World Cup could have been a blessing. Well, it was. For, on the very day the Scottish team arrived in the Bristol, the Scottish newspapers were seized by other sporting news: his bid to effectively put Hibernian Football Club out of business. The *Glasgow Evening Times* had a front page splash of 'Hibs Say No To Sale' and added a quote from the chairman, David Duff, who said the bid was 'wholly unacceptable'. The Hearts chairman had bid 40p a share, which would initially value Hibs at £6.1 million, but taking Hibs' debts into account, would rise to about £13 million. But, leaving aside the finances, it would mean the immediate selling-off of Easter Road, and the demise of a club which, despite its ups and downs, had seemed as permanent a feature of our landscape as Arthur's Seat. So, this person coming into our midst, when nothing was really happening, was a godsend to some.

He was always called Wallace familiarly by the media, which reflected how much he had ingratiated himself to the Fifth Estate. Some even referred to him as the Great Waldo. Some supporters called him a Fat Tory Bastard (amongst other things), which was not the most surprising epithet used. Here was the great controversialist, and indeed highly successful footballing impresario, coming among us with a plan that, to anybody from outside the parochial clutches of Edinburgh, might have seemed eminently sensible. Make the capital a one-club city. That was the way forward to survive at the highest level. Needless to say, the Leith side of the city regarded this as the act of a vandal. They were fighting back. Wallace needed to keep the media on his side. So, given his craving for publicity and his skilful manipulation of the press, he decided to make a pitch to their elite who were, of course, in Italy for the World Cup. With typical grandiloquence, he invited them to a lunch in the very sophisticated narrow inlet of Portofino, which nature had hewn out of the rocks for the benefit of celebrities to berth their yachts beside some of the most celebrated and expensive restaurants in Italy. Rod Stewart had preceded him, for example, and nestled occasionally in one of its howffs during the tournament. The press were more interested in the Hearts man, though. Naturally, those invited by Wallace did not decline. It was there he expounded on the virtues of his initiative. The booze flowed, and so did his charm offensive. He had one objective, which he admitted to Brian Scott of the *Daily Mail*, whose son was a Hearts supporter, when he said: 'Tell the lad it won't be Edinburgh United or anything like that. The club will be called Hearts.'

Not surprisingly, others were on the hunt for him. The supporters of Easter Road, that is. There was no way he was getting out of their clutches. They took their fight to the streets of Genoa and Turin. Frank Dougan, a leading figure in the Hibernian Supporters Association, and a computer manager with British Telecom at the time, organised a party of twenty in a motorcade to travel to Italy to mount their own protest against Mercer.

'We were going to support Scotland, like I had done in all the other World Cups, but this time it was with another purpose. Twenty of us went. There would have been more, but some of the supporters wanted to stay behind and use their money to buy shares in Hibs to try and stop the take-over. And decided to spend their time canvassing around Edinburgh for backing. Now, since I had first been taken to a Hibs game at the age of eighteen months, I was enraged about what was happening. We packed the cars with T-shirts, hundreds of them, with 'HANDS OFF HIBS' on them, and a large banner saying the same. What a reception we got. It was marvellous. We were even getting support from Hearts fans out there. And the World Cup authorities allowed us into the games after we explained what the banner stood for. We took out hundreds of pens so that folk could write support for our petition, and hundreds of leaflets. Only one person refused. And it became so successful we had to get new leaflets photocopied in Italy itself. It was inspiring. Now we were aware that some supporters out there gave Wallace

299

a hard time. But it wasn't us. The instructions were to behave, or else Wallace would gain from any bad publicity. We went to all three games. And it was strange to be out supporting Scotland and fighting for your own club at the same time. And, as you know, we won.'

Many in the media and within the official party thought this was an almost unseemly sideshow to the World Cup. However, although we didn't wholly recognise it at the time, we were in the initial phase of one of the most turbulent periods in Scottish football, in which the national side's hold on the country's psyche began to look distinctly wobbly, as club football gained more traction with the public. Indeed, the passing of time has shown that it was the World Cup itself that was the sideshow. For it wasn't just Wallace's presence, and the salt-of-the-earth reaction by the Hibs supporters in Italy that was an intimation that all was not well back home, while we pursued our dream. Consider what was happening just around the corner from Portofino, in the Scottish camp in the Bristol, at the same time. A controversy had hit Jim Farry. Mo Johnston was refusing to be interviewed by anybody from ITV, including those from STV, whom he knew well.

Johnston's instructions had come directly from Ibrox. It was the product of Graeme Souness's feud with STV, whose cameras had spotted him in February of that year standing at the tunnel at Ibrox being able to pass on instructions to the players, which was a flaunting of the ban that had been placed on him for other misdemeanours. Souness, who thought they had acted in an underhand way, banned his players from dealing in any form with STV and clearly wanted to carry the vendetta to Italy. The head of ITV, Bob Burrows, found himself unable to solve this and was discovering that the SFA could be rendered impotent in certain circumstances.

For even though ITV had paid money into the players' financial pool, no Rangers players went anywhere near their microphones.

So, as Andy Roxburgh and his staff were in their final preparations for the first game, a proxy battle, centring on Scottish football, was about to be fought out under a Mediterranean sun within the precincts of a World Cup. On the one hand, there was the battle to save Hibs, which basically was a resistance to naked financial aggression aimed at destroying community identity. And, on the other, Rangers, defiantly resisting the overtures of the SFA over these days, were merely reflecting their ambition to be independent and succeed in Europe with scant regard to what it did for the national effort. And Celtic, from about then, began to appreciate the impact that the David Murray/Souness nexus had made in the game, and would eventually be forced into copying their acquisition policy, the landmark being the day in September 2001 when Martin O'Neill became Celtic's first manager to field an entirely non-Scottish side in the league.

Contrast all that with the background to Scotland's presence in the World Cup Germany in 1974, on the back of the miners' strike, and the winter of discontent. That had been the first sign of the destruction of the mining industry, which had embryonic connections with much in Scottish football. Now, sixteen years later, with the industry in its final death throes, the native growth of the game, of which the miners' row was one of its symbols, had been replaced by a new model that was merely a reflection of the era of Thatcherism. David Murray and Wallace Mercer were effectively swashbuckling predators imbued with the sense of entitlement that the age seemed to offer them, and however appreciative their supporters were for the various triumphs they respectively

301

acquired, had indulged in business ventures that would speed their clubs towards extinction, although in their different ways, to be saved by fan loyalty. So, over those past sixteen years, as we had battled to reach the various World Cups, in Italy in June 1990, we were now on the crest of a wave which would transform a stable and orthodox footballing society into something approaching that of the social values of a Las Vegas casino.

23

THIRD WORLD TORMENT

Meanwhile, a side had to be picked for the Costa Rica game. It would not be true to say that the Scottish camp was a cesspool of intrigue over team selection. There was obvious discussion, but none of the agonising that had gone on in Mexico over one man, Souness, for that last game. And the presence among the coaches of Alan Hansen, who was allowed to join in all the team talks, was a reminder that they were free of the intrigue that had consumed a lot of attention about Hansen's and his good friend Kenny Dalglish's absences in the previous World Cup. It looked as if it would be fairly straightforward, until voices from outside were heard.

Alex Ferguson, straight from winning his first FA Cup, could not contain himself. He made a public claim for Jim Leighton to be unassailably the first-choice keeper. Such a declaration seemed at odds with his dramatic decision to drop the same man for the FA Cup Final replay against Crystal Palace only a month prior to Scotland's opening game. It was a decision that crushed Leighton. He only played one more game for the club, a League Cup tie at Halifax. More pertinently, it must have affected a confidence that had previously been badly dented by some of his performances in the group games, including conceding that ropey goal against Norway. And there was that rising star in the east coming into focus. Andy Goram was excelling for Hibs. A shot-stopper *par excellence*. Many in the media felt it was now his time. Roxburgh didn't. There was another decision that shocked one man in particular, even though that man, Ally McCoist, was painfully aware of how contentious selections in these circumstances can be.

'I remember Sir Alex phoned Jock Wallace, my manager at the time at Rangers, to tell him he wouldn't be picking me to go to Mexico. The big man went spare and slammed Fergie on the phone. He didn't hold back. I have to say, Sir Alex would probably have given as good as he got. So, it's tough for managers. Now this time I felt reasonably confident that I would be picked for the first game. Mo Johnston and I had struck up a great partnership in the qualifiers. He got six. I got two. And I had scored in that friendly against Egypt. I was feeling fine. I was really hopeful. Well, Andy decided he would meet the different players separately to tell them his pick. He would take the goalkeepers on their own, then the defenders, then the midfield players, then the forwards, and tell them who he was going to play. So, I turned up with the other four strikers and Andy spoke. Now believe you me, this is what happened. He started to talk. He said, as I thought, "We'll play Mo and Ally up front." My heart leapt. People would have seen the look on my face. But, in fact, what he had really said was, "We'll play Mo and Nally up front." He was meaning Alan McInally, but using that "Nally" which, honestly, I had never heard used before. So, while I was showing great pleasure in the announcement, I could see the look on Craig Brown's face. He was obviously thinking to himself, "Fuck me, Coisty's taking it helluva well." For the first three minutes of the team talk, I think I'm playing. Then the penny dropped. I hadn't been picked. I was devastated. Including Craig leaving me out of the '98 squad, these have been the two biggest disappointments in my career as a player. Believe me, I still feel the pain.'

If not exactly devastated, his Rangers club mate, Mo Johnston, was slightly disconcerted.

'We had been working well in the qualifiers and, of course, at Ibrox we had been running in the goals. And you know I like playing with strikers who are like me. Quick on the uptake, fast, can snatch a goal. That's why I got on so well with Ally.'

In fact, in the eighty-two times they were on the field together in league football, Johnston had scored forty-one and McCoist forty. Almost a goal a game.

In talking to Johnston, it was clear that he had nothing against McInally, but you felt he was not overjoyed at missing out on his Ibrox mate. Nevertheless, Roxburgh must have anticipated that there would be some astonishment down Ibrox way. In this instance, it perhaps illustrates what Pat Nevin said to me about Roxburgh and the hard choices.

'Both Andy and Craig Brown were both brave enough to be different. And I do know Andy realised there were players who simply couldn't take to him, and he knew they never would. Indeed, in one game, I was on the bench and, during it, Andy came and told this very senior player beside me to go on. He refused. Point-blank. I couldn't believe it. I ended up having a right row with this man for refusing to go out and play for his country. I'm sorry I can't tell you his name. And no, it wasn't Goughie.'

The man he had chosen in front of Ally, Alan McInally,

was with Bayern. He was a man I got to know well as a co-commentator on European matches and appreciated his firm grasp of the modern game. He had also scored the two goals against Malta in the last match. So, he was the form man, you could say. But he was an entirely different type from Ally. Tall, strong, pacy and powerful in the air, it is that quality which Ally is still convinced swayed Roxburgh's choice.

'What we believe is that the Costa Rica manager had written an article saying that he was worried about the height of the Scottish team and their pace and power in the air. We felt that is what influenced Andy when he either read about it or heard about it. It could have been a double bluff by their manager. You never know. We were also told that their keeper was suspect in the air. That must have been part of the management's thinking. A big part. Anyway, I got on well with big Alan. We were rooming together. Alan hadn't played in any of the qualifiers and I had, and he's picked in front of me. So, I hear him coming into my room later that night and I pretend not to be caring about all this and doing some crossword lying on my bed and he says to me with a straight face, "Get that light aff, some of us in this room will be needing a good sleep tonight." I had to laugh.'

Who could not spare a laugh was Ally's boot sponsor, which had had a newly designed kangaroo-skin pair of boots made for this special occasion. Leaving aside what wildlife protectionists might have thought of this, Ally and they had looked forward to a triumphant baptism of the boots from Oz. The birth, though, had been aborted. As we approached the Stadio Luigi Ferraris in Genoa, after driving through the astonishing linkage of tunnels which had been burrowed out of the majestic mountainous coastline, the general feeling was that they would give McInally a run up front after all, and that the tried, but barely trusted, Leighton would cling to his place. In any case, before an opening World Cup game of this sort, you are never going to do anything other than give a Scottish manager the benefit of the doubt. But, for the writing of this book, Ally asked me to read out the team that was fielded that June afternoon in Genoa, to refresh his memory. I did.

'Leighton, Gough, McLeish, Aitken, McPherson, Malpas, McStay, Bett, McCall, Johnston, McInally.'

'My God,' he replied. 'How could that team lose to Costa Rica?'

I sat there on the commentary platform initially with another feeling of discomfort – which had little to do with team selection. The game against Costa Rica I was about to cover would not be transmitted live by BBC Scotland. We were to offer it as recorded highlights later that evening. When you are about to commentate on a sporting occasion of this magnitude and know that your efforts will not be immediately heard, it's a bit as if you have been asked to drive a Rolls Royce, but not actually handed the keys to do so. The necessary and productive tension that comes with broadcasting live is diluted. You are never sure what is eventually going to be transmitted. The reason for this was a decision by BBC London again. They had tossed a coin with ITV for selection of games, and won. They chose coverage of England's two games in their group, which meant, in balance, that STV could pick up the Costa Rica and Brazil games live. The Sweden match would be ours exclusively. Thanks for nothing, London, we thought at the time. So, our direct competitor had the advantage on us 2–1. We were not amused. However, as things turned out, they were handed a game that, I imagine, left people around the country wishing to throw any object to hand at the screen.

Fortunately, I was to leave a live, steadily unfolding disaster to others to cope with. Unfortunately, in editing the version for night, there was nothing they could do to alter the events of a 1–0 defeat. I remember, when I finished that day I thought of what the producers of *All Quiet on the Western Front* had told Louis B. Mayer, head of MGM, when he disliked the hero of the film, a German, being shot dead by a sniper, and demanded a happier ending. They had to point out that, for a happier ending, they would have to make Germany win the First World War. The disbelief at what happened to us in Genoa almost turned me into a crazed Louis B. Mayer demanding that we bury all this in a sly edit, hiding our shame from the world, and cutting out the hired Costa Rican sniper called Cayasso, the man who floored us with the only goal of the game. It was barely believable from a country that had only slipped into these finals by the narrowest of margins.

At first, all seemed like it would all unfold in a logical way. In the first ten minutes of the game, I thought back to when Zaire trod the turf in Dortmund in 1974, an unknown quantity. There they had come out like frisky newcomers to the game of football itself, let alone playing in the World Cup finals. Costa Rica, you could tell, were entirely different. Apart from any structure they had, which was certainly a scale up from that of those African first-timers, they had a more organised look about them. But individually they looked entirely comfortable on the ball. They were essentially Latin; that is, they played with an ease at times which was derivative of what you could see in any South American, or

Mediterranean country, although certainly not at any exalted level. They had played their football in the CONCACAF area. CONCACAF was to us, at that time, merely an acronym for mediocre, lightweight football.

However, since Roxburgh's major trait was meticulous preparation, the Scottish players were certainly clued up on this opposition, as Mo Johnston makes clear.

'Oh, we knew all about them. But look, let's get this straight. We should have won that game. Easy enough to say now, of course. But don't forget I hit the bar and the post about three or four times in the game. So, I blame myself. I should have scored at least a couple of goals that day.'

It was perhaps ominous that the Scottish subs picked the wrong bench before kick-off and had to be shooed away to their own roost. It was neatly symbolic of a day in which everything seemed misplaced. I do, of course, recall Johnston's great strike, midway through the half. It was a brilliant move; Gough racing into the box to meet a high ball and heading it backwards to Johnston who struck it venomously only to see Conejo, their goalkeeper whose pre-match profile, as percolated throughout the media, suggested he could not get a game for the Brownies, saving brilliantly. Conejo, whose name means 'rabbit' in English, looked more like a swallow in the remarkable way he threw himself at the ball to parry it, and left Johnston looking astounded. Afterwards, he told us all in the media, 'It was the best save of my life.'

Of course. We seemed to inspire goalkeepers. And his colleagues seemed to be enjoying themselves as well. As Roy Aitken put it succinctly to me, 'It was their Cup Final.' And yes, about the time of the Conejo save, doubts were beginning to rise. Here was a goalkeeper about to play the game of his life and here was a neat, reasonably skilful team, thwarting

Scotland with ease. For Johnston was missing the right kind of prop: McInally was making no impact. He strode about to no effect against a defence that seemed diminutive by comparison, but showed no signs of intimidation. A header by Gough just before half-time, and a twenty-five-yard shot by Roy Aitken, who had perhaps his best game for Scotland, both going narrowly past, was just about enough to suggest that, with time, the goals would come. But then there was the half-time episode.

Arriving back in the dressing room, Richard Gough, who at times had looked our most impressive attacker coming from the deep, told Roxburgh that he could not continue, his injury having become intolerable. The frigid relationship between Roxburgh and Gough had now reached its climax. Even a few hours before the match itself the manager was heard uttering derogatory remarks about his defender, in language not normally associated with him. It was about his suspicion that Gough was not coming clean about his injury and that he was merely playing to attain his fiftieth cap and any associated sponsorship enhancements as a result, since the wearing of boots in a World Cup means cash. This was about lack of trust. In a way, it mirrored the suspicions that had surrounded the complexity of the Ferguson/Dalglish/Hansen turmoil before Mexico, four years earlier.

Craig Brown puts it into the context as seen through the management's eyes. 'I got on very well with Richard, and still do. He was a great player. Now, in Malta, in the friendly before we came to Italy, we had asked two players if they would be fit enough to play in the tournament: Davie Cooper and John Robertson. They both said, after much consideration, that, no, they wouldn't be. Andy loved Davie Cooper and it hurt him that he wouldn't be able to make it. Now, it takes a lot for a player to come clean and deny himself the chance to play in the greatest football tournament in the world. But from Richard we heard nothing. Now, we knew he had a toe injury, but he was going to play on with that. So, I have to say, I was not surprised when he told us that he couldn't carry on in the second half. Not only that, he told me he was leaving the camp the following day, but he didn't tell Andy. So, in a sense, he left without permission.'

The player saw it, not surprisingly, from another angle.

'Let me put it this way,' Gough told me. 'I had this chronic injury which I was getting injections for to keep me playing. It had been going on for some time. Andy, as far as I can recollect, never mentioned this to the press. Contrast that with how Bobby Robson treated the manner of Bryan Robson's injury with the England team in 1986. He always talked about it at press conferences. He made sure the public were aware of Bryan's fight to keep playing. That was different from the way I was treated. As soon as I knew I couldn't fight on and the pain was so intense, I had to give up. And as for leaving the camp after the Costa Rica game, that was organised by Graeme Souness, who flew me directly back to Harley Street for essential treatment. Nothing other than that. And would you believe I ended up in the same hospital as Bryan Robson?'

Yet, on the back of a defeat and that sudden withdrawal, those who associated Gough with an Ibrox regime continually at odds with the SFA developed the notion that it was a purely selfish act to play with such an injury, merely to get to that milestone in his career, with little regard for the needs of the country. To tell that to Mo Johnston is like lighting a fuse.

'Goughie gave everything for Scotland. It was great to be in a dressing room with him. He gave you a lift just by being

311

there. Yes, he might have had differences of opinions with Andy, but that happens the world over between players and coaches. Players just don't always see eye to eye with managers. And yes, he wanted to play in this game. I was there seeing him getting injections in the dressing room, with a needle the length of my hand, right into his toe and he was screaming with pain. He was that desperate to play. We weren't playing for Andy Roxburgh; we were playing for Scotland. As for him leaving the next day, tell me something, would you walk out for nothing, with Sweden and then Brazil to play? No chance. You would kick your grannie to stay in the World Cup. I played with him in countless number of games. He was a fighter, a winner. Desert us for no reason? No chance. The injury had become too bad.'

Within four minutes of Gough having been replaced by Stewart McKimmie of Aberdeen, Scotland effectively lost the game. We had been warned about one player in particular. Juan Cayasso, who had sixty-one caps to his credit. He had floated around the game looking elusive, but hardly menacing. His was the only name we had discussed in terms of threat. But, in fact, his strike was a team goal. However, they were given an unintended assist. Roxburgh had banked heavily on McInally. What he could not have expected was the poor effort of his striker to hold on to the ball in their half, give it away cheaply and then initiate the move for the only goal of the game. Taking it from the striker, the wing-back Marchena flowed forward to the edge of the box and cut a short pass to a tricky winger named Jara, who impudently, cunningly, back-heeled it to the unmarked Cayasso, who chipped it past the onrushing Leighton.

At one behind with plenty time left, you must always feel there is a way back. The efforts became more predictable, the misses almost a certainty. You felt the equaliser was not part of this script. The 10,000 Scots in the stadium knew it too, with their irritation becoming all too evident and probably exacerbated by their enforced alcohol abstinence. They watched in increasing sullenness as Scotland continued drawing blanks.

In the post-match press conference, the statistics offered by Roxburgh – 'we had ten corners to their three' – seemed like a plea for mercy that he knew would not be forthcoming. It was true of him to say, in effect, that they had been caught by a sucker-punch from a team that had counter-attacked intelligently, and had come across a goalkeeper who would have stopped an Exocet. The much-travelled Costa Rica coach, the Yugoslav, Bora Milutinović, who had only been in his post for a few months, was the least surprised at the result when he revealed his self-confidence by declaring, 'I had promised I would walk home if we hadn't won.'

If this weren't enough to irk Roxburgh, he had to contend with someone who asked if he should apologise to the Scottish supporters. It is the first time I saw him really riled at a press conference, snapping back at his questioner to remind him that he was a Scotland supporter as well. When Roy Aitken came on the scene, he blew away a questioner who had reported that Rod Stewart had said that if Scotland couldn't beat Costa Rica by four then they had no chance against Brazil and Sweden. The captain disposed of him by replying, 'I don't listen to what Rod Stewart says about football, only my manager.' They knew in this first meeting with the media that they would now run the gauntlet until the next game. But, seventeen years later, when I talked to Roy in the quiet of a Glasgow hotel, after his travels around the world as a coach and manager, he pointed to one salient fact.

'We have a parochial mentality. Costa Rica were a decent team. It wasn't just Third World stuff. They could use the ball well. Individually, they were talented. But we just believed they had no right to beat us. Yes, we shouldn't have lost. We learned another harsh lesson about ourselves. The world of football was changing. And you had to wonder, were we falling behind?'

24

PRESS POISON

Less profound questions were being asked by the press about a scene that developed later that night. We had retreated to Rapallo and made for the bars. Solace and sobriety are not best mates. The piazza in the middle of the town was packed with people simply out to take the air of a balmy evening and to relax. And drink. A substantial portion of the Tartan Army there were in good order, fighting off despondency in time-honoured manner. Then, sometime later, members of the Scottish squad, attracted by the natural gaiety of the piazza, entered the scene. This was risky. There were undoubtedly men in tartan who had spent a fortune to see what they perceived as a disaster, who would like to have seen most of the squad behind bars with the keys thrown away. In fact, everything was noisy, boisterous, but eminently civilised. In the entire time we spent there, I saw nothing that would have shocked the Women's Guild. I saw several players, including the two who roomed together, Mo Johnston and Jim Bett, all composed, calm and relaxed. They had all been given the night off. Had a survey been taken amongst the Tartan Army, they would have preferred to have had them stay in and play cards, or watch Italian television without subtitles, given they felt some kind of penance would be in order. But Roxburgh was a sensible man who felt they needed the tension lifted, not intensified by moping players hanging around their own rooms. So, he was right to release them. Then, of course, there were others, who were aware nocturnal misdemeanours of the past were prowling.

Roy Aitken was witness to how Johnston and Bett ended up on the front page of *The Sun* (English edition). 'They had been asked to pose for photographs with some local girls. That's all. They did it innocently. It was all harmless. Yes, they had drinks in their hands, and it was champagne, but that was not against the orders for the night. It all passed over without any fuss.'

Craig Brown recalls an ensuing telephone call. 'It came in the middle of the night from Andy to my room, which was unusual. He told me that we were going to be on the front page of *The Sun* the following morning. They were splashing a story about Mo, in particular. But I can tell you the players did not break the midnight curfew, despite the stories that circulated eventually. Andy and I always took shifts checking the rooms to make sure. We did exactly the same that night. Nobody broke the curfew.'

But that front page of *The Sun* was toxic. A defeat, considered in general to be ignominious, followed by champagne and girls and Mo beaming out of the front page of a top-selling tabloid, fitted the picture of moronic behaviour with little sense of shame for failing at the first hurdle. But all was not what it seemed. The players felt they had been targeted. It was a set-up. According to Mo himself, it is the media who bear a certain kind of responsibility for the way they handle a squad, without having to be uncritical cheerleaders.

'Let me take you back to where I think the press started to hound me. I was shattered by being told I wasn't going to Mexico in the World Cup before this. I couldn't believe it. There was a lot of rumour and wild talk in the background about what happened in Melbourne, where we were for the play-off. For instance, I was supposed to have rapped on Ernie Walker's door in the middle of the night and woke him up and caused a disturbance in the corridor and all that. It was baloney. About twenty years later, I came back to Scotland for a Hall of Fame event at Hampden. And who did my wife and myself walk into on the stairs but Ernie Walker. And I'll never forget what he said to me: "Mo, I've never said a bad word about you. I never accused you of anything. I can assure you." I could hardly believe it. And I had missed out on a World Cup in Argentina I had been desperate to go to. It just didn't make any sense. So, we get to the World Cup in Italy and then we get slaughtered by the press. They're not looking to support us. What good do these distortions do? Where's the common ground to make us successful? We are our own worst enemies. We were allowed out for a drink. We did nothing wrong. Some of these papers think I was an easy target and was always irresponsible, a bad character. Listen, I've lived in the States since 1996 and I haven't even had a parking ticket.'

However aggrieved he felt, there is little doubt that the English edition of *The Sun* succeeded in putting the entire Scottish squad in the dock. The fact that both BBC and ITV showed that scene in various reports led to us feeling that we were being too readily caricatured in the south as unman-ageable Scots based on incidents in the past dating back to the night Bremner and Jinky went AWOL. At the time, it felt so bad that it seemed to contradict that old dictum of the PR business, that there is no such a thing as bad publicity.

The criticism crashed against the entire Scottish camp in towering waves. There is no doubt that the Scottish media

317

can be very creative when their ire has been raised. Journalist Alex Cameron could do apoplexy like nobody else in the business and his piece in the *Daily Record* was headed, 'Worst In The World' and he warmed to his task of invective by stating categorically, 'They were a disgrace.' And this from a man who had been round the world with me and suffered, like me, on other occasions. He was merely writing the words the punters were using in the streets, and he knew it. The *Glasgow Herald* simply stated, 'Our Task A Mission Impossible' and James Traynor, underneath that banner, reflecting on the aftermath, wrote, 'In various parts of the city, groups of bedraggled figures trudged the streets. Their gaudy tartans, which had been perceived before the early kick-off in the Stadio Luigi Ferraris as celebrations of Scottish confidence and optimism, looked garish and someone's idea of a cruel joke in the aftermath of defeat.' The *Evening Times (Glasgow)* front page looked forlorn with 'Show Us The Way Home'. And, in its sports pages, poetic imagery had deserted it with 'Frankly We Stink', to which Alan Davidson added his impeccable distaste, 'Scotland have joined the unwashed in world football and not even the cologne of their five-star headquarters on the Italian Riviera can camouflage the stench of putrid failure.'

I had expressed somewhat similar sentiments in my commentary, which, for the record, did not please an overly authoritative BBC figure back home. He objected to my candour. I objected to his myopia. It was the beginning of my departure from BBC Scotland. But, did all of this mean turning our backs on Roxburgh completely? Generally speaking, you felt as if we were by his graveside muttering, 'Alas, poor Andy, I knew him well!' I had come through this all before, of course. I had learned that outrage can be short-lived in a

318

World Cup, and that the final game in Argentina in 1978 had provided us with a lesson in not to jump ship before it's fully berthed. And, indeed, there was a clue to that kind of controlling of the emotions in another Alex Cameron sentence, in the midst of the vitriol, when he rightly claimed, 'There is no question they had dreadful luck at times.' This was echoed in the more solemn editorial in the *Glasgow Herald*: 'Oh, well. Oh, dear. Once again, the Scottish football team has dumped the nation into depression. You cannot really blame the players. They tried their best. They were unlucky.'

They were. The result was awful. The feeling, terrible. The hard-luck stories now feeling almost fossilised. But had the performance been the worst I had seen from a Scotland side in the World Cup? In fact, it was scintillatingly brilliant compared to the Scotland–Iran game in Argentina in 1978, which almost destroyed the will to live, even though it was drawn 1–1. There were weak elements in the Costa Rica game, which you felt could be repaired.

The first time we saw Roxburgh at training again, he looked strained, not surprisingly. Never one for merry, spontaneous quips, this was like watching a man trying to mask internal wounds. Many decades later, Craig Brown, friend and colleague, pointed to what he thought might have been a personality flaw.

'Andy was an extremely serious man. He was meticulous in everything he turned his hand to. Nothing was left undone and he could go into incredible detail to organise and prepare for games. In a football context, especially with a match looming, Andy didn't appreciate much humour. Me? I could face up to some adversities with a joke or a quip, to lighten the situation. We weren't exactly complementary opposites, but sometimes the more serious Andy became, the more fun and banter I tried to introduce. But he didn't have a sense of humour. Andy had none of that in him. It would have helped him if he had. So, in fact, I was good for him. I could see the other side of things that weren't as dark, and in the dressing room I could put in some banter, which helped.'

But there were clearly pointed failures about which most of us agreed. McInally would go. No argument. Bett had been incognito. Obvious. McStay had underperformed, again. Little dispute. Gough had vanished. Who would he turn to now? There was a whole variety of combinations coming to mind. In their first training session after the defeat, a goodly number of supporters turned up to watch them in an atmosphere that seemed flat and spiritless. The players were now barred from consorting with fans as a result of the snare that caught Mo Johnston. So, it was with a sense of relief, to be able to slip away from all that, take a camera and go further west down the coast to the tiny fishing village of Camogli, where the Swedes were based. We were after Tomas Brolin.

The Swedes were in the World Cup finals for the first time in twelve years and had set up in a hotel on a promontory jutting into the Med and oozing with class. The swimming pool was fit for Esther Williams. To our advantage, everybody in the Swedish party spoke English almost impeccably. Well, Glenn Hysén, the Liverpool player, did have a Scouse lilt to his tongue. The player we wanted to talk to though was twenty-year-old Tomas Brolin, who had scored against Brazil in Sweden's 2–1 defeat. It was a goal, and a performance, that was to see him sign for Parma in Serie A immediately after the finals. To be honest, up close, he looked more like a small Eagle Scout come to knock at your door for Bob-A-Job week. His rotund face gave the impression that he had not yet got rid of his puppy fat. That tendency for his body to broaden was to handicap

320

him in future years. Everybody, of course, was after him for interview, but frankly he wasn't interested in us. He sloped around the place obviously enjoying his newfound fame, and clearly didn't think a BBC camera would add one molecule to that. He deserved the spotlight after his recent performances in scoring three goals in five internationals and proving a waspish force against the Brazilians. He was fast, skilful and tenacious, despite his innocent boyish appearance. The South Americans laid into him, but he never winced and looked after himself so vigorously that he was booked eventually.

It was clear that, among both players and Swedish journalists, they still hadn't fully grasped the reality of that Scottish defeat. We managed to pin down their manager, Olle Nordin, who could not yet believe the Costa Rica result. 'I am honest with you. Some of our party did not see the game and thought we were joking when they heard the result. This is not to be taken as any sign of weakness by us. I know what Scotland can be like.'

So did his cosmopolitan players. Ten of them played outside Sweden. Hysén was well known to all of us, not only because of his residence on Merseyside, but also because of the superb defensive combination he had formed with our own Alan Hansen, who was now advising the Scottish manager in Rapallo. At thirty he was the oldest in the side. Jonas Thern of Benfica, at twenty-three, was already establishing himself as a central midfielder of renown. He was to come to Rangers for a short spell and will be remembered for a spectacular goal he scored at Ibrox in an Old Firm game in April 1998. Roland Nilsson was the darling of the Sheffield Wednesday crowds and was to become the sixth most capped player of his country. Anders Limpar would be signed by Arsenal at the end of the tournament and become a key player in the

321

Gunners, winning the title that next season. Stefan Pettersson, the man who scored for Gothenburg against Dundee United to win them the UEFA Cup, was now with Ajax, where he also won that same Cup. Klas Ingesson, then only twenty-one, was to play for six different European clubs, including Sheffield Wednesday, where he got a culture shock by telling a journalist once that he had to deal with players who 'went straight to the pub after training but are still able to run like wild animals come Saturday.' Only one of these players I've pinpointed was older than twenty-four. So they were fresh and strong, as they had looked in the Brazil game.

Nevertheless, when you watch a typical Sweden side, at their best, they don't excite; they impress. They play by the book, as it were, but it's one that follows the lines carefully. They were still running strong at the final whistle and could have scored more than their one goal against a Brazilian defence that was chaotic at times, but lost, essentially due to counter-attacks. They did seem eminently beatable to me, though. When we returned, we heard that Roxburgh had been hinting at bringing in Murdo MacLeod to join Stuart McCall in midfield. Nobody demurred at that suggestion. Thirty-one-year-old former Celt, MacLeod, stocky, unflinching, was now cosmopolitan, playing with Borussia Dortmund, and had helped manager Horst Köppel win his first trophy, the German Cup, the year before. When I reflected on his international career, he made it patently clear to me he was indebted to Roxburgh.

'It's easy to explain why I like him. He picked me. Remember, I was at Celtic for eight years before I got a cap. Jock Stein had me on as a sub in a game against England at Hampden in the Rous Cup in 1985. I came on for Gordon Strachan for the last nineteen minutes. And that was all.

Then it seemed I had been forgotten. So, along comes Andy and picks me to play from the start in Dublin against the Republic in '86 in a 3-5-2. When a manager does that for you, you back him. And, in any case, I saw nothing in the preparation for that first game in Dublin that suggested to me he was not up for the job.' For the rest of us, watching that goalless draw in the Republic was like sucking gooseberries, but he had proved to his manager that he was a source of solid reliability. In shaky times that can never be underestimated.

So, to 16 June, in the Stadio Luigi Ferraris. The Scottish crowd outnumbered the Swedes. It is a game I play back many times in the mind. Indeed, I have a special affection for it, if only because it was my last live commentary for BBC Scotland. It was also one that I felt immensely satisfied with because I believed I could not have performed any better. There were four changes in this side:

Leighton,
McPherson, Malpas, Levein, McLeish,
MacLeod, Aitken (*captain*), McCall, Durie,
Fleck, Johnston.

The Swedes, as we expected, had their captain, Glenn Hysén, back in the side after injury. They played:

Ravelli,
Nilsson, Schwarz, Larsson, Hysén (*captain*),
Limpar, Thern, Nilsson, Ingesson,
Brolin, Pettersson.

Neither McCoist nor McInally had been picked. Something that Ally felt was worthy of a comment to his tall room-mate.

323

When he and McInally went back to their room, after having heard the team selection, the Rangers player asserted himself.

'To be honest, big Alan was hopeless in the Costa Rica game. So, remembering what he had said to me in my room after he had been picked before me for that game, and wanted a good night's sleep, and because we were now both out, I waited until we got back to my room and then threw my crossword puzzle down on the bed and said, "I think you'll be able to help me with that tonight!"'

Durie and Fleck were in there to add undoubted pace to the attack. Aitken was to play wide on the right, MacLeod and McCall were to show they were no blushing violets in midfield for a game that would certainly be British in a sort of way. And Levein added to a defence that had been caught out by pacy counter-attacking in the first game. In the tunnel, lined up alongside the Swedish players, came a display of disdain for their opponents that came straight from being inspired by a certain film, as Stuart McCall recalled.

'We had an ugly team. I played 998 competitive games in my time, but that game against Sweden is the only one that I can say was won in the tunnel. Roy Aitken led us out. He and Alex McLeish and Jim Leighton, without his falsers, looked ferocious and they were going 'Aargh' into the Swedes' faces in the tunnel. Wee Robert Fleck didn't have any teeth either – half of our team didn't – and he was standing beside the big male model Glenn Hysén, who played centre half for Liverpool, telling him what he was going to do to him. It was like being on that *Braveheart* battlefield. We weren't the bonniest team to go to the World Cup, and we clearly frightened them to death. Honestly, I thought they were shrinking in front of us. They refused to make eye contact with us; they were staring at the ground. We were pumped up.'

So was Andy Roxburgh. I noticed he was prominently wearing a tartan scarf. I actually found myself being distracted by that. Here you are, building up an atmosphere for a major game, and yet you find yourself internally debating what that was all about. A superb gesture of bonding with the legions in the stadium, or simply a request for sympathy? I think I recall saying something in the nature of him wearing his patriotism round his neck, and I am still not sure whether there was a gentle mocking tone about that. He was certainly sticking his neck out. Then a raging team started the game. Murdo MacLeod remembers the astonishing reaction to the whistle.

'We were running around like madmen. Right from the start. We were hassling, tackling, getting at them. It was just a relief to be part of it among players who desperately wanted to make amends.'

It is true. From the TV platform I could sense it was tigerish by comparison with the previous game, which looked merely as if they had only been going through the motions, not exactly kittenish, but certainly far from bullying. Fleck and Durie were bothering a defence where Hysén looked shaky throughout. Fleck had already given Hysén a runaround in a club game before the World Cup, and it looked as if the experience had left its mark. Nothing was passing MacLeod in midfield. McCall was breezing his way through the game and performed as well as he ever did for his country. At the back, the expected strong running of the Swedes was being handled calmly by Levein and McPherson. And the much-vaunted Brolin? He was somewhere on the field, but significantly showing a trait that was to plague him throughout his career, despite his intrinsic skills: inconsistency. Only early in the second half did we see him revealing his pace on the left to bring out a fine save by Leighton.

325

And then the first goal. When I look back on it and the kind of reaction I had at the time, it becomes even clearer that watching a Scotland goal in the World Cup is a phenomenon quite different from any other context. McCall's goal in the tenth minute was the eighteenth I had commentated on since 1974, all of which made you feel as if you were looping the loop, but this one with a particular sense of relief, for two reasons. Firstly, it came after two days of hell, living with the ignominy of that first result. Secondly, it was without doubt the scrappiest goal of all eighteen witnessed.

A MacLeod corner in the tenth minute was flicked on by McPherson at the near post. There were many takers for it thereafter, defenders and attackers; in the quick flurry of a thicket of legs to get a touch, Stuart McCall stretched and stabbed at it and, to exultant celebrations, it found its target. Afterwards, I learned that the English commentator, Brian Moore, a personal friend of mine and a highly accomplished broadcaster, could not avoid attempting to dampen Scottish fervour for those listening to him when he said, 'The scorer of that goal was born in Leeds.' At that moment he could have been a morris dancer as well, in his leisure time, for all we cared.

His colleagues were looking rejuvenated. Sweden were certainly not cowed, but looked much less adventurous than they had against the Brazilians. This was looking good, even though we had to be thankful for a wonderful Leighton save from a Jonas Thern, low free kick, in about eighteen minutes, which was an early indication of how well the keeper was going to play, particularly in the second half. Now, it should be pointed out here that the Scottish captain, Roy Aitken, had taken some critical broadsides in the lead-up to the finals. He was never an immaculate ball player. What he unquestionably provided, when sometimes needed, was power and thrust. With only ten minutes left in the game, he picked up the ball wide right, the area he was patrolling, and went on what turned out to be a fateful run deep into their half and then towards the penalty area. He was eventually challenged by defender Roland Nilsson.

'I charged into the box, moving diagonally towards the left and I thought I had got just beyond him, into a position to shoot. It just put me off balance. And I went down.'

Not with a trip, but more of a slight nudge. Admittedly, on my platform, I was surprised to see the Paraguayan referee pointing to the spot because I had seen many slight collisions in the past that had been denied Scotland in other World Cups. My words at the time, as far as I can recollect, perhaps erred on the side of absolutism. A penalty. Without a doubt. The word 'softish' hovered in my mind, but never left my lips.

Then I saw Mo Johnston picking up the ball as the players went through that fevered reaction of accepting the reward, but not really knowing what would come next. In my *Sunday Mail* column the following day, I admitted this: 'I don't think I have ever faced up to a more terrifying few seconds than watching Maurice Johnston step up to take the penalty kick.' After all, I had watched Don Masson miss a penalty in Cordoba, which, had it gone in, would have altered the entire course of our World Cup history. A kind of communal holding-of-breath seemed to mute the Scottish crowd as Johnston prepared himself.

'Actually, I wasn't the penalty taker,' Mo told me. 'It was either big Roy or Coisty, if he had been on. I took it because I wanted it more than anybody. I just grabbed the ball. Of course, I knew that if I was to miss, it might haunt me for the rest of my life. Then I began to think, I'm just twelve yards out. What better chance can you get to score? Then it was just another penalty. So, I put it the opposite way the keeper was moving, that was all.'

He makes his fourteenth goal in thirty-five internationals sound like he had yawned at the same time.

But although we all felt that sense of relief, it lasted only four minutes. What was to happen was to resurrect those few ghastly moments that we suffered at Hampden when Norway equalised with about a minute left. Certainly, when a Roland Nilsson 'Hail-Mary' kind of ball, high into the box eluded everybody except the toe of substitute Glenn Stromberg, who simply poked it into the net to make it 2–1, there was an almost eternity of five minutes left. Leighton again had looked nervous, having failed to come off his line for it. So, the hanging-on was infinitely worse. At times like these it makes men feel weak and emboldens others. The Swedes seemed taller, faster and more accomplished in those last few minutes than they had throughout the entire game. They sensed another kill. This was the dysentery level of 'squeaky-bum time', as the ball would flash across the Scottish goal in those minutes. Scotland held on. The supporters at the end erupted like they had been emancipated. Andy Roxburgh danced on the touchline holding his tartan scarf aloft. You had to feel he deserved being reprieved from any more wrath, but at the same time worried that the security people might mistake him for a supporter initiating a pitch invasion, and pounce. But he seemed to be exemplifying the 'we fear no one' bravado of the hordes who made that evident in the streets of Genoa that night, even though the next stop was Turin, where old adversaries were waiting for us.

25

ARRIVEDERCI

We all went north towards the Alps. Scotland were to settle their base in the foothills in a place called Saint-Vincent in Valle d'Aosta in the north of Italy, which was 2,000 ft above sea level and so much cooler than the humid climes of Rapallo that you could at times feel chilled to the marrow. All we did then in reports was to emphasise again how close they were to qualifying. If they were to achieve a draw against Brazil, Scotland could qualify in second place. If perchance they could win in Turin by 2–0 , they would win the group outright. There was no sin in thinking that was possible. But, even if they were to lose narrowly, it would still leave them a chance of qualifying as one of the four best third-place nations. It all had a familiar ring to it, but it was enough to put a spring in the step.

I hadn't been near the Brazilians so far. A visit to their training camp was essential. It seemed the same on the surface this time, although I was handicapped by not having Peter Pullen from the London Brazilian embassy to help me out as he had in Germany in 1974. He had retired and had even written to me, asking if I could get him some work at the BBC, as his civil-service pension was poor. I couldn't, and never saw him again. But a multi-lingual Brazilian television commentator made it clear to me he was not at all happy with what he had seen so far. He told me of his worries after having watched two uninspiring games, particularly their 1–0 win against Costa Rica, and that by a deflected shot by Müller, whom he thought might be replaced by twenty-four-year-old Romário, the great PSV goal-scoring machine who was to score 165 goals in 167 games in the Eredivisie. Romário was also the epitome of coolness, who had a special relationship with his club manager at the time, Guus Hiddink, who said of him, 'If he saw that I was nervous before a game, he'd come to me and say, "Take it easy, coach, I'm going to score and we're going to win". And incredibly, in eight out of the ten times he told me that, he really did score, and we did win.'

He had been on the bench for the first two games, although there were fitness concerns, considering he had broken a leg with PSV only a couple of months previously. So, was he being conserved specially for Scotland? A non-committal shrug for that one from my interpreter, followed up by him pointing out that the real threat to Scotland would be Careca from Napoli, where he played alongside Diego Maradona. In the previous World Cup, he had ended up second to Gary Lineker in the Golden Boot rankings with five goals. And, in his first game in the tournament, he had scored two superb breakaway goals against Sweden. He was on fire.

The temperature in Saint Vincent at the Scottish camp was much cooler though, nestling there in the Alps. Alan Ferguson didn't like the place, nor did some of the players after the relaxing warmth of Rapallo. It didn't seem to fit the mood of triumph that certainly had followed the Sweden result.

'They really should have stayed down there in Rapallo. It wasn't a huge distance to Turin. Up there in the hills, it was downright cold at times. I don't think it suited the circumstances.'

Whether it was a dampener or not is difficult to tell. We're into the AMG territory again. Was it a detail that ought to have been taken into consideration?

Down they came from the hills and entered the Stadio delle Alpi on 20 June on a day when, surprisingly, the rains came. All day, and into the evening kick-off time of 9 p.m., there was a downpour. I had been told by other journalists, who had been there previously, that the Stadio delle Alpi was impressive. It was: impressively soulless. It was a prefabricated concrete monument to civic blindness. The owners, the local authority, had failed abysmally to satisfy the real needs of football people. It was a stadium which housed both Torino and Juventus, but was never to be filled to its capacity of just over 68,000, despite the fact that Juve have the biggest support in Italy. Yes, from my commentary position, you could see views of the snow–covered Alps. After the intimacy of the stadium in Genoa, this was going to be like watching Subbuteo pieces way down below. Even in the middle of an Italian summer, the concrete bowl seemed to me a chilly, futuristic folly. It seemed Juve thought the same, because the team eventually sought out more intimacy with their support in another new stadium.

The team sheet handed to me before kick-off was going to be particularly useful in identifying the Brazilian midgets I would be spying down there on the pitch. Scotland's selection was:

SCOTLAND
Leighton,
McKimmie, Malpas, McPherson, McLeish,
MacLeod, McStay, Aitken (*captain*), McCall,
McCoist, Johnston.

BRAZIL
Taffarel,
Jorginho, Branco, Ricardo Rocha, Ricardo Gomes,
Mauro Galvão, Valdo, Dunga (*captain*), Alemão,
Careca, Romário.

Levein was injured. McPherson moved to centre back and McKimmie came in at full back and Ally McCoist, having come on as a sub in the previous two games, got his start at last, with Fleck dropped to the bench.

McCoist was inevitably delighted. So were his boot sponsors. He was pointed in expressing his feelings about that.

'Now you may think I would say this anyway, but I think Andy picked the wrong team against Costa Rica. It's as simple as that. If he had played me alongside Mo it might have been different. I honestly do. It might have made all the difference right at the start of the campaign. That first game was vital. It could have put us on the right road. Put it this way, was I more likely to score against Brazil than I was against Costa Rica or even Sweden? I don't think so.'

On this occasion, the voluble Scottish fans were having to compete with the constant throb of drums and chanting from the large Brazil contingent, supplemented by the locals who, in World Cups, always tend to favour the South Americans. But the atmosphere was tinny and distant, compared

332

to the engulfing sounds in the Genoa stadium. So, for me, this game was to remain difficult to pin down and get close to throughout. I have never been able to rid myself of the impression that I was watching the poorest Scotland/Brazil encounter ever. The Brazilians were minus recent giants like Eder, Sócrates, Zico and Falcão. Indeed, their more European set-up was exemplified by the presence in midfield of Dunga, the ACF Fiorentina player of German and Italian descent, whose style of play was described by his own Brazilian press as 'thuggish', and they dubbed that more plodding period when he was an influence as 'Era Dunga'. It almost sounds like an expletive. So, Brazil had become more Europeanised in 1974, and by all accounts were resorting to that now through the guidance of their manager, Sebastião Lazaroni, who was defying the public mood of demanding to see a more creative formation with three being played up front. All this emboldened the budding politician in Romário to let loose an opinion to journalists when he said of the great Pelé's criticism of the side, 'Pelé is right. Lazaroni is making mistakes with this line-up. Brazil cannot win the World Cup with that formation.'

However, down there on the field, players might not have agreed with me. One was Mo Johnston.

'You know, at times I thought they had twelve or thirteen players on the park. Their movement and pace was tremendous. They seemed to be everywhere. We were chasing shadows for a lot of the time. I thought they were brilliant.'

Roy Aitken was of similar mind.

'They could keep the ball away from us well and then they could turn the play quickly. The counter-attacking was breathtaking at times.'

Yes, it was ... at times. Undoubtedly, we saw some fluid

moments from them. However, I just felt, for the major part of the game, too many Scottish players were slightly in awe of the Brazilians who, dare I say it, they might have been overestimating. After all, in their previous two games, the South Americans had looked, by their standards, very ordinary. I suppose it is possible that if you are playing against those yellow jerseys for the first time you might feel they carry a cachet of history that intimidates. Brazil of the past was certainly on the mind of Ally McCoist, who was overjoyed at his first start in the competition. 'I didn't think Brazil were at their best. But, on the other hand, I can't recollect an international I have played in when we had so little possession.'

But he also concurred with my overall impression.

'What did surprise me was that, although they were brilliant technically, there was a lack of urgency about the way they played. I don't know why. They just looked easy on the ball but without any real bite. And let's not forget they could defend and they were tough. I honestly can say I didn't get a real chance to score in that game.'

Twice in the game I can recollect him almost getting on the end of crosses from wide play which, unfortunately, was not a regular pattern. Certainly, Brazil were instantly on the front foot. Stewart McKimmie came close himself to scoring, but against his own side, when early in the game he headed a wicked cross from Jorginho over his own crossbar after a Brazil movement which had been initiated just outside their own penalty area, with the ball swept from Gomes to Valdo to Romário to Jorginho. Just like that, the way it reads – slick, classy. But much of their play was across the field interspersed with quick thrusts, which Scotland looked to be defending well, even though there was a slight air of desperation about it at times, like an Aitken tackle on the prowling Careca as he was about to lay boot to ball. At that time, Scotland were holding their own in the physical struggle in midfield because, with Dunga and Branco in the side, they could not afford shirkers in there. Aitken and Macleod, in particular, were staunching any attempts at intimidation, which, let us not forget, was the gristle in Brazil's current make-up. MacLeod, for instance, in order to claim ownership of his area, laid into Jorginho and, unsurprisingly, was booked. Calamitously, this fortitude was depleted in one fell blow.

Branco had already taken a free kick, which had knocked Johnston off his feet early in the game. This time, six minutes from half-time, a repeat of his venomous thrust struck Murdo MacLeod fully on the side of the head. He remembers the blow, but nothing much else.

'Everything went blank. When I recovered, partially, and got to my feet, I knew I couldn't even tell which way we were playing. I had to go off. Now I tell you I cannot remember a thing about the game or about the day before, or the day after. I sat in the dugout not knowing where I was. I didn't go to hospital, as perhaps I should have. Do you know that it wasn't until I got back to Germany that I was given a full proper check-up? Nowadays, of course, I would have got immediate attention.'

Gillespie came on in his place. Frankly, the game became stalemated. Brazil pressing. Scotland resisting with barely a structured move forward or making a genuine threat that penetrated their penalty area. And how was I feeling about it in the commentary platform? Tom Shields, in his daily diary in the *Glasgow Herald*, seemed to capture the essence of my mood when he wrote, 'Archie's most eloquent moment came when the cameras focussed on a young Brazilian lady, dusky, dark-haired and wearing tight jeans and skimpy top. "Oooh!" he said, in his rather flawless English.' At least it was better to look at than that exasperating Mexican Wave, which had begun to uncoil around the stadium, signalling, as it always does, playful impatience.

Leighton never had much time to look at the crowd. Initially, he had been steady, saving from a Romário header in the first half at full-stretch, and, in the second, diving to parry Romário at his feet after he had been put through from the most delicate pass by Branco, the slayer of Scots obviously. When you are holding a Brazilian side at 0–0 towards the last quarter of the game, you might feel that things are going to plan as, after all, a draw would have done Scotland handsomely. I didn't feel all that comfortable about it. Remember, I had seen it all before, and the Ghost of World Cups Past was sitting beside me; silent but menacing. It's just a way of saying I did feel we were on the brink of another disaster. Easy to say now. But truly the feeling wouldn't go away. It didn't even lessen when the feckless and unfit Romário was replaced by the sturdy but less accomplished Müller in the sixty-fourth minute. And, almost with a degree of incredulity in my voice, only eleven minutes later, I described Scotland almost scoring. McCall from wide right crossed to Aitken, who met it with a strong header, only to see it cleared off the line by Branco.

Then the ghost on the platform gave me a nudge as, with only nine minutes left, something stirs. That moment is now ever present in the mind. Alemão has the ball. He is moving forward. It is the edge of the penalty area. He shoots. Leighton dives. Stops it. The ball spins away from him. Two boots lunge at it to intervene. Careco and Gillespie. The Brazilian wins. The ball rolls towards the far post and looks like it will trundle past harmlessly. It doesn't. Müller reaches it and steers it into an empty net.

Into an empty net. It is one of the most forlorn descriptions in football. It implies some kind of negligence. A net should always be guarded, come what may? Easy enough asked. It was yet another goal that almost suggested there was some strange cosmic power which, by any means possible, orders closure on Scotland's efforts. Think of Johnny Rep's stunner which prevented us from progressing in Argentina; Russia's ludicrously gifted goal in Malaga in 1982 and Stevie Nichol's glaring miss in the Nexa against Uruguay in Mexico. And now a goalkeeper makes one of the most fundamental errors anybody in his trade can make; gifting a ball to a renowned striker. The pattern seems remorseless. But the immediate corollary to this goal in Turin made this sinister intervening force seem even worse.

For Scotland, to their credit, did not surrender. In a sweeping combined move that showed more fire than they had in the previous ninety minutes, McKimmie on the right centred for Malpas to head the ball to Fleck, who couldn't make proper contact. It fell to Johnston, only six yards from goal. It was his for the taking. But the cosmic power had other thoughts. It might not have whispered in Mo Johnston's ear, but it looked like it.

'Dying seconds and I miss a fricking sitter. I smashed it and, what do you know, it touches the top of Taffarel's shoulder, rises up, hits the crossbar and goes over. Yes, it was his shoulder, but it must go down as a great save. But honestly, I could have put it anywhere. Nine times out of ten I would have. I just lay there thinking "Our World Cup's over." That's the one I always think about. It never goes away.'

With seconds left, I looked down mournfully on the pitch and, lo and behold, recognised again Herr Kirschen, the East German referee who had added those incredible minutes in Cyprus. Ironically, he was now a linesman, his stopwatch only on standby. And so it ended 1–0.

With a familiar numbness, we made our way to the media centre to verify that we could still qualify for best third place overall, depending on results between Uruguay and South Korea and the two games between England and Egypt, and Holland and Ireland. Not for one moment did I meet anyone who believed that it would work out in our favour, despite every responsible media outlet feeding that remote possibility to the public. Of course, it wasn't going to happen, and it didn't, because, wholly in keeping with our cosmic deficiency, Uruguay scored in the third minute of stoppage time to win. And the Republic of Ireland drew 1–1 with Holland. Both results were heard like a creaking sound of another ship sinking. Once again it was airport time.

I was now engaged in the process of coming to terms with my fifth World Cup exit and my head was reeling with the wholly incomprehensible nature of our defeats, given that, in practically all instances, even in Argentina, we only just fell short. By this stage any more hard-luck stories seemed unfit for human consumption. What we perhaps were witnessing, in fact, was an overall decline in the quality of players we could take to a World Cup. And indeed, given the changing domestic conditions, which would lead to an increasingly more cosmopolitan make-up of Scottish clubs, then the almost depressing thought was emerging that the decline could be accelerating.

There were the usual visceral calls for the SFA to get their act together and do something about it, leading to the news headline in the Glasgow *Evening Times* 'SFA TO ACT OVER OUR EARLY EXIT'. There was no dancing in the streets about that declaration as it seemed like a weary, tuneless old song they were singing. 'Oh, it's all down to the teachers' strike in the past and when jannies stopped taking school-teams any longer.' That is one of the most durable refrains I have heard through the years about the dearth of emerging talent. Still do. We are major exponents of over-simplification when we self-examine. It's much more complex. It was a developing age in which too many young minds were domesticated by fingertip technology and sucked indoors away from competitive hassle. Their living conditions, thank heaven, were better than their fathers and grandfathers. They could now do many other things than kick a ball in the street. There were other leverages to a better life than just signing an S-form for a football club. Our general social betterment in many ways bypassed football; made it merely an item that competed with other more alluring activities. My own kids could ski, whereas I considered ice and snow as one of the most loathsome jokes nature could play on the only game that mattered to me at their age.

And, inevitably, Andy Roxburgh faced hostility. He continued in his post until Scotland, failing to qualify for the World Cup in the USA in 1994, he quit. This intelligent, articulate man who could not have been faulted for lack of diligence, had to take the ultimate responsibility for failure. Would a hairy monster have done any better? Many people liked to think so. It's all hypothetical. But he did get to the States eventually. For decades later, when I heard him on video introducing himself to the New York public as technical director of the New York Bulls, after almost eighteen years as technical director for UEFA, he sounded in his

339

element. Like he was back to educating, back to his natural environment, informing a less enlightened audience about the relationship between coach, players and public in this sport they call soccer over there.

In the country to which Scotland would be heading for their next World Cup, they simply call it *'le foot'*.

THE 1998 FIFA WORLD CUP

FRANCE

26

VIVE LE TARTAN

On 10 June 1998, the entire Scotland squad for the World Cup walked out on to the Stade de France pitch wearing kilts. This would have come as no surprise to the readers of the renowned French newspaper *Le Monde* for, on the eve of this World Cup opening game against Brazil, they published a special supplement with the banner headline: '*Renaissance d'une Nation*'. They were writing of Scotland, with the perception that we were a nation in the process of rebirth. Although *Le Monde* did clearly recognise the vote on 11 September 1997 was for devolution, you gained the impression, in their detailed sixteen-page summary of the economic and political forces at play, that they believed ours was a nation capable of going even further. They proceeded to commend Scottish produce in citing their appreciation of our whisky, fish, beef, cloth – right through to their headline '*Le Shortbread, biscuit par excellence*', with the news to their readers that the French consumed twenty-million francs of these special delights from one Scottish producer alone.

And they reminded their readers of the Auld Alliance, the ancient bonding between the two countries based on *Le Monde*'s cute reminder, 'The enemies of my enemies are my

friends.' England, one presumes, being the unnamed cata-
lyst for that. It beat the Entente Cordiale hands down. You
could tell from the non-Scots around me expressing delight
in seeing this traditional dress, proudly displayed on the
new turf of the recently built spectacular stadium, that they
were witnessing, and sympathising with, a defiant statement of identity. That empathy with the Scots permeated the
French media and public in general. John Collins, who had
been playing in French football for Monaco since 1996, lends
testament to that.

'The French get on very well with the Scots. Wherever I
went, I felt warmth towards me, no antagonism. And at the
time, listening to the people and what was written, the French
wanted Scotland to do well because of the atmosphere the
Tartan Army could bring to the country. Believe you me, the
French wanted us to qualify for the later stages.'

So much so, that on the basis of what I heard myself in
Paris working there, and on the sort of analysis of where we
stood in the world by *Le Monde*, it forced me into compli-
cated explanations to my colleagues in Eurosport, for whom
I would be commentating on the tournament. They failed to
understand that we were not an independent country. They
simply could not grasp the concept of devolution, particularly
since they saw these men in the tartan kilts as representing
a nation that had played its football independently, as such,
for over a century. So, you could hardly divorce yourself
completely from the historic constitutional changes taking
place in Scotland. For there was also one man prominently
there in Paris to remind us of a country trying to make up its
mind about which way to travel in the future: Alex Salmond
was in attendance.

In one sense, there was nothing unusual about the leader

of the SNP being there, for since his early days in Linlithgow, he was keen on football and had more than a fondness for Hearts. But he was not there just to raise a voice for the lads. With Sean Connery in town as well, he was to attempt to dominate a special gala evening on the eve of the Brazil game in front of a well-heeled celebrity audience. That evening was memorable for the way in which football and politics came together in an almost brazen manner, as we shall see later. His presence simply reminded me of how much Scotland had changed since that flight I took with the Scottish players from Glasgow to Brussels back in 1974. It also left me in no doubt that the performance of this Scottish squad, one year before the establishment of a new parliament, in an era of heightened political sensitivities, would interest those who thought they could benefit from a national feel-good factor on the back of any success in a tournament which had been increased in size to include an unprecedented thirty-six nations.

Nonetheless, in common with the cosmopolitan crowd inside that massive stadium, which housed 80,000 that day, I was genuinely stirred by the sight of the kilts, and the striding figures wearing them with a self-confident ease that gave the impression they were part of their normal wardrobe and had not been brought out of storage, as for a wedding. Although it has to be pointed out that the kilts idea had come from the players themselves, who had a deal with the manufacturer, who would lob a sizeable sum of cash into the Players' Pool. Yet, it was full-blooded, as compared to the solitary wearing of that tartan scarf by Andy Roxburgh in Genoa, which, after his initial defeat, had seemed like a defensive afterthought. And it clearly chimed well with the French in the crowd, who, even before a ball had been kicked, were now more resolutely on the side of the underdog.

But, although they were clearly charmed by this tartan presentation, you could hardly say all Parisians were making it easy for the tartan hordes to come to terms with the city. And hordes there were. Without doubt, this was the largest congregation of Scots in a single city I had ever experienced. From the leafy suburbs, to the pavements of Montmartre, the forecourt of the Louvre, the pleasure boats on the Seine, the parks, the bistros, the queues for the Eiffel Tower, they were unavoidable. But what they had not reckoned on were the French unions. In the years I had worked around Paris, there was barely a month in the nineties that did not have a strike in operation. The World Cup offered no exemption. For instance, if you arrived for the tournament at Charles de Gaulle airport, panting with anticipation for the event, and hearing you were lucky to get there because Air France pilots had decided to ground all flights from that midnight, you would also be panting with the exertion of having to humph your own luggage from the aircraft to a six-mile queue for a taxi – for the airport handlers were also out. Then, when you got to the centre of the city eventually and discovered that the Metro, their subway, wasn't in operation, because there was solidarity throughout the Parisian unions, it felt as if you had signed up for an edition of the fondly remembered comedy TV programme, *It's A Knockout*.

We can only guess at the number of Scots who came into the city for that opening game, the vast majority of whom were ticketless. It is said about 60,000. Who knows? They seemed to have ousted the local population and even dwarfed the Brazilian support, which normally is supplemented by local sympathisers. The draw for the Finals had been made, for the first time ever, in a stadium hosting games in the tournament, the Stade Vélodrome in Marseilles. So, although Norway and Morocco had been drawn against us, it was the name of Brazil appearing in our group again that sparked the excitement. From that very day of the draw on 4 December 1997, the desire to get there, to see this being staged in one of the most famous capitals in the world, became a national obsession.

Once there, insanity seemed to prevail. The vast majority had come without tickets. So, they all wanted tickets. They all expected to get tickets. And they would try anything to get their hands on tickets. You could not walk a few yards before they were clutching at your arm virtually begging, with a desperate 'brother-can-you-spare-a-dime' look on their faces. Even on the famous Champs-Élysées, there were tartan wanderers crowding the pavements with the plaintive look of the unemployed of the Depression. And after the claim by the French authorities that they had the ticket distribution as closely under scrutiny as an Egyptian relic in the Louvre, the touts were in fact so brazen, sauntering up and down the Champs-Élysées, phones clamped to their ears and doing deals with each other and handing out their phone numbers to potential clients, that it was manifestly evident that the black market was in full throttle. One demented tout told a group on that fabulous stretch, very picturesquely, 'Tickets are as scarce as rocking-horse shit!' Not once did I see a Scot coming away from them with a smile on their face. In all the time I had been around the world to these tournaments, these couple of days before this game came nearest of all to revealing the almost primal hunger to see a football match. This had been exacerbated by the official announcement that Scotland would be allocated a meagre 5,000 tickets.

347

I was not immune from the ticket wrangle myself, even though I was heading for the commentary platform with my new company, Eurosport. I had been assured by a man I trusted that six tickets for family and friends would be handed over to me. They never were. So why was I scrabbling about for match tickets when I should have been focussing like a laser, night and day, to the exclusion of everything else, on one of the great occasions in the history of our World Cup appearances? Because, at heart, I was no different from those thousands trawling Paris for their gold nuggets. A ticket had become a status symbol, and I wanted to show I was empowered to get some. I failed. And so did others, hugely.

Take the experience of Paul Davidson of the highly successful glass firm, Glencairn Crystal, who, like many other business people, saw this as an opportunity to entertain clients, be associated with this prestigious event and have a ball. It didn't quite work out as expected, as he recalls.

'There was a whole tribe of Glasgow people who had travelled together for the game. We were all staying at the Hilton. A bus came to pick us up. In the company were many Glasgow businessmen, including James Mortimer, highly successful in the restaurant trade, Kenny Dalglish and Alex Ferguson, plus many executives from Coca-Cola and Tennent's for example – a Who's Who of leading Glaswegian and national figures, well-heeled and eager to see the game. The majority ticketless. Of course, they had been guaranteed them. So, they took off to a very fashionable restaurant for a tuck-in. I even saw the man who used to be inside Barlinnie Prison's Special Unit there: Jimmy Boyle. Then I felt a tension developing towards the end of the meal. Where were the promised tickets? About fifteen minutes before the meal finished, the word came out. There were no tickets for anybody. None. And that even included the very top Coca-Cola executives. They were all going mental down in the foyer because of that. You can imagine tempers were rising. It was a very angry group now. Time was slipping away. It was getting near kick-off. We all started padding our way down towards the stadium about a couple of miles away. James Mortimer had two phones to his ears, walking and talking, negotiating. You could hardly believe it. We were getting close to the stadium and still nothing. Then he shouted, "We've got tickets. They're £1,500 each." What? I couldn't believe it. The face value was between £15 and £37. But that was it: take it or leave it. Those who could had to stump up. But these tickets that had been fixed had been dropped off at the restaurant and a couple of us had to run back to get them. I tell you, we just made it. Some of us got in just before kick-off. But here's the thing: many of the party didn't get tickets at all. Even some of the big shots from Coca-Cola. There just weren't enough. It was a disaster.

'And to make matters worse, after the game, when we packed into the bus, for some reason there were more inside than we had started out with. So, the bus driver refused to drive us, saying that it was overloaded. We stuffed a lot of money into his hand to bribe him to take us. He did. Only for part of the way, though. Because when we came to an area that honestly looked a bit like Beirut to me, he refused to go any further and told those standing he wouldn't move any further until they got off. So, he handed the money back to us and ordered them out. He meant it. No further. So out went Kenny Dalglish and Alex Ferguson into this godforsaken part of Paris in the middle of nowhere, like the rest of us. And to this day I do not know how they got back to the Hilton.'

So, even though this tournament was beginning to look

simply like a corporate junket, as we had expected, not even those in the know, and with well-lined pockets, could beat the over-stretched system. The paradox behind all of the mayhem to see a football match, is that Paris is not really a football city. It has catered for every taste, pleasure and sin imaginable through the centuries, but football has never been able to flesh out its appeal through the myriad of cultural alternatives and sensual attractions to stamp some of its personality on the city. When you watched Paris St Germain playing at the Parc des Princes, you felt there was too much going on in Montmartre, or along the Champs-Élysées, or in the dens of the Left Bank, for the rest of the city to pay too much attention to what was going on out in the suburbs; this despite the efforts of one of the greatest sports newspapers in the world, *L'Équipe*, to shed consistent light on what was considered a less illuminated spot in the City of Light.

As the football historian, Pat Woods, a lover of the city, says, 'PSG is just a fashion accessory for the great and the good in the city.' When they won their first European Trophy, the Cup Winners, two years before the World Cup started in 1998, in a season that saw them defeat Celtic 3–0 at Celtic Park, the people certainly did go out on the streets to celebrate. But that was habitual. The Parisians do like a street party and couldn't resist carousing for a club's success that probably many of them wouldn't even know which Metro to pick for the Parc des Princes.

It's not as if Scots did not try to popularise the game there. 'Gordon FC' was a club formed by expatriates in the early 1890s in Paris and, in his book *Sport and Society in Modern France* Richard Holt writes, 'In 1891, "White Rovers" were begun by Jack Wood, a Scotsman, and the rest of his team was largely made up of his compatriots. A contemporary witness later recalled that, "Sunday games followed too closely on the excesses of Saturday night for many of the players to produce their best form.'"

That reminds me of the pub teams I used to watch as a kid on Shettleston Hill pitches on Sunday mornings, which were the bleary-eyed versus the incapacitated. But Holt goes on to observe, 'Scottish customs of a rather different kind proved to be an obstacle for another young player called Howatson, whose Presbyterian father would not tolerate his son amusing himself on the Sabbath by playing football. The unfortunate boy did not dare to take his football strip out of the house on a Sunday and had to play under an assumed name in his ordinary clothes.'

Oh, how the game's image might have soared had Howatson and his mates caught the eye of a contemporary of theirs called Renoir! A painting of a football match getting hung in the Salon de Paris would have brought the game in from the periphery of French culture. So, although the opening ceremony and first game was to be staged in this vast stadium in this capital city, to feel the genuine pull of football in a community, fans would have to go to places like Marseilles, St-Étienne, Lyon, Lens, where you sense football is just around the corner.

However, if you had walked around another corner off the Place de la Concorde, on the eve of the opening game, where they used to guillotine the aristocracy during the Revolution, you would have seen Scottish supporters thronging the pavements. A gala dinner was being held for a celebrity audience to offer spiritual support for the Scotland team. In other words, any excuse for *haute cuisine* in the very place where the phrase was born. Through the Tartan Army's mysterious but effective grapevine, the word had spread that certain well-known Scottish personalities were about to enter the Buddha Bar, just behind the world-famous Hotel de Crillon, which astonishingly had been allowed to retain some of the bullet holes in its façade as a reminder of the French Resistance's battle for Paris at the end of the war. They were not disappointed. Sean Connery had promised to be there. So had Ewan McGregor and Ally McCoist, about whom there was much chat concerning an incident in Paris's 'Auld Alliance' bar, in which it was alleged he had been witness to Stan Collymore apparently 're-designing' his girlfriend Ulrika Jonsson's features. That last piece of tittle-tattle was the very stuff of pre-World Cup gossip, without which you could not have kick-off at all. But the crowd outside had not come just to gape, but to barter with these personalities for tickets for the game. The partygoers included writers, actors, journalists, broadcasters, business tycoons and editors of Scottish newspapers, all of whom ran the gauntlet in the ticket frenzy. Connery was no exception.

After we had all assembled in the bowels of this restaurant, which had a grand flight of stairs that would have done justice to the Palace of Versailles, they made an announcement that Scotland's most famous man – Connery, that is – had arrived. There were about 300 guests at tables about to be laden with Parisian cuisine at its finest. Then Sean appeared at the top of that grand staircase. But not alone. As we all rose to our feet to acclaim him and started to applaud, we noticed, as he slowly, regally, made his way down the stairs, that he was accompanied by Alex Salmond, who had left his table and sped upstairs, having been told the great man was about to enter. You have to credit Salmond. What a performance! What an entrance! They made their way downstairs in tandem, as if they were about to present their credentials at the Court of St James's after Scottish independence, and the well-oiled company rose, as to a man, and cheered them to the rafters. Salmond was beaming, and had a proud look on his face, as if Sean had whispered to him that he could get him the role of Q in the next Bond film. Milking it for all its worth, Salmond brought the great man to our table.

To his credit, Sean appeared slightly taken aback by all this fuss, and all of us who felt slightly queasy about this quasi-political stunt at what purported to be a footballing event were assuaged by the man himself. Sean grilled me about Scotland's chances on the morrow. You say kind and hopeful things in these situations without really hearing yourself say anything worthwhile. But the contrast between the genuinely perplexed Sean, worried about a game against Brazil, and the assured polish of the screen Bond was stark. Sadly, later that evening, the political overtone rebounded, for, after much drink had been taken, Sean took over the microphone and delivered an incoherent rant about independence which ended up with him being roundly barracked. Arguing about whom Craig Brown should pick to face Brazil was clearly more important than being reminded of the Declaration of Arbroath. Nevertheless, when they came to assess the tournament, the *Daily Record* was in no doubt about the effectiveness of Salmond's presence, publishing the headline 'There Was Only One Winner'. They described his street appearances in full tartan regalia as, 'more like a pudgy bricklayer than a politician in his outfit, but the SNP believes their leader has brought back hundreds of new supporters with him'.

The kilted figures down there on the pitch, who had been insulated in their hotel from the cauldron of beseeching figures and raucous assemblies all around the city, were becoming aware for the first time of the exalted sense of occasion. Tom Boyd, of Celtic, a now established figure in Scotland's defensive system, since making his debut as a sub against Romania on 12 September 1990 and coming off the bench to lay on the winning goal for Ally McCoist in the 2–1 win, was facing the Brazilians for the first time, and felt this emotional lift clearly.

'I could tell it went down well. The response made us quite emotional. You could tell the Brazilians were going to be out-shouted and out-sung by our support. It was incredible. However, I have to say the kilts weren't suited to the kind of day it was: hot and humid. I was sweating under the heavy jacket as well. So, it wasn't all that easy walking out there. Yes, it caused a right stir, but it wasn't the ideal way to get ready for a game.'

There was another reason for that. Gordon Durie of Rangers, who made his debut for Scotland under Andy Roxburgh in the game against Bulgaria in November 1987 when he provided the pass for Gary Mackay to score the only goal of the game – which ironically qualified the Republic of Ireland for the European Championships, and effectively kick-started a profitable era for the Irish – remembers the immediate aftermath.

'We came off the pitch sweating. And then we found we couldn't get back on to the pitch before kick-off because the opening ceremony was taking place and we were stuck in this big underground room somewhere trying our best to prepare and loosen up. It was far from ideal. Then you walk into that huge stadium and you're beside these yellow shirts for the first time. One of the biggest games we ever had to play and we couldn't warm up properly because of the opening ceremony. Maybe that might have caused a lapse of concentration so soon in the game.'

The SFA officials had decided blazer and slacks would be the preferred option, as if kilts were for a younger generation. In the middle of the group strolled Craig Brown, the Scotland manager, whose outwardly relaxed figure simply hid the fact of his full awareness that the buck would eventually stop with him.

27

NERVY NAVIGATIONS

The first time I had seen Brown walk on to a football pitch was at Laigh Bent, the playing field of Hamilton Academy where he was a stalwart of the school's first eleven. In my student days, I refereed many school games and I was assigned to officiate at a cup tie involving two Lanarkshire schools. I remember little of the game, but I still sustain the image of a very committed, energetic player who seemed to cover a lot of territory, in the slightly uncoordinated style of schools' football, as it was then, back in the fifties.

Craig was brought up in a household that lay great stress on academic and footballing achievement. They seemed to have been twinned. His father, Hugh Brown, was then Principal of the Scottish School of Physical Education at Jordanhill. His strong personality led him to be called 'The Bomber' by his students. He had been a friend of the innovative and legendary Wolves manager, Stan Cullis, and liked the style he had established in the Midlands to win league titles and become the youngest manager to win the FA Cup. Indeed, when Cullis and other managers from the south came to look at talent here, they would never come straight into Glasgow. They preferred discretion, and knew that porters on the trains were being given backhanders by the press to let them know if a significant English manager was on the hunt. So, they would get off the train at Motherwell to be met by Hugh Brown, who would act as their go-between. Thus, Craig was immersed in talk about the great and the good in football from an early age, and certainly had his first taste of criticism from a father who could roast him for a poor performance as a boy. Curiously, as a youth, Craig went to Rangers from Coltness United. Curious in the sense that his father had an aversion to Rangers, based on his criticism of their 'Iron Curtain' philosophy of the 1950s, which he felt stunted creativity in the game. But obviously money swayed matters.

He was only there for three years, though, and failed to reach the first team. He became the first signing of the wily Dundee manager, Bob Shankly, and, in his four years there, played in every game in the side that reached the European Cup semi-final, but was ruled out at that stage because of a knee injury which was to plague him for the rest of his career. So, we are talking about a playing career spanning only nine years, marred by a knee problem which surgeons operated on no fewer than five times. But inside the dressing room at Shawfield, as manager of Clyde, as he was for nine years, from 1977, he would have said little about the fact that he was also the holder of a couple of degrees in education, and had moved from being a headmaster to become a college lecturer and, in between, had written academic books.

It is hard to determine whether he was in the mind of the SFA International Committee when Andy Roxburgh decided to resign as team manager shortly after drawing 1–1 with Switzerland at Pittodrie stadium on 8 September 1993, an outcome that meant that Scotland would not be going to the

USA in 1994. It had been a long reign after all. Roxburgh's sixty-first game had equalled Jock Stein's record, but at the age of fifty he certainly was not a candidate for the wilderness. The feeling among many of us was that Roxburgh had jumped before being pushed, even though, at the time, the rather po-faced Jim Farry gave us one of those maddeningly cryptic SFA statements: 'It is not the intention of the international committee to alter the function of the national coach.' But specifically, about the managerial post, there was nothing. A few days after that statement, Roxburgh resigned.

Brown admits himself that he did not think he was an automatic successor, even though he had a long coaching record with the SFA, a quality recognised as such by Alex Ferguson, who took him to Mexico in 1986. Attention might also have been paid to his great success with Scotland's U16 side, which reached the FIFA World Cup Final at Hampden in 1989 against Saudi Arabia, which drew a crowd of over 50,000 to the national stadium. 2–0 up at one stage, Scotland were pulled back to 2–2 in the second half, with the game ending in a penalty shoot-out, won by the visitors 5–4. Craig Flanagan, one of the squad then, and now on Rangers staff, who like the rest of players thought the world of Brown, is one of those who felt that what beat them were the suspect birth certificates of a more mature-looking, and physically stronger, Saudi team.

'I would put it this way,' Flanagan told me, 'when the civic authorities offered us a reception after the final, the team went properly to the City Chambers for that. The Saudis went to Victoria's nightclub.'

Yes, these were just Scottish boys and there were undoubtedly some cynical observers who thought that was as relevant to promotion to the senior post as someone who had served kids from a Mr Whippy van. That is why, within the ranks of the SFA international committee, there were still some in doubt about Craig Brown. In the discussions I had with people at the time, it seemed that two members of the seven-man committee were opposed. You couldn't really pin it down for sure, but the suggestions that they would wait to judge him after he took charge as interim manager for the game against Malta in Valetta, which was meaningless in terms of qualifying for the USA, would have been unfair, as he was having to field a team minus six regulars, who had pulled out at the last moment. However, they came to the decision to appoint him to national team manager on the day of the match on 17 November 1993. Gary McAllister remembers it well.

'They came in and told us that Craig had got the job. I felt I had to say something. I gave a little speech in the dressing room. We liked him. We got on well with him. And I think what I did was appropriate.'

It was. The players applauded. None of them had ever heard such a thing in a dressing room before. Brown was almost overwhelmed. But that certainly did not satisfy critics of the SFA, who felt that the Roxburgh period had been an experiment that had failed. And that he had now been replaced by a clone. Or so they perceived. In fact, as I have pointed out in previous pages, Brown and Roxburgh's personalities were quite different. Indeed, on another occasion, when I had written an article implying there really wasn't much of a difference between them, Brown was quite surprised. What annoyed him was this blanket phrase 'Largs Mafia', which was used to dismiss a cadre of men who, down on the Clyde coast, just above the holiday resort, in the Inverclyde National Sporting Centre, dwelled in their own little world of fantasy football and wished to stamp rigid control over all development in the game, in ways that were infantile to professional players. And they were all clones. That's how it was portrayed, by the less enlightened, from pub to boardroom. Still is, to a degree.

He believes the degrading implication behind that phrase stemmed from Steve Archibald. The former international had wanted to be fast-tracked for a coaching award to get the job as manager of RCD Espanyol in Barcelona. He successfully completed only half the course and obtained a fast-tracked UEFA 'B' licence, when an 'A' was required for the job. Brown and his colleagues refused to expedite matters, as that would have been grossly unfair to those who had completed the requisite examination. The Spanish management took one look at the lesser qualification Archibald was showing them and rejected him. So, he lashed out, Brown claims, at what he termed 'the Largs Mafia'. The phrase was quickly taken up by others and is even mentioned today by some of the Tartan Army I have spoken to.

Gary McAllister, his former captain, is adamant that Brown was no clone, and points to his period with Clyde, when he won two Second Division titles.

'I know a lot was said about how he had never played the game at the highest level or never managed a major club, but he had been in a professional dressing room dealing with all the problems that arise from that for several years. And that's why I think he was different from Andy. In my view, he certainly did have a harder edge to him.'

Thankfully, the more discerning in the media concurred with that. Hugh Keevins of the *Daily Record* interviewed him frequently.

'Craig could tell funny anecdotes about his time as manager.

Lots of stories. He seemed more of a man of the people to me than Andy, who was far too serious at times. Indeed, Andy was the nephew of Jack Steedman of Clydebank, a car salesman, a wheeler-dealer, an aggressive personality. You could hardly believe they were of the same family. And Craig had already dirtied his hands in the game, having been a club manager. So these two were very different.'

Colin Hendry, eventually Brown's captain, admired his articulate qualities. 'He spelled everything out well. Everything was laid out for you to think about. And he was well-disciplined himself. The only time I personally saw him in a deeply emotional state was at Wembley when England beat us in Euro96. He showed it then, in the stadium and the hotel afterwards.'

However, Brown, with his well-documented academic status, was deemed unfit for purpose by some critics. One journalist, in particular, pursued him with a vengeance throughout his entire career, almost like Inspector Javert shadowing Jean Valjean in *Les Miserables*; relentlessly critical, impugning his status and hell-bent on bringing him down. I came across Brown one day in Charles de Gaulle airport in Paris, where he must have been on a recce of sorts. He was incensed after another beating in print from this man. I knew he was really upset, because he began to speak about how well he had managed his future with healthy insurance schemes and that he was well prepared for the future, if this man had his way. Apparently, much of the hostility derived from the fact that Brown did not pick Richard Gough in his sides and refused to give this writer reasons for that non-selection. Week after week it went on, with the clear-cut journalistic objective of being able to boast that he had helped the manager change his mind. Brown, rightly, would have none of it.

Now there were others who were surprised by Gough's omission, and may have commented one way or another about it. It was definitely worthy of discussion and criticism. Personally, I wouldn't have minded him being picked, given Gough's stature under Walter Smith at the time Brown took Scotland to England for the European finals. But it wouldn't have been right to use my misgivings about that as a bludgeon to continually question the manager's entire credibility. Indeed, he told me he had met this journalist as he was returning from a defeat once, who told him that he was going to savage him in a column. 'Nothing personal, you know,' he was told. When he complained about the insensitivity of that remark, the response was, 'That's showbiz!'.

He had been placed in the same category as his predecessor, an easy target, unlikely to say 'Fuck off!' over the phone and slam it down on people. Too gentlemanly by far in face of this rough journalistic trade? More probably just simply being civilised. An oddity for some. Brown, in fact, had settled in well with the players, who performed creditably under him in the European finals in England in 1996. They fought a no-scoring draw against Holland at Villa Park, were defeated by England 2–0 at Wembley and beat Switzerland 1–0, again at Villa Park. They failed to qualify for the second stage because Patrick Kluivert came off the bench with only twelve minutes left to score a goal for the Netherlands when they were trailing England badly by 4–0, that single strike clinching the play-off place through goal difference. It was the sort of experience that could mummify a manager. He took it on the chin, but certainly would have known the Scottish public had witnessed the organisation and effort he stimulated, and that he had secured his immediate future. But, now that he had experienced in Mexico, Italy and England what we can easily describe as that special Scottish early-exit anguish, handed down like some hereditary disease, he thought he was now ready for anything. But he really couldn't have bargained on the bizarre happenings within their World Cup qualifying group of Austria, Latvia, Sweden, Estonia and Belarus. After a no-scoring draw in Vienna against Austria, followed by a comfortable 2–0 win in Latvia, Tom Boyd recalls another evening of palpitations on 10 November 1996:

'We met Sweden at Ibrox. I'll never forget it. It was one of the most one-sided games I've ever experienced. Sweden battered us. It's a game Henrik Larsson hates to talk about to this day. He came on as sub in the second half and he still can't believe we won that match. But I'll tell you how we won it. Jim Leighton. It was one of the best goalkeeping displays I can remember for Scotland. He was saving them from all angles. Now I know he had been criticised severely after Italy, but he had rekindled his form with Hibs, and anyway, I honestly don't think the manager thought Andy Goram was in the best physical state for consideration judging by what we saw when he turned up for training sometimes. So, in terms of reliability, I think everybody knew, including Andy, after a performance like that, that Jim would be in goal in France. But, take it from me, we got a big fright that night.'

Even though John McGinlay of Bolton Wanderers scored the only goal of the game for a valuable three points, it was the kind of contest that forced us to re-examine our assessment of this squad. It was the kind of game where you were asking yourself, 'Have we been found out? Were we seriously lacking? What happens when we get to the big time?' Not for the first time, we were being quizzical about our status before a major competition, despite the fact we had won.

Paradoxically, it was actually another sequence of events that might have scuppered their chances of qualifying.

The problem originated on 9 October 1996 in Estonia. John Collins, now established as one of the crucial figures in midfield, who was playing football in Monaco and had scored with a direct free kick when he made his debut for Scotland at the age of nineteen against Saudi Arabia in a friendly on 17 February 1988, talks about that like he can still scarcely credit it.

'They wanted to play the game in the evening under the lights, which we complained about. They were just very poor. FIFA backed us and ordered the game to be played in the afternoon in good light. So, would you believe, they didn't turn up, as I thought they would. The referee told us we had to go out and get ready for a real game. So out we walked in line with the officials, all going through the motions of a real game. Then he blew the whistle and the game was over. So, I jumped up in the air and shouted "YEEES!" like we had won a cup.'

FIFA did not award the points to Scotland, as most people thought they should have, but ordered the game to be replayed at a neutral stadium, which turned out to be the Stade Louis II in Monaco, on 11 February 1997. Unfair, unjust and annoying it might have been but, on the face of it, it did not seem to represent a huge challenge. But, although this game has virtually been written out of history, in the long term, it was in fact something like a hidden rock not mapped on the charts, which could have wrecked the ship. For a start, it was like playing a game in a morgue.

Tosh McKinlay, of Celtic, who played in defence in all ten

of these qualifying games, in which only three goals were conceded, agrees.

'It was awful: small crowd, unreal atmosphere and we were terrible. We just couldn't get going. I suppose we felt it's a game we shouldn't have been playing. Maybe the awful decision of FIFA not to award us the points from that non-game affected us as well. We shouldn't have been there. I remember too that they had a chance late on in the game when they could have scored. Honestly, it was an awful night. And what's more, when you think back, the no-scoring draw at the end of the day might have knocked us out of contention.'

Tom Boyd still bridles at the thought of that. 'I can't tell you how awkward that night was. I remember I hit the bar with a shot. That's really all that stands out in my mind. But it's not just that; when I look back, I start to think of what might have been, and how dropping two points in a game that should never have been played could have ruined our chances of qualifying.'

However, Colin Hendry points to another feature of that night: a rather truculent Tartan Army. 'The supporters were normally right behind us, as you know. But that night, some of the supporters had an issue with Duncan Ferguson, who was with Everton then. There was a bit of to and fro between him and some of the supporters and that seemed to sour the atmosphere. It was very unusual.'

What was also in the minds of the Scottish players, eventually, was that this utterly stalemated game was to emerge later as a possible pitfall for qualification.

But firstly, there was one game looming on the horizon that caused some concern: Scotland had to travel to the young nation of Belarus to play them for the first time in unknown territory, after having lost to close rivals Sweden 2–1 in Gothenburg on 30 April 1997. A win was imperative. It offered a monumental challenge to one man in particular. For, in the fiftieth minute of the goalless game in Belarus on 8 June 1997, Cakir, the Turkish referee, awarded Scotland a penalty.

28

DAD'S ARMY

It was their first penalty since Wembley 1996, against England. The one that was missed. The one that made me feel like my entire savings had gone down the drain in a trice. The one that was made even worse by a remarkable English goal, which followed immediately in its wake. The one that made a group of the Tartan Army sound like saboteurs for their recurring shameful booing of one man. The one that none of us would forget, including Gary McAllister, the Scottish captain, a patriot to the core. Tosh McKinlay watched him closely at that moment in Belarus.

'There was no hesitation. Gary stepped up to take it. You can imagine what was going through his mind. He missed that penalty at Wembley after which England ran up the park and scored. And he got stick from the Tartan Army for some time after that; totally unacceptable, but that's what happened. So, here's another penalty, and we desperately needed a win to get to France. This was the toughest of the games left for us, or so we thought. It tells you something about Gary's character that he didn't flinch in stepping forward.'

When you talk to McAllister about this, you come away with the impression that the Wembley penalty in particular was so superimposed on his mind, that any penalty he ever had to take after was like a re-run for him, with hopefully the right outcome. How could it be otherwise, given the wholly ignorant barracking he received from part of the Tartan Army after the miss? I actually heard one SFA official trying to explain the aftermath of that Wembley afternoon by saying that, in some eyes, McAllister was associated too much with English football, as if he couldn't do the dirty on some mates, like a Quisling in the ranks. If that ridiculous notion held sway in certain minds, then we could present to them two other Quislings – Denis Law and Graeme Souness – who played their entire professional career south of the border. No, this was a case of a model professional who was deeply hurt by the reaction, but maintained a restrained and dignified response to the hullabaloo, and had no inhibitions about that moment in Belarus.

'You know, before the game I can't remember if anybody had been chosen to take a penalty. My first instinct was to step up and take it. Don't get me wrong. I didn't want to take it to make myself a hero. No way. It was just that I took penalties. It was in my upbringing. As a boy, at Fir Park – indeed in all my football life – I took penalties. It's just one of these things; it's just in your nature. And I've scored more than I've missed. And, to be honest, that day in Belarus, I'm not sure if there were many people wanting to take the penalty anyway. I can't remember fighting people off. But, after I hit it, I just wasn't sure if I had got it right. Now, I put it high up to the keeper's left-hand side, but I had directed it towards an even smaller space than the postage-stamp corner we talk about. There was a wee moment when I thought it would hit the post or the bar and come back. You can imagine my relief when I saw it in the net.'

And with only the slightest nudge from me, he lapses into that other indelible memory, one penalty on top of the other. 'Firstly, there was no doubt in my mind that we were in the ascendancy at Wembley that day. So, I definitely understand how the fans felt about the miss. I tell you, it was weird. There was something I could never understand: there was movement on the ball on the spot. It's something I've never really discussed with press, but the ball seemed to move. That's how it looked to me. Well, I did something I never did with penalties: I blasted it. I usually went for placement. But in that millisecond, when I planted down my left foot to hit with the right, it went through my mind that, if that ball is moving and I hesitate, I might make a real mess of it. Do I just avoid it altogether? No, I had to keep going. So, I put my laces through it. And the rest we all know.'

To those who don't know McAllister, that might sound like some hallucinatory excuse. To those who do, like myself, it is a narrative that comes from a man whose tall stature on the field was a reflection of his innate integrity. He had won the day in Belarus, much to the satisfaction of Brown, who said afterwards of the game, 'The players were running on empty at the end. Their legs had gone, their brains were numb, but their hearts were huge.' And it was with sadness that he accepted McAllister's ultimate retirement from the international scene, for fear that the ignorant booing of him by some of the Tartan Army would negatively affect the team as a whole.

Without him in the side, Scotland played their last game in the group on 11 October 1997 at Celtic Park, winning 2–0 against Latvia. It wasn't just the qualification and scoring the second goal of the game that Gordon Durie remembers, it was the crowd of 47,613.

'The noise was unbelievable. We just had to make sure we didn't do anything stupid that night and the crowd gave us an incredible lift. Celtic Park produced the greatest atmosphere I have ever experienced in playing for Scotland.'

Choice words, coming from a Rangers player.

But, after two wins against Belarus and Latvia at home to clinch qualification formally, Scotland went into the draw in the Stade Vélodrome on 4 December 1997, which, of course, linked us with Morocco, Norway and, for the benefit of the black-marketeers in the ticket business, the blessed Brazil. An intimidating thought for some? Not for John Collins. 'As soon as the draw was made I thought, ya beauty! Opening game. Brazil. Paris. A beautiful new stadium. A huge Scotland support. Our families able to see this great event. It was the perfect draw for us.'

Brown had brought in as his assistant Alex Miller, the player who helped Rangers win the European Cup Winners trophy in 1972 and, as Hibernian's manager, had won the Scottish League Cup in 1991. He was hugely respected in coaching circles. When I asked Brown to look back and make a comment about his overall player selection, he was enthusiastic about his choice, but surprisingly candid about a mistake he thought he had made. 'I had a good squad. Maybe not as talented overall as some of the others preceding me. But there is one player I should have taken and didn't. And to this day I still regret that.'

Here are those who did get the nod.

Jim Leighton (Aberdeen) Age 39/Caps 86, Jackie McNamara (Celtic) 24/6, Tom Boyd (Celtic) 32/55, Colin Calderwood (Spurs) 33/28, Colin Hendry (Blackburn Rovers, **captain**) 32/32, Tosh McKinlay (Celtic) 33/19, Kevin Gallagher (Blackburn Rovers) 31/36, Craig Burley (Celtic) 26/25, Gordon Durie (Rangers) 32/40, Darren Jackson (Celtic) 31/24, John Collins (Monaco) 30/49, Neil Sullivan (Wimbledon) 28/3, Simon Donnelly (Celtic), 23/8, Paul Lambert (Celtic) 28/12, Scot Gemmill (Nottingham Forest) 27/13, David Weir (Hearts) 28/5, Billy McKinlay (Blackburn Rovers) 29/25, Matt Elliott (Leicester City) 28/3, Derek Whyte (Aberdeen) 29/11, Scott Booth (Utrecht) 26/16, Jonathan Gould (Celtic) 29/0, Christian Dailly (Derby County) 24/10.

Brown did not shirk from informing me of the player he now regrets omitting: Ally McCoist.

'I decided to tell him to his face. I travelled into Glasgow and met him at Parklands Leisure Centre in Newton Mearns. Stuart McCall was there as well. When I broke my decision to Ally he was devastated. Looking back, I still try to reckon what made me do it. I think it might have been because I thought his form had shaded off that season and it could have looked like an old pal's act. It must have been that. Anyway, I should have taken him; not only because he was a scorer of goals, but also because his personality would have been a great benefit to the dressing room.'

In fact, Ally was approaching the end of his playing career with Rangers and was about to move to Kilmarnock. Walter Smith had even put him on the bench for the Scottish Cup final at Celtic Park against Hearts on 16 May, just before the World Cup finals. But I do understand why Smith and Brown, in their different circumstances, had the nagging afterthought that this was a player you could not dismiss lightly. This he proved when he was brought on at half-time in that final, and went on to score Rangers' only goal, his 355th for the club in all competitions. On top of this, according to most press

371

reports, he ought to have been awarded a penalty for a tackle near the end of the game, which would have saved his club from a 2–1 defeat. It's that which I think occupied Brown's mind for some time – that here was a player who may have been out of form, but nevertheless could still snatch, steal, smuggle, grab or magic a goal out of nothing. So, the regret still lingers.

But his squad, like the German side, which was the oldest in the tournament and won Euro96, was seasoned and experienced – the first name, forty-year-old Jim Leighton, signifying that. He had been reborn at Easter Road. Certainly, if you take the team that Brown chose for the opening game against Brazil, you will see just how mature it was:

Leighton,
Burley, Boyd, Calderwood, Hendry (*captain*),
Lambert, Jackson, Collins, Dailly,
Durie, Gallagher.

Seven players were thirty or over. Only one player was under twenty-five. Compare that to the first match in 1974. Scotland fielded only two players over thirty, Billy Bremner and Denis Law, and had six players aged twenty-five or under. Many people have judged that youthful squad in Germany to have been the best Scotland ever had. I think their view is influenced by the fact that the World Cup was new to all of us back then, and that the squad returned unbeaten after prophecies of doom. But there was another factor: it was that many of them were just embarking on their careers and carried a youthful freshness which was one of the reasons that we believed then that Scotland would have a long run in World Cups. This was not the case in 1998. This, by comparison, seemed like the homestretch World Cup for many men, almost certainly experiencing this for the last time, regardless of what would befall Scotland in the future.

Kevin Gallagher was both angered and stimulated by some of the comments he read. 'I know they liked to call us Dad's Army and all that, but they weren't taking into account what we had actually achieved. We were experienced, and that was a factor that was going to be invaluable in a World Cup.'

It also demonstrated, not just the faith Brown had in these players, by the numbers of caps they had been awarded, but also the reality that there were not many viable alternatives in key positions. In comparison with previous years, Brown's choices had been severely limited. He was choosing worthies, dependables, and that expressed itself in team solidarity, as Tom Boyd points out.

'We bonded well. We were never defeatist. If you look at the qualification games, we were a difficult team to beat. We hadn't lost many goals in the qualifiers. And we had some fine technical players – think of Paul Lambert and John Collins in our midfield. And compare it to Scotland selections now. Are many playing at the top level in England now? We had players playing for the top teams in England at the time; first team regular players.'

That certainly put a hard, professional edge to the squad. And, in terms of European experience, Lambert had helped Borussia Dortmund win the Champions League final the year before as a defensive midfield player who significantly subdued Juventus's Zinedine Zidane, and also provided the cross for Karl-Heinze Riedle to score the opening goal for them to win 2–1. Collins was with the Monaco side that had beaten Manchester United in the quarter-final of the Champions League to reach the semi-final. And Collins could not talk highly enough of the players in front of him.

'Kevin Gallagher, Darren Jackson, Gordon Durie. They were all fast and, above all, they were unselfish runners. Run all day for you. They could get in behind defences.'

But there was one thing which had begun to annoy the new captain, Colin Hendry, who again had only started his international career at the age of twenty-seven: it was the 'Braveheart' tag which had been attached to the squad, to connect it with the historically phoney Hollywood film of the same name.

'I'm sick to the teeth of Scotland being thought of as Bravehearts,' he told a press conference prior to the finals. 'We no longer wait for the roar of the crowd and charge forward. Yesterday's approach is history and should remain there. Of course, we still play with passion but, under Craig Brown, we have grown up and gone forward to embrace a more European style of play. The fans have come to terms with the fact that Scotland do not rely on one, or maybe two, big-name stars.'

This was no false modesty, but a genuine analysis of how to cope with the limitations that the passing of time had imposed on the current Scottish manager. You could say it was also a tactical awareness of how to try to dampen down the lurid expectations that still remained in the DNA of some of the Tartan Army. Hendry was a born leader, a powerful and courageous presence. But nobody was happy with the enforced absence of their previous captain, Gary McAllister. McAllister still talks wistfully about it.

'I damaged my cruciate before the squad was selected. Normally a major operation would keep you out at that time, but I also knew that some people had tried remedial exercises to get round it. So, I set out to work on it. I tried desperately hard, but I had to give up. I just had to admit to myself and Craig that I wasn't going to make it. But, to Craig's credit, he decided to take me along anyway. He felt my presence might be good for morale.'

This was a serious loss, as John Collins admits.

'We were going to miss Gary McAllister. He had wonderful balance and poise, and a full range of passing. A great striker of the ball. Elegant. That's the word I would use about him. What we could have done with that quality at a World Cup!'

Tosh McKinlay, who had made his debut against Greece in 1995 at the age of twenty-nine, and became a regular during the European Championship period, admitted to me that he was never quite sure if he would make the final selection, although he was the type that would have played anywhere for his country. He seemed to exemplify, as well as any, the work ethic that was now clearly the redeeming feature of the squad. But it had taken some time for him to get international recognition. On that subject, he made a frank assertion that sounded very much like an echo of 1974 when Peter Cormack, originally with Hibs, but then with Liverpool, claimed that teams outside the Old Firm were low down the pecking order for selection – something endorsed by Willie Miller of Aberdeen when he reflected on his time in Spain in 1982. McKinlay is quite adamant about that.

'I was playing one day for Hearts against Aberdeen at Tynecastle. I had a great game that day and we won 2–1. I was outstanding. Everybody admitted that, including the press. I knew Andy Roxburgh and Craig Brown were sitting in the stand. So, I said to myself, if I don't get a cap after that performance, I never will. But I wasn't picked. Then somebody asked me when I thought I would get a cap and I said I knew I would get a cap the minute I signed for Celtic. And I did.'

Perhaps the most astonishing selection was that of Darren Jackson.

'In September, the year before the tournament, I was having pains in the head and they discovered I had water on the brain and surgery was imperative. They drilled a hole in my head and then lasered another passageway so the water flowed the right way. I was out for nine weeks. But, when you think of it, I've been out longer with a hamstring problem. However, when Scotland played a friendly against France in Saint-Etienne in the following November, I wasn't allowed to play. Nevertheless, Craig took me along, just to keep me part of the group, and I made a full recovery. He really did appreciate my work-rate for the team.'

Those whom Brown had eventually picked to play Brazil were seen walking on to the turf, not only in the stadium by an audience of 80,000, but on several large screens throughout the city and around the globe. It was the biggest television audience of all time for a sporting event, estimated at about five billion people and utterly dwarfing that of the Olympics, for both the opening and closing ceremonies. Because of this unique global reach, and the attraction of Brazil, it is certain that many people around the world would be watching a Scotland side for the first time. The technology involved was of the same magnitude. There would be seventeen cameras in every stadium and, for this stadium in St-Denis, an eighteenth overhead balloon camera to provide 360-degree panning capability. Two of these cameras would be solely involved in a hi-tech super slo-mo innovation, which the French claimed would be so effective it would show dandruff falling from hair. And, take note, even with all this available, FIFA was still adamantly refusing to exploit it to clarify controversies on the field, defying the advance of technology. For, two days before we kicked off, Sepp Blatter became the new FIFA president – the start of a contentious reign.

Two days before the game, I dutifully turned up at the Brazil training camp. It was the same kind of carnival atmosphere as before. Except, in the middle of the media storm, which entails fighting to gain vantage points in the press conference, sat their manager Mário Zagallo. Throughout the next twenty minutes or so, observing him, I could not help but see that image Burns created of Kirk Alloway in *Tam o' Shanter* where, 'sat auld Nick, in shape o' beast/ A towzie tyke, black, grim and large ...' Zagallo fitted that bill perfectly. Here was a perpetually sour man in charge of the tournament favourites, blessed with some of the best individual players in the world, probably insuring himself against ever worrying about how to make ends meet, and yet he performed like someone sent from the nether regions to excoriate humanity. A Brazilian colleague there told me that, in the press conference before the friendly game with Germany, prior to the tournament starting, he had been asked, because of his irate manner, if he was in a bad mood. He replied, 'Yes, I am. And I was in a bad mood in '58. I was in a bad mood in '62. I was in a bad mood in '70 and '94.' Thus, he shot down his questioner with an oblique reference to his triumphs as a player and coach with the national side through the years. He didn't mention his coaching failure in 1974.

Through the years, I have fantasised about how he would have fared in a confrontation with the formidable Aggie, the tea lady at St Johnstone.

But there were other factors colouring our views of this

Brazilian side. Something of the *joie de vivre* of their expressive football seemed to have been compromised by the deal they had struck with Nike for various gear, which would net them something like £120 million over ten years. But it left them in the clutches of a ruthlessly commercial power that strictly controlled exactly where they had to play games. The team were also at Nike's behest to attend promos when necessary. The great Tostão of the 1970 Brazilian team uttered a howl about all of this. This medical doctor sensed that Brazilian football was developing a sickness when he said, 'The power of Nike over this Brazil team is damaging the team technically. The World Cup has already been won by the multinationals and all the emotion and excitement is being taken away.'

But in Paris that day, the average Scottish fan, clutching a ticket in his hand like it was a satnav to the Holy Grail, was blissfully unconcerned about such predatory commercial matters; he wanted to see how Scotland would cope with the great Ronaldo.

29

HONOURABLE HEROICS

He was the poster boy, the symbol of continuity in Brazilian style that would link him with the greats of the past. Tall, powerful on the ground, like a flying bear in the air, he seemed to have everything at the age of twenty-one. He was the beaming antidote to the sullen Zagallo. Waves of adulation from the Brazilian press splashed around him for being *O Fenômeno*, the FIFA World Player of the Year and Serie A Player of the Year that year and Golden Boot holder the year before, with thirty-four goals in La Liga. Little were we to know that this young giant of the game had a physical vulnerability which was to be revealed sensationally in the weeks ahead. Brown had been primed though; Bobby Robson, who had been Ronaldo's coach at Barcelona, warned him that man-marking would be fruitless against the best striker he had ever known. The tactic was to cut off the supply to him, which came mainly from Cafu on the right.

I put it to Colin Hendry, however, that despite tactical planning, the public were looking forward to a personal duel between him and Ronaldo. He responded, 'Not a bit of it. We had watched videos of the entire team and there was to be no man-marking. For heaven's sake, look at the rest of the talent they had. They could come at you at all angles. And the best player I ever played against, Romário, couldn't even get a game for them now.'

This was to be the fifth time I had to commentate on a Scotland–Brazil match; I had started with the friendly at Hampden in 1966, which ended 1–1. My experience of those previous matches left me with less apprehension in Paris. To further ease the tension, Brazil's recent form had come nowhere near the level of the Gods of Mexico in 1970. Certainly, they had beaten Germany 2–1 in a friendly some weeks before they arrived in France. But, on the form of the past year, that had seemed like a one-off.

Then, just before kick-off, I was handed the Brazilian team and that old, familiar unease began to stir inside me again.

Taffarel (Atletico Mineiro),
Cafu (Roma), Roberto Carlos (Real Madrid),
Júnior Baiano (Flamengo), Aldair (Roma),
Giovanni (Barcelona), César Sampaio (Yokohama Flugels),
Dunga (Jubilo Iwata, *captain*), Rivaldo (Barcelona),
Bebeto (Botafogo), Ronaldo (Inter Milan).

What was not to admire in scanning these names? However, note the clubs they were attached to. Only three players were based in Brazil. In 1974, covering my first World Cup game against them, every single player in their squad was home-based. A revolution had taken place in Brazilian football over that period. Basically, the economic circumstances of their country made European football much more attractive. And, to us in Eurosport, it was no surprise that the quality players were fleeing the country. We had become disenchanted with Brazilian football by having to commentate on their club games, via satellite, something we had taken on with initial enthusiasm. We expected the full range of pyrotechnics to be on display – the tricks, the control, the slick passing, the spectacular shooting. Certainly, there were instances of that, but more often we came away from games with the over-whelming impression that it was one of the crudest leagues we had ever seen, played mostly on dire pitches and with fouls that would bring tears to your eyes.

Four days before the game, I had written in my column for the *Glasgow Herald*, 'Scotland's players could not boast of being a performing troupe, but when they go into the Stade de France on Wednesday facing a much more awesome task than some people are making out, if honesty and dedication are great virtues in this world, then they need fear nobody.'

This is something that was echoed by the thoughts of Darren Jackson. He still reflects on the steely resolve of the entire squad. 'I wasn't in the slightest bit nervous. I was probably more nervous when I started off playing games for Meadowbank. And I was certainly nervous before an Old Firm game. But there I was, standing beside Ronaldo, the most famous player in the world, and yet I felt like I was privileged to be there. Not a single nerve did I feel.'

His devotion to duty on the back of that was to cost him the first yellow card of the tournament – for overenthusiasm,.

Looking over the immensity of the Stade de France, and aware of the huge global interest in this match, you had to feel this was not like any other Scotland game I had witnessed before, but more like an attempt to turn the people's game into the Greatest Show on Earth. It remains the dominant image of all the eighteen Scotland World Cup games I covered. I was bracing myself for the potential threat of, say, the left foot of Roberto Carlos, whose thundering banana-bend free kick against France the year before had baffled physicists and scared the bejesus out of many a defender; or the left foot of the Barcelona genius Rivaldo, whose skills had helped his club win the Spanish League that season; or Cafu's leggy runs at the speed of a gazelle down the right; and not to mention Ronaldo, who could do anything at any time. So, it was perplexing to have to analyse something as mundane as a corner kick and of the huge sense of anti-climax that it brought crashing down on us, so soon after kick-off.

For Brazil were awarded a corner kick on the left only four minutes into the game. Bebeto, who was to be one of the meekest of their players on the field and replaced eventually, swung in what seemed an innocuous cross. It was met by César Sampaio, close to the near post, and, uncontested, he glanced it into the net. At first it seemed like a neat header. It wasn't. It was his shoulder. Really? Were there no limits to the ways we could concede a goal in a World Cup game? Whatever part of the anatomy was used, a negligent Burley and a static goalkeeper could have snuffed this out. We expected to be vulnerable to genius, but not to the kind of goal I used to watch in the Lanarkshire Primary Schools final. This was the first time in the fifty-six goals conceded in seventy games during the Brown reign that Scotland had conceded a goal from a corner kick. A memory suddenly flashed through my mind of that moment in Seville in 1982 when, early in the second half, Júnior had taken a corner and Oscar, with embarrassing ease, had headed the ball into the net, putting Brazil 2–1 in the lead. After that had come the deluge. Not again, surely? Tom Boyd still suffers.

'We certainly prided ourselves in not conceding many goals from set pieces. We were well organised about that. So, yes, it was a big blow for us, so early in the game. But we didn't crumble. Perhaps Brazil thought that they had beaten Scotland before and now they were in easy street with that early goal. Did they take their foot off the pedal? I don't know, but we actually got a grip of the game right after that.'

Gordon Durie then realised he was now facing up to a huge workload.

'We were set up in a kind of 4-5-1, with me as the lone striker. We accepted that they would have a lot of the ball, but we were determined not to lose an early goal. So, I remember looking round at the boys after that corner and thinking this could get very, very bad for us. But, remember, the squad had character. No superstars. And we worked ourselves back into the game.'

Scotland, overall, did look organised. At no time did there seem to be a breakdown in communication with one another. I was impressed, and slightly surprised, at how quickly they picked themselves up, despite another early scare when Colin Hendry headed past his own left-hand post under pressure. Craig Burley was playing wide right to counter the menace of Roberto Carlos. It was not a position Burley relished, and one with which he was never really comfortable. The manager simply rated other midfielders better than him, like Lambert, Collins, McAllister and Billy McKinlay – and Burley was indeed effective in that wing-back position.

Darren Jackson in midfield was to aim to get forward and support Durie and Gallagher, his work rate under-appreciated by some in the media. Lambert, now an accomplished holding player, and Collins, with his technical excellence, would naturally supplement defence and attack respectively, and they certainly were not being overwhelmed by Brazil's midfield. Taffarel, in goal, carried the reputation of many of his predecessors, in that given the cultural background that

383

nobody ever wanted to be a goalie on Copacabana beach, his position was always the weak link in a Brazilian team,. Knowing this, Christian Dailly was primed to take advantage of high diagonal balls to the far post; the young man, playing only in his eleventh international, was superb in the air. So, they were bouncing back. It was getting smoother. And where was Ronaldo? Hendry and Calderwood were blunting him. The Scottish captain now sounds quite taciturn about the challenge he faced then.

'The most important thing we had to do was compete, man to man, against a better side. And what helped me was that Ronaldo was nowhere near as good as I thought he would be. I can remember one run in the first half. He came down the right-hand side, between Colin Calderwood and I, and he cut inside. I got a little bit exposed, and he was able to get a shot which Jim Leighton palmed past his right-hand post. And I thought, if he could do that then we were going to be in for a very busy afternoon. But, honestly, that was that. That was his only output.'

Ronaldo seemed to be effectively leaving the stage to the wonderful play of twenty-six-year-old Rivaldo, who had a left foot that was like a wizard's wand. He twisted and teased the Scottish defence, particularly in the first half. This was the real stuff from him, despite attention focussed on the star up front. This was a personal throwback to the good old days.

Kevin Gallagher was not so surprised about Ronaldo's apparent impotence.

'We were being fed a lot of information by the media on his personal life, and how he had problems with family and that he had trouble with his coach and with the sponsors, Nike. This must have been preying on his mind.'

Yet, in midfield in particular, Ronaldo's colleagues had the lion's share of the ball, as expected. But, at the same time, they were reminding me of the easy-looking, almost languid style I had seen in Turin in our last game in Italy in 1990, which meant they were posing only a minimal threat, largely due to the excellent thwarting work of Calderwood and Hendry and the blunting of Ronaldo's supply by Dailly.

It's something Tom Boyd rightly boasts about. 'We were good defensively and we limited them to very few really good scoring opportunities'.

As a result, Scotland were now looking confident and strong towards the end of the first half. They were not creating any great openings, but eight minutes from half-time, Durie rose to a cross from Burley and knocked the ball to Gallagher coming across the penalty area. César Sampaio brushed against him. Gallagher fell forward. Penalty. Of course, the heart rate increased in the way it did at Anfield in 1977 when Robert Wurtz pointed to the spot. I would have seen other referees simply ignore that, but the Spanish referee, José María García-Aranda, almost leapt into his decision. My response, frankly, was puzzled elation, because it did look like the referee had suddenly turned benevolent. Had the fates, never on cosy terms with us, at last been seduced by the display of these kilts? Kevin Gallagher began his narrative to me about that with an almost impish quality.

'It was the first time I ever dived in my career,' he told me.

I thought, for his sake, that comment deserved further elaboration. So, he put his remark into context. 'I remember when we played Sweden in one of the qualifying games. I recall being pushed in the back, but I kept on my feet when I should have gone down, so we lost possession and the ball went out of play. I thought back on that and how we had missed an opportunity because I stayed on my feet. Against Brazil, there definitely was a push. Normally, I would have tried to keep on my feet and keep going, but there was something hanging around in my head after that Sweden game. And I knew if I had kept on my feet I would never have reached the ball before Taffarel in goal. So, I went to ground. But the thing is, as soon as I did that and the penalty was awarded, I suddenly wondered who was going to take the penalty. I kind of panicked. Would I have to take it? But, fortunately, I noticed John Collins peacocking it, with his chest stuck out and the ball under his arm. So, I felt relieved because John had the ball and nobody was going to take it off him.'

The considerable Scottish crowd had erupted and it was now up to Collins to take the most watched Scotland penalty in their entire history. For I think it is safe to say that, from Copacabana to Carnoustie, time seemed to stand still.

'I was the designated penalty taker', Collins told me. 'We hadn't been awarded one for a while, but I was up for it. The first thing you think is, ya beauty, we've got a chance to get back into the game! You know, at the time, I had no nerves. Anyway, the night before the game, I had thought about the possibility of a penalty for us and it was then that I picked my spot in the net. So, I put it to the keeper's bottom right. That's where I always liked to place it. And the basic rule is "never change your mind, keep calm".'

Tom Boyd watched with mixed feelings.

'I never turn away from watching penalties, although at times it's hard. Now, it wasn't the greatest penalty John has ever taken. He placed it as he always did. He never leathered his penalties and Taffarel guessed right and almost got to it. But he didn't, that's the point. John's accuracy with the kick paid off. What a boost!'

The ball just avoided fingertips, just like Davie Cooper's penalty against Wales on the night Jock Stein died, 10 September 1985. I wondered at the time if it would have the same significance. For it was clear from the early period of the second half that Brazil were seemingly incapable of mounting the massive assault on the Scottish goal we had expected, having lost a goal softly so early in the game.

John Collins asserts that. 'They didn't batter us and create a lot of chances. Yes, they had lots of the ball, but Jim Leighton hadn't really to deal with too much.'

In an effort to break the deadlock, Bebeto was replaced by Denílson and the hapless Giovanni by Leonardo, which gave the team more artistry and pattern in the middle of the park, but no more edge in attack. All credit to the defensive qualities as set out by Brown. Plus, their opponents could not take lightly the pace of Scotland on the counter-attack. Halfway through that half, for example, the speed of Gallagher caught out their defence and his ball, low across goal, would only have required a tap to put Scotland in the lead. Nobody had been available.

The game unfolding was no great spectacle, and the only beneficiaries of such a state would be Scotland. Brazil were simply not being allowed to play in the manner many had turned up to see. The sense of wonderment I had experienced at the outset, because of the nature of the occasion, was changing into a sober appreciation of the way Brown had laid out his stall and how his men had gone about it. Until…

Ah yes, until!

Long before this game, I had always considered Cafu, the right back playing for Roma at the time, as one of the most attractive defenders in world football. He was a joy to watch at times as he rampaged from one end of the field to the other, skinning players with ease and either getting to the goal line for a cross or getting himself right into the box – which he regularly did. But he had a flaw. He couldn't pull the trigger. In many ways he was like Scotland's Danny McGrain in that matter. Both superb in the way they could penetrate defences, but with a reluctance to strike themselves. For all the menace they carried when they went forward, McGrain had only scored four for Celtic in 460 games and Cafu fifteen in 428 games for six different clubs. So, when the Brazilian went forward late in the second half on a run that took him into the box, it did not seem like our defence was about to crumble under his flighty presence. Tom Boyd had his eye on him on the seventy-third minute.

'Cafu came strongly into the box from the right. He was flying. Ronaldo, in the process, was slightly deeper, but coming to make a front-post run. I blocked him, as you could do at that time, using my arms. He stopped. He couldn't go anywhere. So, OK, I thought I could get to a cut-back from Cafu and keep my eye on Ronaldo. I put myself in an area where I could do both. There was nobody else near me. Cafu then doesn't cut it back, but hits it towards goal. Jim, in goal, palms it out and, in my effort to get back, the rebound hits me in the chest and goes toward the net.'

It is not a mournful man telling me this, but a fine player who was utterly blameless for what then happened, and recounts it almost in a dispassionate manner that suggested, rightly, that there was no need for regretful apologies.

'I don't know if Jim could have got a stronger hand to it. If he had, would that have gone straight to a Brazilian player? That was probable. Could I have held off a little bit, rather than getting into that position? I just can't tell. At the point of impact, I saw Colin Hendry coming into my vision on the periphery, and I was hoping that Colin had pace I'd never thought he had before and would get to the ball. But I knew it was a forlorn hope. It hit the net and I was gutted. I have conceded own goals before, like when you head it back to the keeper and he's not there, like I did for Celtic with Gordon Marshall at Pittodrie one day. This was totally different. And, do you know, almost twenty years later people still have a wee dig at me about that. But, it's never been hostile. It's always good-natured banter.'

The gutted defender and the rest of his side could have capitulated but kept going. Near the end, a John Collins free kick saw Dunga seem to put out his hand to deliberately block it inside the box. It could only have been that the referee didn't see it, or that there was little chance of him awarding two penalties against Brazil, which was at least a plausible reason put forward by some of the cosmopolitan media immediately after. Naturally, the players were aggrieved, but when Craig Brown addressed the press conference afterwards, he reflected on the 2–1 defeat positively.

'There is no denying that Brazil were the better team, but it was a game we shouldn't have lost. We conceded two very bad goals and really, as the match was played, we should have come out with something. I'm told pictures back home show Dunga handling the ball at the free kick and, if we'd got the penalty and drawn, it would have been a fair result. But the fact of the matter is that we are at the bottom of the table, trailing Brazil, Norway and Morocco.'

Generally, they got a good press. Except the headline in *The Guardian*, 'Boyd Gifts It To A Ruffled Brazil', suggested an act of treachery, until you read the explanatory text below. The *Glasgow Evening Times* came out with a kind of world-weary acceptance in stating, 'Another Cruel Twist Strikes The Knife Into The Scots Again'. The *Daily Record*, with a typical pun concerning the early goal for Brazil, sighed, 'Shoulder To Cry On', and, more encouragingly, 'Hold Your Heads Up High'.

Equally, not a single supporter I talked to that night in Paris, many of whom had watched the game on giant screens in the city, would have disagreed with that. You could describe the mood as one of muted satisfaction. After all, weren't we only to play Norway and Morocco next? Then, a day later, came this admission from Dunga to the Brazilian press.

'I touched the ball intentionally. I admit that. But only to protect my face.' The paradox is that viewers around the globe saw it, although the Scottish bench couldn't, from their angle. Indeed, only one Scottish player, Billy McKinlay, protested to the referee at the time, because he was closest to the incident. But most of the media had been comparing that incident with the hugely controversial one the following day when Lucien Bouchardeau of Niger awarded a penalty kick against Chile in the eighty-fifth minute, after Ronaldo Fuentes's right hand seemed to get in the way of a free kick taken by the great Roberto Baggio. To most onlookers it had seemed unintentional. Bouchardeau awarded a penalty to a great uproar, since Italy had been trailing 2–1 at the time. The journalists around me seemed more interested in that one, since it involved one of the world's great players and also gave rise to the notion that Italy had been helped by a savvy referee, simply because they were, well, Italy. The new president of FIFA then decided it was high time he met the world's press to defend the standard of refereeing.

30

VINTAGE IN BORDEAUX

Two days later, I took myself off to *Le Méridien*, the FIFA hotel in Montparnasse – a huge, towering slab of a building – where Sepp Blatter was to hold his press conference about refereeing controversies. There I saw a figure so distinctive that it wasn't until years later that I could put a name to him. He was round and huge, with so much hair about his head and face you felt he could only have been cleaned up by a combine harvester. He was hugging and backslapping people like they were long-lost relatives. His American voice soared above the heads of the crowded lobby. Of course, I now know this was Chuck Blazer, the CONCACAF General Secretary at the time. That day, in that grand setting, he and the rest of the FIFA delegates conveyed the impression of a fraternity gathered together to implement policies that would lead to the betterment of mankind. Little did we know at the time that this fat figure embodied the deep-rooted corruption of the organisation. As we were later to discover, Blazer had failed in a bribery attempt to win Morocco the right to host this very World Cup, a ploy scuppered by the voting of 12–7 for France in the first ballot. In their sights was Sepp Blatter. Remember him? The man who was once President of the World Society of Friends of Suspenders, to protest women replacing such belts with pantyhose? He was now President of FIFA, having beaten Lennart Johansson of Sweden by 111 to 80 votes in the final ballot, amidst rumours of open bribes to certain African delegates. There were other European investigative journalists in the hotel that day, who, even then, thought FIFA stank from top to bottom.

But there Blatter was, only recently in office, making a general statement to the assembled media, with the usual hearty optimism, about how the tournament was proceeding. That day they were to deal with the media's concern about the trend of harsh refereeing. The media had every right to be concerned, because in thirty-six first-round games, fifteen red cards were to be issued, in comparison to that same number for the entire tournament in the USA four years previously.

But, beside Blatter was a Scotsman, who was later to address the throng about the refereeing performances. I had known David Will well through the years, from his work originally with the SFA. He was now the head of FIFA's refereeing committee, and, for me, was still the amiable, conscientious wee solicitor from Brechin, with a demeanour and manner that suggested a kind of Presbyterian rectitude – quite incongruous beside the presidential smoothie with the charm of a huckster. To his credit, and true to his character, he did eventually become a harsh critic of Blatter. That day, though, he delivered a stout defence of the referees in general, placing emphasis on the fact that, if they weren't supported, then anarchy would prevail. I tried to ask him a question about the Dunga handling, but there were forests of hands up and I wasn't called. Then Blatter took over and virtually pushed Will to the side. I recall that one Frenchman did ask him, eventually, about the use of television to help referees, but was treated as if he were deranged, and dismissed with a sober endorsement of the sanctity of refereeing and the primacy of the human in charge.

For years this King Canute obduracy reigned. It took almost twenty years for Gianni Infantino, the President of FIFA, to announce, in April 2017, that video refereeing, of a sort, would be used at the 2018 World Cup in Russia. One wonders what effect such a technique would have had in France in some of the games. For, paradoxically, with eighteen cameras on the ground, an incident in a penalty box in the Brazil–Norway match, on the day Scotland played Morocco, which might have had huge ramifications for the qualifying process, was missed initially by the cameras and led to perhaps the most controversial refereeing decision in the entire tournament – one which forced David Will to come to the referee's rescue before he was lynched by the media, as we will see later.

Meanwhile, Scotland had repaired to their training camp in the soothing climes of the south of France. Defeated, but certainly not bruised nor battered, they were in fine spirits. They had chosen well in St-Rémy-de-Provence, near Avignon, where they had the hotel to themselves, and with perfect training facilities nearby. What enhanced their sense of well-being, having acquitted themselves splendidly against the world champions, is that they felt they knew a great deal about their next opponents, Norway, who, impressively, had come through their qualifying group unbeaten and conceded only one goal. They certainly were familiar with the players who frequented British football. The choirboy face of Ole Gunnar Solksjær comes to mind even now, as masking a ruthless desire to do damage to defences, as proved by the seventeen goals he had scored for Manchester United in his very first season, to help them to their fourth consecutive title. He could make a dynamic partnership with towering Tore André Flo, who had scored fifteen goals in his debut season with Chelsea. Bjørnebye was a stalwart of Liverpool, and Alex Ferguson had acquired the services of Henning Berg to join Ronny Johnsen at United to form a formidable central defensive partnership. And, furthermore, all were doing handsomely in the capitalist system to which their manager, Egil Olsen, had an aversion. For, in defending himself against some criticism of his social views in co-authoring a book about the history of Norwegian football, he dispelled any dubiety about his political stance by declaring, 'I am not a socialist. I am a communist.'

I commentated on Norway during the 1990 World Cup in the States and 'Red' Olsen had developed a style of football that was as appealing as reading Lenin in the Cyrillic alphabet. Their elimination, after a record of one scored and one conceded in three games, was a cause for quiet celebration among commentators who had run out of the variety of words you can use to convey boredom. And yet, in May the previous year, they had beaten Brazil 4–2 in Oslo, principally down to the performance of Tore André Flo with a couple of goals. Their 2–2 drawn game against Morocco, on the opening day of the tournament, revealed little new about them. So, my mood sensors in the Scottish camp were indicating quiet confidence among management and players. On the other hand, there was no way of telling how players would react to virtual seclusion in pleasantly rural France, far from the bright lights, but just the overwhelming sense that the real world was far distant. It was something that fascinated one journalist, Hugh Keevins. 'Players were definitely changing at that time. We'd been used to players getting out of hand, being found in bars when they shouldn't have been, climbing over walls, getting found with a bird in the room. That's what we do! But there was I, walking into the Scottish camp and seeing Craig Burley, who had been outstanding for Celtic that year, coming towards me with his hair dyed peroxide-blonde. I asked him why he had done it. "Ach, I just got bored, so I did it." You get bored and so you dye your hair? It certainly was different to what they used to get up to in the past when they got bored.'

His new white head lent him a kind of extra-terrestrial lustre that might have been a subtle act of rebellion, which Tom Boyd alludes to. 'There was a wee bit of an animosity between Craig and the manager. Burley was a central midfielder and was Scotland's Player of the Year, in that position for Celtic. But he was being played as a wing-back by Craig.'

I had to leave the Scottish camp, mulling over selection for the next game, as Eurosport had assigned me to commentate on the England–Tunisia game in Marseilles, the day before Scotland played Norway. Arriving at the central station mid-morning on the day of that game, I thought of walking to the Vélodrome stadium, but changed my mind when I saw the hordes of England supporters choking the pavements. As a veteran of the Old Firm clashes I had witnessed since I was a boy in the East End of Glasgow, I could sense that violence was simply biding its time. I tried to walk down the back streets and hail a taxi when I heard a roar and the sound of breaking glass. Then a stream of opposing supporters came rushing down a side street, shouting and screaming at each other. The olive-skinned Tunisians, their flags draped around their waists, were giving as good as they got. They were throwing anything they could get their hands on at each other, so I made a diversion away from the magnificent harbour area and managed to find a taxi, the driver of which, curiously enough, was a Barcelona supporter, and suggested that these scenes were occurring in pockets all around the city. Marseilles was effectively under siege. The Vélodrome was therefore a point of refuge.

The game itself was uneventful and I suppose I was perhaps a little over-enthusiastic in describing the goals by Alan Shearer and Paul Scholes, in their 2–0 win, to prove that I could detach myself from my cradle-born inclination to enjoy England being beaten at almost anything. Then I had to try to reconnoitre a city which was in mayhem, with riots breaking out in the areas where there had been big screens placed. They had simply become the sources of the worst trouble. My companion in skirting as much of this as we could was the great sports writer, Hugh McIlvanney. He was with the *Sunday Times* at the time, although, for me, he always seemed to abide in the mind as an *Observer* writer. He was hoping to get out of the city to get to Alex Ferguson's French residence somewhere, no doubt at the beginning of their collaboration on the autobiography. So, we were two Scots witnessing this very English football crowd phenomenon, and yet I cannot recollect there was any gloating over the fact that the Tartan Army was now a peace corps by contrast. I think we were both saddened by the thought that decent professional players were going to be held ransom by behaviour that had nothing to do with them. Nevertheless, we parted with the hope that Bordeaux would be carnival time in comparison.

It was. When I arrived the next day and walked through the city, the Norwegians and the Scots were behaving like they had a common heritage, although some of the Norwegians with the horned-helmet costumes reminded me that we hadn't taken too kindly to Vikings in the past. It wasn't exactly Seville of 1982 all over again, but you could tell from the chants that the bonding was strengthened by their distaste for what had taken place in Marseilles. Flags and drinks were exchanged, impromptu eightsome reels were danced. Anybody would have felt completely at ease in this environment. The mix was a joy to behold. So, by the time I sat in the commentary position again and looked at the team sheet, I did feel quite relaxed in the Parc Lescure, whose shape, although completely modernised, did remind me of a Scottish First Division ground of the sixties – say, a Pittodrie or a Tynecastle. However, do not imagine that the double-speak of politics, which includes reference to the 'known unknowns', doesn't apply in football. We always know something unusual is going to happen, but are never quite sure what. This time it was an injury, which in itself was a 'known', as in any game. The 'unknown' was that, if it hadn't occurred, Scotland might not have seen this game through.

SCOTLAND
Leighton,
Calderwood, Dailly, Boyd, Hendry (*captain*),
Burley, Lambert, Collins, Jackson,
Durie, Gallagher.

NORWAY
Grodås (Tottenham Hotspur, *captain*),
Berg (Manchester United), Bjørnebye (Liverpool), Eggen (Celta Vigo), Johnsen (Manchester Utd),
Riseth (Lask Linz), Solbakken (AaB), Strand (Rosenborg), Håvard Flo (Werder Bremen),
Rekdal (Hertha), Tore André Flo (Chelsea).

397

Just consider the huge English influence in their side. The danger of a kind of British stalemate was never far from our minds. There was nothing to surprise us about the selections. Brown could hardly have changed the Stade de France side, even though they would be confronted by an entirely different style of football. The Norwegians, I learned from their journalists, were grieving over the absence of the injured Solksjær. At the time, I did not come across a Scottish player who thought they could lose that game. Not like the false assumption which led to the spectacular downfall in Argentina against Peru, which was simply based on the fact that Ally Mcleod, in particular, didn't know enough about the South Americans. As Tom Boyd confirmed to me, this would be different.

'We knew a lot about Norway. Some were doing well with English clubs, but there was nothing unusual about them, nothing special. We knew how they would be organised, what shape they would take and, because of that, we were definitely more attack-minded in the game.'

Colin Hendry was impressed with them, but only up to a point. 'Henning Berg was reliable. He was a 7/10 man every time he played for Blackburn with me. So, he was a strength. As for Tore André Flo, I never really had any difficulty playing against him in my career. Overall, we had better players to pick from than they had.'

Despite his captain's lack of concern about Flo, Kevin Gallagher was fully aware the opposition would have done their homework. 'They had watched how we had played against Brazil and I knew they would play with two big men up front and send long balls up to them. That was predictable.'

So was Scotland's preparation. It had been impeccably

planned out. Except we have to consider that it was Scotland in the World Cup, and practically nothing ever ran quite to order. It certainly wasn't about to be smooth-going for me as the game got underway, for Eurosport had informed me, a couple of days previously, that my co-commentator would be Bryan Robson, the former England and Manchester United captain who had been one of the best exponents of box-to-box play in the world. I had really been looking forward to rubbing shoulders with a great player and was intrigued as to how he would handle his comments about Scotland. When he joined me about fifteen minutes before kick-off, he was in a rather flustered condition. As a well-known English icon, he had to push his way through the epicentre of the Tartan Army to get into the ground. He admitted he got what he called a 'good-natured grilling' from the crowd outside. There was one exception: a fan tried to 'dip' him. Robson grabbed the invasive hand from his jacket pocket and pushed it away, and was about to take aggressive action, when he thought the better of it, given that he might have been sent 'homeward' by the patriots around him. But then he added to me, 'Would you believe, the bugger then asked me for my autograph!'

Apparently, it was refused. He was decent enough to see the funny side of it all, and I thought he was on his toes. I was wrong. I would have got more analysis out of the Old Man of Hoy. For instance, Scotland were looking bright and brisk from the outset. My enthusiasm for this was evident to anyone listening. It was an opening that required a tension in the voice, a feeling that at any moment something significant would occur. I was maintaining that sharp tone of voice to reflect the team's enterprising start, hopefully keeping the viewer poised and expectant. I was soon to realise that beside me was a man who was about to put a dampener on proceedings. Early on, for example, John Collins was stamping class all over midfield, and in my view turned out to the most influential player of the match. In a sudden, darting thrust, in the fifth minute, he curled the ball from the right towards the advancing Dailly, who, as per instructions, had to make these accompanying runs. The wing-back leapt and headed the ball towards goal. It's the sort of action that any commentator loves; a flowing move with an explosive ending. Except it wasn't the end result I had hoped for. The ball scraped past the post. But it raised the temperature, with my voice soaring in a mix of expectation and then anguish. I handed over to Robson.

His reaction was like a man who had just been asked to comment on the Corn Laws of 1815. The voice was down-beat, uninterested, flat and short. I was so taken aback I struggled to know what to say after that. Slightly shaken, I recall picking up and started to praise our initiatives up front and then, at one point, concentrated on the early performance of Colin Hendry at centre back. Remember, he was playing against two giants up front and, pre-match, we had all been particularly apprehensive about Tore André Flo. In fact, Hendry, against the occasional counter-attack of the Norwegians, was handling any threat with almost majestic ease. Their aerial strategy was nullified brilliantly by him. I doubt if he lost a ball in the air in that first half. And on the ground, several times, those thrusting legs of his blocked out attempts by Flo and Rekdal. The compact defence around him made Norway look utterly predictable. Towards the end of the half, Strand did bring out a save by Leighton, but it was distinctly against the run of play. I had no other choice than to ask Robson about Hendry's performance in the early part. 'He's doing all right', was all he could say. Now, you don't expect a piece of analysis during a commentary to be as long as the Gettysburg Address, but you at least want it to stretch longer than a sneeze.

I was by now realising that I was on my own in trying to interpret this game. I didn't mind that, because I was watching a really dominant Scotland side. The Norwegians' long-ball mindset was having little impact on the Scottish defence, and I nearly left the seat in exasperation when the immensely troublesome Gordon Durie was brought down by Stig Bjørnebye in the sixteenth minute, only for the referee to judge that it was just outside the box. Brown told us afterwards that Durie had felt he was inside – 'I can't say any more or I'll be in trouble with FIFA.'

Durie himself was relishing the contest. 'The difference in this game was simple. We were getting a lot more of the ball and with Kevin Gallagher beside me and the speed both of us had, we knew their big defenders were toiling against us. But we couldn't score. That's the point.'

And this was despite the fact that, with Dailly supplementing the attack with those long-legged runs of his, and Collins in particular threatening all the time to penetrate from midfield, a goal always seemed imminent. Darren Jackson tried hard to supplement that forward drive.

'Let me make it clear. We did not take Norway easily because of how we had played in Paris. We had them on the back foot all the time. My job was to get in behind their defence and I did get into these positions and I had one chance, not a great one, but the goalkeeper saved it anyway. Although, that sort of tactic of running from the deep was to pay off for us eventually. And, don't forget, they were a decent team and they defended well.'

401

Scotland went in at half-time flushed, not with success, obviously, but with the knowledge that they had been the better side by far, and having encountered nothing they ought to fear. But being judged the better team at half-time in football can so often be a prelude to an unpleasant forty-five minutes to follow. This is how it appeared when Norway took the lead only a minute after the restart. It was an act of stealth, countering what had been Scotland's admirable attacking strategy, with Dailly as the defender getting forward when he could. Vidar Riseth, who was to sign for Celtic that season, took possession on the left of the penalty area, went past Calderwood and crossed to the area which was to be patrolled by Christian Dailly. Except he wasn't there; Håvard Flo was. The Norwegian did not let his surprise muddle his thinking, because he had the simplest task to head into the net. It pained Dailly, as he was to tell us later. 'I should have been marking him, but I was conned by his run and was left a couple of yards short. It isn't something I'm especially proud of.'

Not surprisingly, the Norwegians, one up, rose in stature for a period immediately after that. And where was my co-commentator? Beside me, managing the odd word, but in no danger of verbal diarrhoea. At first I thought this was some kind of reluctance to unleash his views on his traditional rivals. It wasn't. Because, later in the tournament, he was to accompany me to St-Étienne for the England–Argentina game that saw David Beckham sent off and England lose 4–3 on penalties. He was even more subdued in that game, for some unaccountable reason, which led me to being criticised by Simon Reed, commentator organiser for Eurosport, and brother of actor, Oliver, for not doing enough to get him to comment. I told him that the only way out was for me to become a ventriloquist. Meanwhile, Norway were beginning to buzz around the Scotland penalty area much more than they had in the first half. Then came the 'known unknown'.

For want of another explanation, call it fate, I suppose. For, when Colin Calderwood sustained an injury, with half an hour to go, it seemed a matter of concern, but not earth-shaking, since David Weir was a reputable replacement. However, it meant infinitely more to another player on the field, as Tom Boyd explained to me.

'As I said, Craig Burley hated playing wing-back. He used to say, "Central midfield is where I like to play, that's where I should be playing." Now I don't know the process that went on at that very moment, but the substitutions (McNamara had come on two minutes later for the yellow-carded Darren Jackson) meant that Craig could move into the position he much preferred in the centre of midfield, where the manager was reluctant to play him. And within four minutes of the second substitution, Craig scored the equaliser. That meant a lot to him. You could tell by the celebration and the look on his face. It was like telling the manager something.'

It was a gem. The sub, Weir, had been told to play long passes against a defence that was lop-sided, in that the right-footed Berg and the left-footed Bjørnebye, were defending with the 'wrong' foot. He chose his moment and unleashed one through the middle, which flat-footed that pair. With the goalkeeper coming towards him, Burley, whose new peroxide-white head might have been visible from the Inter-national Space Station, surged forward, now re-emerging as the real deal, his identity as Scotland's Player of the Year unmasked again, utilising the bounce of the ball in front of him to loft it with astonishing accuracy over Grodås in goal. Watching it droop tantalisingly towards the bar, then just slipping under it, to end in the net, was like waiting for a roulette wheel to come to rest and seeing your number come up. In the context of what Tom Boyd admitted about positional disagreements, the Scottish players celebrated with him like it was the return of the prodigal. England's former captain gave me a thumbs up in recognition of a strike he would have been proud of himself. That act was more eloquent than anything of his that had preceded it.

In the remaining twenty minutes, Scotland seemed eminently capable of adding to that. Just before the end, Burley again, playing like a man who had thrown off shackles, drove in a shot that narrowly went over, and, judging from the grief he showed, he knew he ought to have done much better. That final disappointment did not deter the Tartan Army from seeing the players off the pitch with rousing acclamation, which elevated a 1–1 draw into something of a triumph, and you knew that there would be few voices raised in criticism of the overall performance.

Indeed, my good friend Alan Davidson of the *Evening Times* was almost beside himself when he wrote, 'This was as fine and as professional a performance from our national side as I have seen over twenty-five years of pleasure and anguish witnessing the vagaries of those who carry the hopes of the nation.' He then added in conclusion, 'Maybe, just maybe, Scotland's time is about to come.' Oh, how often I had heard that before, and his wise use of the caveat reflecting the uncertainty of any prediction about a Scotland team. For the situation had the potential for head-scratching complication. Scotland would qualify for the second phase if ... *they beat Morocco and Norway failed to beat Brazil ... or drew with Morocco and Norway lost to Brazil by two or more goals ... or drew 2–2 with Morocco (or 3–3, 4–4 etc.) and Norway lost 1–0 to Brazil ...*

and if by chance Scotland and Norway were tied on points, goal difference and goals scored, lots would be drawn.

I kept reading these possibilities like reading instructions on how to cope with an aircraft making an emergency landing on water. These things only happen to other people, not to you. For nobody, surely, would end up having to draw lots at a World Cup! But, as the hours, then the days passed, before the third game in St-Étienne, I was already bracing myself for any outcome, given a radical change that was beginning to alter my perception of the Scotland team. For I was with Eurosport and, more often than not, away from my ain folk.

31

SUCH SWEET SORROW

In the previous World Cups, as part of our herding instinct, and the need to release pent-up emotions, the Scottish media would group themselves into their respective filial packs and hold post-mortems, usually in or near a bar. Usually with a lot of drink. Usually into the wee sma' hours, which I have alluded to previously. But we were always staring into the familiar faces, friends, colleagues, adversaries, all of us with the same rooted prejudices about players, managers, tactics and with the feeling that we could be reading off a script printed in Germany for us in 1974. It was all so incestuous. Throughout all the years of following Scotland, these group therapy sessions were nevertheless invaluable and I wouldn't have missed them for the world, for they carried brutal truths about how we felt about one another, apart from how we felt about the team. They were stimulating, mostly entertaining, sometimes rowdy, and really, the only benefactors were the manufacturers of Alka-Seltzer.

But my duties with Eurosport had taken me away from much of that and placed me in a totally different sphere of dispute and discussion. For I was mixing with commentators from countries around Europe. From time to time I was socialising with French, Dutch, German, Italian, Spanish or Portuguese men, totally detached from the Scottish camp. They hailed from different football cultures and, thankfully, as English was the common language, it was a new experience for me to be in the middle of a kind of melting pot of views, totally divorced from the views of the parish I was accustomed to.

Some of them admitted to me that it was the first time they had paid much attention to a Scotland side, because obviously they had to be watched playing the world champions on the opening game. Some had never even seen a Scotland game live before. The pity is that most of them had infuriatingly bought into the *Braveheart* analogy, even at a time when the Scottish captain was trying to disavow it. I think this was because the French press had latched on to it, taking their cue from our own domestic media, who had been handed a convenient Tinseltown cliché to cling on to. To augment that, they were still queuing up to see the film, which was still running in a cinema just off the Champs-Élysées. So out would pour the words of encouragement to me. Brave, courageous, spirited, patriotic, proud; all the descriptions of the Scottish players that fitted the perception of triumph against massive odds. Actually, they were being patronising. The more they chatted, the more you realised they really regarded the Scotland side as only in France to make up the numbers. It was sobering to hear such trenchant views outside the Scottish bubble.

Then there were the interpretations of a man I found it immensely rewarding to work with, Graham Taylor, the former England manager who covered some other games with me for Eurosport in that interim period. He was a superb analyst – one of the best I had ever worked with. His stories of how he had been hounded by the English press and had been characterised once in the back page of *The Sun* as a turnip, made our own Scottish press' style of occasional trenchant criticism seem like an output from the Samaritans. One night in our hotel in Paris, with many of the commentators from other parts of the continent enjoying themselves around the bar, including Johnny Rep, of Mendoza notoriety, he started to talk about Morocco. I had only seen their games on video, but there was nothing much in the 2–2 draw with Norway in their first game, or their straightforward 3–0 defeat at the hands of Brazil that had caused me any torment. Taylor, though, seemed to know them well, because he was apparently still involved in looking at players interesting English clubs. The name he particularly picked out was Noureddine Naybet of Deportivo La Coruña, their central defender, who was eventually to end his career at White Hart Lane. According to Taylor, he was the stabiliser of the side: tough and intelligent. But it wasn't just a case of identifying players of worth, like Mustapha Hadji, the midfielder who was interesting several English clubs, it was the thoughtful cautionary tone he adopted, in that he thought there may be a doubt about Morocco's temperament, but that, if they set their minds to it, they could really play. And, they were fast on the counter-attack. That he emphasised. It wasn't as if Craig Brown would not have known this himself, but coming from someone on the outside, it probably got through to me in a way I didn't particularly relish listening to. And he did air the view that, given the ages of some of Scotland's key players, and the hectic season most of them had come through, they might struggle physically in this, their third game at this intense level of commitment.

They had a formidable coach in Henri Michel, born in the south of France, who was to go on to manage no fewer than twenty senior clubs in his lifetime and was popular with the French crowds because he had coached the national team to third place in the World Cup in Mexico in 1986. So, there was little doubt that, when he got to St-Étienne, the Tartan Army would have to be in full throat to dominate the proceedings against a vocal local support for the North Africans. It probably didn't merit too much attention, at the time, considering the pedigree of nations from better-known areas, but they were African champions after all, and in a country of something approaching thirty-five million in population, football was a major passion for them.

Both managers were wary of trying to predict the manner in which the game in St-Étienne would be played. At a prematch press conference before the game, Craig Brown gave the impression that he was addressing his remarks directly to the Tartan Army when he declared, 'There won't be any need for some kind of "Braveheart" approach. We won't need that. We need steely determination. And we will get that from these players.' But the past was still on his mind, and if not actually haunting him, was at least whispering in his ear, when he spoke this way. 'Ideally, I'm looking for the type of performance we gave against Switzerland in the last game of Euro96. We had to win that one and we did so, and it was only a late Dutch goal at Wembley that knocked us out. But we did what we had to do and that has to happen again here in France.' But there was a significant afterthought when he said, 'I am not concerned about Brazil resting players against Norway because I know they have a squad of twenty-two very talented individuals.' That thought had passed through the mind of many of us.

St-Étienne. It's a name that used to send a chill through clubs in Europe if they were drawn to play in that atmospheric stadium. The last time I had sat there was watching the immensely talented French side play Rangers in a European Cup tie in 1975, the season St-Étienne reached the final of that tournament to lose 1–0 to the reigning champions, Bayern Munich, at Hampden. The place had pounded with vitality that night, as the most successful club in the history of French football beat Rangers 2–0. Alas, St-Étienne had fallen on bad times through various financial scandals, and the club was now languishing in the French second division. But the World Cup officials in France recognised the great footballing heritage there, associated strongly as it had been with the once-thriving mining industry, like Scotland, and were sure that tapping into that would produce a crowd with the right kind of atmosphere. It did. There were just over 35,000 in the Stade Geoffroy-Guichard that evening as the players trooped out.

Of course, we had our minds on the other game in Marseilles between Norway and Brazil, and there is nothing worse for a commentator than being aware that what you might say about progress in the tournament of Scotland and Morocco in St-Étienne could be rendered ridiculous by what has happened in the other. And yes, it could have been embarrassing, given that we had made many rash assumptions about the outcome of that other game, which ended with the most dramatic, and controversial, refereeing decision in the entire tournament. And hardly anybody I talked to thought the Scotland side was weakened by the inclusion of Weir and McNamara, when the team selection reached us.

Leighton,
McNamara, Boyd, Weir, Hendry (*captain*),
Burley, Lambert, Collins, Dailly,
Durie, Gallagher.

Morocco had made a couple of changes themselves from the Brazil game, but they were merely names without any flesh and blood meaning to me. In the final analysis, I felt it was about how Scotland played that mattered and, looking back, admittedly, there was an element of disrespect in my attitude. For the record, their team was:

Benzekri,
Saber, Triki, Abrami, Naybet (*captain*),
El Khalej, Amzine, Chippo, Hadji,
Hadda, Bassir.

Of all the eighteen Scotland games I covered in the World Cups, this was the strangest of all. Not even with the assistance of some of these players, reminiscing with me about that night, can I reach a clear understanding of why one highly professional performance was followed by something that showed Scotland unable to cope with a team of merit, but hardly of great repute. But, of course, I am minded of what Alex Smith said to me earlier in this narrative about the need to be cautious in anticipating what a Scotland team would do against any opposition, in a world of improving standards all round.

At first there was no sign that anything untoward would take place in an opening phase. Scotland looked competent enough and, in fact, were playing on the knowledge that

411

Driss Benzekri, the Moroccan goalkeeper, was believed to be vulnerable. He flapped at a corner from Kevin Gallagher in only ten minutes. And then, barely recovering from that, he looked very static and vulnerable again as Gordon Durie met a John Collins free kick, only to head just wide. The Tartan Army were not to know then that what they had just watched was the beginning of a meagre diet of attacking football they had to swallow thereafter. The Moroccans did look fast on the break and moved the ball around well, to the delight of the locals. They were creeping into the game and now seeing more of the ball in that first quarter. It represented no great danger, because they weren't creating clear-cut chances. But they were alert and sharp. Then came a goal of sudden simplicity. They knew how to travel Route One as per the instruction manual. In the twenty-second minute, a long Naybet ball seared through the twin pillars of Hendry and Weir, Bassir got behind them and hooked a shot between Leighton and his right near-hand post, to put Morocco in the lead. From my angle, the shot looked saveable. Its suddenness provoked me into looking for a scapegoat and the goalkeeper looked the most likely, although where was the defence? They were there, but clearly flat-footed. Gordon Durie underlines the raw significance of that shock.

'In all of the games, we conceded the first goal. As a result, we were always chasing. I've often wondered what we would have been like in that game if we had got in first, for it was depressing trying to catch up again. Third time? It now seemed more difficult.'

They were shocked and it showed. They got to half-time without sustaining any more damage, but were only sporadic going forward, although Craig Burley, in his favourite position, did bring out a solid save from Benzekri with his usual powerful right-foot shot before the interval. I recall at half-time trying to get reports on how the game was shaping in Marseilles, not just content with hearing the 0–0 scoreline there. Were Brazil taking it too easily? It had been a mediocre first half in St-Étienne, but we were learning quickly that Morocco were no slouches. They proved that only two minutes into the second half. Again, it was a long ball forward, which was picked up on the left just outside the penalty area by Abdeljalil Hadda, who had suddenly materialised behind the Scottish defence. He hit it at some pace, but straight at Leighton, who could only push it high in the air, but with such a trajectory that it looped behind him and, struggle though he did to get back, saw it nestle in the net. Again, it all seemed so eminently avoidable. This promoted the period in which scribes were beginning to mull over words of damnation for this performance. For, at 2–0, the Moroccans had taken over. There was a kind of contentment in their accurate passing, which was beginning to make Scotland look ponderous. And there was nothing ancient and creaking about Burley's tackle from behind on Bassir in the fifty-fourth minute that would have got the referee the sack if he hadn't red-carded him. I still see his walk to the pavilion vividly. It seemed like a gallows walk, epitomising the depressing mood seeping into all of us.

His captain, Hendry, was not well pleased. 'You do not tackle like that when you are two down. It deprived us of a goal threat because Craig was a great player and could give us a goal anytime. Now we were crippled.'

What had been galling for the manager is that, before they had left for the World Cup, he had asked Hugh Dallas to lecture players on the danger of red cards for tackles like the one Burley had just perpetrated. Overall though, Tom Boyd admits that Morocco's style had surprised them.

'We just didn't expect they would play the long ball the way they did. I suppose they maybe saw a weakness and got their tactics right.'

There was no way I thought Scotland could come back from 2–0 behind and I said so, because I was looking for some surge, some anger, some renewed belief. I couldn't recognise it. There is little doubt that, in the aftermath, in the media, there would be a discussion about ageing. The 'Dad's Army' label could now be seen, by their long-term critics, to be dangling round their necks. For the immediate and over-simplistic analysis was going to be that some of the legs out there were not up to it any longer, particularly against such a lithe opposition as the Moroccans. You could hardly dismiss it from your perception, watching what was going on. Nobody, as we all know, likes to be told they're past it. Especially not Colin Hendry, who was deeply offended by the suggestion that some of the joints out there were creaking.

'We were certainly long-in-the-tooth and we'd all had a long hard season, but it wasn't that. No, they were just so much better than we thought, especially when they got the start they did, then it was always uphill for us. Always a struggle to get back.'

Whatever the reason, the Moroccans were in cruise control now, and, with only six minutes left, Bassir scored a sublime goal by hooking the ball over Tom Boyd's head, on the edge of the box, before sweeping the ball home, aided by a slight deflection off Hendry. This was going to be the first time that a Craig Brown side was to lose by a clear three goals.

And it mystified Tom Boyd.

'We prepared exactly the same way. We were set out the

same way by Craig Brown. We were up for it the same way and, even though we didn't know all that much about their players, we were confident. If we beat them, we would be the first Scotland team to qualify for the next round. It was all so close. And, looking back, perhaps we were over-confident, although we knew that Morocco were higher in the FIFA rankings than we were.'

That was a statistic that had been barely mentioned in many previews of this game. In fact, they were sixteenth, their highest ever status. Scotland were thirty-sixth. It's not that FIFA rankings are necessarily accurate barometers of form on any particular day, but you could hardly ignore that sort of gap. However, Colin Hendry was much clearer in his mind about what went wrong.

'There were two things. Firstly, we did underestimate them. I don't think there is any doubt about that. They came from a different part of the world. I hadn't really played against a team from Africa in my whole career. Secondly, I don't think we turned up as a team. There were too many times, as I remember, when there was bickering and arguing – all about positional play, whose job was it to do what, etc. That was never the case in any of the qualifying games, or the first two games in France. We just didn't turn up as a team. That's the worst aspect, because you can underestimate opponents, but you still take them on by solid teamwork. That was the real failing. We didn't turn up.'

Nothing could be more damning in football than the phrase 'didn't turn up', and especially damning coming from the captain of a side, who, of course, doesn't exonerate himself. It might be considered by some as a cliché, a cop-out from some deeper analysis, but anybody in football would know what he's talking about: this strange absence of conviction that without any particular reason seems to visit some teams at times. A classic case of 'not turning up' was when we met Iran in Argentina in 1978.

In the press box Hugh Keevins will never forget how some of the Scottish press were reacting.

'I have to tell you that when the third goal went in, there was cheering. Yes, cheering. Cheering by some of my colleagues. It was as if we all had had enough of this. We couldn't take any more of it. Time to get out of here. Time to go home.'

Given what they knew about past World Cups, it's almost as if they had come all this way, half-expecting an ending like this. And they would hardly have disagreed with Karl Marx's saying, 'History repeats itself, first as tragedy, second as farce.' For Scottish football seemed to be testing that theory to the point of exhaustion. In the midst of it all, it required a special personality to show some respect for the sufferings that the vagaries of football can heap on men, for different reasons, on just a single game. For Scotland's captain Colin Hendry actually found it in himself to feel sympathy for his opponents. 'If you think we were gutted, you should have seen the Moroccans. They were jumping up and down like they had won the World Cup because they thought they had qualified. Then they heard Norway had beaten Brazil and they were out. They looked suicidal after that.'

In fact, Esfandiar Baharmast, an American referee of Iranian origin, had awarded Norway a penalty in the last minute of the game, which everyone in the stadium thought was an astonishing blunder. TV coverage had not clarified the situation, and the following day he had to seek the help of David Will to help him stave off all the hostility in the media, particularly inspired by Brazilians. In fact, astonishingly, he got a telephone call from his wife the day after, from the USA no less, to say she had seen shots from a camera behind the goal on American television, which had not been used at the time. The camera footage did in fact reveal that Tore André Flo's jersey had definitely been pulled by Júnior Baiano in the box, which vindicated Baharmast completely for awarding the penalty in the 2–1 win. *Referee Magazine*, in the USA, called it one of the best refereeing 'calls' of all time.

So, we had endured an embarrassment that in the end didn't count, even for the men who had made us suffer it anyway. Indeed, it was an evening that made all our final games in the preceding World Cups seem valiant by contrast, even in failure. In Germany in 1974 I witnessed, not dying embers in Frankfurt, but the glow of burning conviction right to the end. In Mendoza in Argentina in 1978, there was the evangelistic triumph of a great goal that converted all the unbelievers to a renewed pride in our game, transient though it proved to be. In Spain in 1982, there was recovery from a farcical muddle to the scoring of a goal that might have been a salvation. In Mexico in 1986, the goalless draw against ten men at least showed a team with spine, which could face up to brutal opponents. In Turin in 1990, we had rendered the Brazilians toothless for much of the game. And now there was St-Étienne. However good Morocco had turned out to be, it is still something of a mystery why Scotland had seemed to shadow-box, rather than compete effectively. The players I have spoken to can't paint a coherent picture, as much as they try. For years after, they talk as if everything is clouded, ill-defined, like they still cannot grasp why they should have been rendered so impotent. It is possible, of course, that the disappointment of the night distorted our own views and that perhaps Scotland were not as bad as the scoreline suggested. A 3–0 defeat can tend to skew opinions, and we might have been blinded to some positives in the game. This is something that intrigues John Collins to this day.

'The scoreline suggests they battered us, but my recollection isn't that at all. Remember, we had to win and go for goals. My impression is that they caught us with counter-attacks when we were pushing forward.'

Brown concluded, with dignified acceptance, that a better team had beaten them. Hugh Keevins, in the press box, simply said to himself, as representative of his colleagues, something he repeated to me years later with a simplicity that would chime with the realists among us. 'We were just not good enough, that's it in a nutshell.' It certainly chimed with the *Daily Record*, stating in its leader column, 'Scots used to boast, "Here's tae us, wha's like us?" Now the toast is "Sorry, but we're not very good actually"', although he did add, tellingly, later in the column, 'Just being there was the achievement.' But, of all the other comments, the one which came nearest the mood of the Tartan Army was by Brian Meek in the *Glasgow Herald*; he chose a whimsical Cole Porter to sum it all up, 'It was great fun/ But it was just one of those things.'

That fun had expressed itself mostly in the stands and the streets of France to the fulsome praise of the locals, who greeted the Tartan Army, at times, like they were a liberation battalion marching in to put a smiling face on the grim pursuit of success. John Collins certainly found some consolation in looking around him that night at the supporters, who clearly had not forgotten the courage of Paris and the professionalism of Bordeaux. 'It was amazing,' he told me. 'We were out of the World Cup, and yet they were greeting us like heroes. They were cheering us off that pitch. I'll never forget that. I felt so sorry for them.'

But that didn't prevent them from easily lapsing into inquest mode. No journalist nor broadcaster, with a public face, could avoid running the gauntlet of supporters after that night; they demanded to know what went wrong, as if answers were all that easy to fathom.

You could not avoid looking all the way back to 1974. The evidence in St-Étienne was the product of a gradual decline in quality of player through the years. 'World-class' is a phrase we could genuinely have attached to some of our players in the past, but it has slipped from our vocabulary in recent years. Put another way, I doubt that, after the tournament in 1986, there were any players in the Scotland squad whom an opposing coach would rather have had in his side. That was the reality. Willie Ormond could feast on talent. Roxburgh and Brown, in particular, had to dine modestly. As Brown was scorned that night in St-Étienne by some of the Tartan Army, so had the others been, to different degrees in the past, for, in the final analysis, they had all stumbled fatally at the end. Ormond, buttressed in particular by Bremner, returned undefeated and brought an almost innocent decency to management. And since the 1974 World Cup was so new to us, we thought it was something of a triumph. That spared him. Ally MacLeod's sufferings were in a different dimension from the others. He was hoisted by his own petard with his bombastic populism, which he could never hope to live up to. Stein, greatly protected from outright wrath because of his immense reputation, faced a more cerebral criticism. And, bluntly, we saw in him then a failing figure bereft of his former majesty. Sir Alex was a temp, pure and simple. He was never going to be judged the way the others were.

Roxburgh, from the day of his appointment, faced an almost inevitable firing squad. Brown's Euro96 record garnered an affection among the public which St-Étienne didn't wholly erase, although, from then on, he knew life was not going to be a bed of roses for him.

Lump them together and you can come up with statistics of their respective managerial careers that simply set the head reeling. Ormond, 47% success rate; MacLeod, 41%; Stein, 43%; Ferguson, 30%; Roxburgh, 38%; and Brown, 45%. Frankly, they are only fit for a question-master in a pub quiz. They tell us nothing about the changing circumstances through the years, the range of quality of player available, or the disproportionate numbers of games to take into consideration as new nations emerged in later years, particularly from the break-up of the Soviet empire. But, as managers, they did hoist us into contention one way or the other. And the overall feeling that emerged from my conversations with people across the whole spectrum, from players to supporters, was this overwhelming sense of privilege at having witnessed it all, even though we had all suffered too many cruel anti-climaxes for the good of our health. It's what came with the admission ticket. We all bought one in our different ways – from the man in the street to the hovering politician, all of us irrevocably affected by events. Few would wish aversion therapy for our memories though.

I have panned for gold in this narrative, and hopefully found some nuggets amidst the sediment, to enhance my initial identification of these years as a glittering era for our national sides. One such is the admission of how deeply affected players had become in striving for success, and how precious an experience it all had been. I sensed that particularly in the words of Colin Hendry, the Scottish captain, a